Everyday Data Visualization

Everyday Data Visualization

DESIGN EFFECTIVE CHARTS AND DASHBOARDS

DESIREÉ ABBOTT

MANNING
SHELTER ISLAND

For online information and ordering of this and other Manning books, please visit
www.manning.com. The publisher offers discounts on this book when ordered in quantity.
For more information, please contact

> Special Sales Department
> Manning Publications Co.
> 20 Baldwin Road
> PO Box 761
> Shelter Island, NY 11964
> Email: orders@manning.com

Manning Publications Co.
20 Baldwin Road
PO Box 761
Shelter Island, NY 11964

Development editor:	Doug Rudder
Technical development editor:	Michael Petrey
Review editor:	Aleksandar Dragosavljević
Production editor:	Keri Hales
Copy editor:	Lana Todorovic-Arndt
Proofreader:	Jason Everett
Typesetter:	Dennis Dalinnik
Cover designer:	Marija Tudor

ISBN: 9781633438408
Printed in the United States of America

For my husband, who thought **Graphs Gone Wild** *was what I should name this book.*
For my mom, my most ardent and constant cheerleader.
And for Lyra.

brief contents

contents

preface

When I was in college deciding what I wanted to be when I grew up, I had no idea that data visualization was even a thing. It wasn't yet a major or a discipline, and it certainly wasn't something to which young minds might aspire. I loved the beauty of outer space, and it turned out I was pretty darn good at math, so I decided to pursue physics to study the makeup of the universe.

For those who might not know, physics is really hard, and you basically can't do physics as a career unless you get a PhD. After spending 25 years as an A student, I landed squarely on academic probation after my very first term of graduate school, with two Cs and a C– in my three classes.

Thus began a bit of an existential crisis, and after two years of torment, I realized I had turned into the type of graduate student I'd seen all throughout my college career—the one who hates their department, hates their work, hates physics in general, and ultimately hates themselves—even though I'd vowed that would never be me. I decided to finish out my third year of grad school with a master's degree instead of continuing to pursue a PhD, and then I would "go into Industry" to make money and be happy. (Spoiler: Missions accomplished!)

Since, as we've already established, one can't really "do physics" with such a paltry degree as a master's, I had to get creative to find a job that I could do that would pay well enough to allow me to begin paying down the mountains of student loan debt I'd accrued and still put food on my table. I landed in analytics at a small tech company in San Francisco, where my critical thinking skills and my experience with data and experimentation were exactly what I needed. I learned SQL on the job, and the real-world adventure began!

About a year and a half later, I first caught wind of data visualization. In 2014, I started hearing about this program called "Tableau" that was supposedly great for analysis and reporting, but I'm not much of a bleeding-edge type (not because of a fear of new things, but more like a fear of disappointment), so I didn't pay it much heed until I started working for a company that had Tableau in their analytical tech stack. Sure enough, it was way easier to create automated reports and share the results of statistical experiments in Tableau than it ever was in Excel. And so, I was hooked.

As I used Tableau more, my stakeholders would ask me to incorporate this or that into their dashboards, and thanks to my manager at the time, I learned to figure out a way to accomplish what they wanted rather than say, "I can't because I don't know how to do that." So, as I encountered things I didn't know how to do, I would read blogs, follow tutorials, and scour forum posts to solve each puzzle.

In 2015, I jumped at the chance to attend my first Tableau conference where I could learn even more about this whole "data viz" thing. I came back with a fervor for making better charts and graphs, fueled mostly by attending a session titled, no lie, "Pimp My Viz 2: Electric Boogaloo." I learned how to add some whimsy to make a graph fun to look at and how to clean up my tooltips so my users wouldn't be confused. By mid-2016, I was ready to focus purely on visualizing data, and so I did just that. As it turns out, data viz suits me very well by marrying my love of beautiful things to my love of math—much better than physics ever did.

As time went on, I got more involved in the data viz community, and my skills continued to grow. In 2019, my Tableau public portfolio caught the eye of some folks at the University of California in Davis. They asked me if I would help them overhaul a course they had on Coursera about the fundamentals of data visualization with Tableau, so I did. In the following six months, I wrote all new scripts, built all new assignments, and crafted all new quizzes myself. Then we recorded the videos in their studio over the course of two days that fall, and finally, they added the finishing touches and published the course in the spring of 2020.

Two years later, I got an email from Manning Publications, who had seen my portfolio and that Coursera course, asking to meet with me to talk about the needs of the tech community—it was such an unsuspecting message that I very nearly wrote it off as spam, until it dawned on me that Manning is a legit publisher and I even owned and loved one of their books already (*D3.js in Action*, in fact). I agreed to the meeting, at the end of which they asked if I might want to write a book about data visualization. My response was a no-brainer: "Um, *yes*, I want to write a book!" But I didn't want my book to be specific to a particular tool, and while I aspire to be artistic, that is not where I have done my best viz work. Instead, my strength lies in the *everyday* stuff.

Analysts don't just write code or wrangle Excel anymore; the lines are blurring between analyst, designer, and developer. Data visualization is busting out of the spreadsheet and into the app, the game, the heads-up display on your car. We are surrounded in our everyday lives by data—data about how we spend our time, how much we sleep (or don't), how healthy we are (or aren't), how bad the traffic is, how we've scored in the games we play, how much money we've saved, how much money we've spent. *That* is what I wanted to teach about, and so here we are.

I give you this labor of love, *Everyday Data Visualization*.

acknowledgments

Writing a book is a colossal amount of work, which I think everyone knows, but you don't really know it until you endeavor to do so yourself. When you inevitably begin to wonder what on earth you were thinking when getting into this mess, you find that there is a community of people around you who love and support you and help you keep going even when it seems like you're never going to finish and never going to have a life ever again.

I'd like to thank my special community of people.

My mom—besides the obvious, where would I be without you? You have been my loudest cheerleader and most dedicated proofreader for as long as I can remember. Words can't capture how much your constant love, strength, and support have always meant to me.

My husband—for always making me laugh and pushing me to keep going even when I was quite literally going to quit. You are my rock, and I thank you for being okay with eating premade microwavable meals for entirely too many months straight.

My brothers, Jeffrey and Bradley, and a multitude of friends (Armela Keqi, Ali Mansheim, Ryan Applegate, Claire Kahrs, Erin Ferrari, Kyle Yetter, Samantha Li, Alexandria Washington, Maya Sandler, Carol Dunn, Gloria Schultens, Damien Watson, Andrea Millea, Patrick Browning, Mike Hanks), who always asked me how writing was going and listened attentively as I droned on about this or that chapter or some part of the writing process or just listened as I complained about how much I missed going to Home Depot.

The rest of my family—Frank, Dad, Selena, Kimberly, Frankie, Lauren, Caleb, Hannah, Ben, and young Frankie. You are the best gaggle a girl could ever want, and I'm so grateful for all the laughs and fun we have whenever we're together.

Nik Hanselmann, my dear techy designer friend—for so patiently putting up with my weird data viz questions and prattle over the years and so graciously helping me with the interaction design chapter to make sure I wasn't misleading or misguiding.

Neil Richards and Anabelle Rincon—for volunteering at TC23 to take time out of your very busy lives to read my book and then singing its praises on social media. I was terrified to ask this of anyone, and the fact that you both volunteered means so much to me.

My NorCal Slalomers—for their love and support in the year-plus it took to write this book. There are too many to list everyone, but a special shoutout to Eugene, Aprajita, Megan, Bryce, Marco, Peter, Avra, Luis, and Boris.

My technical editor, Michael Petrey—for meeting with me and changing your style of feedback to suit this noob writer and for keeping me in line.

Finally, my development editor, Doug Rudder—you have been amazing through this past year-plus, and I'm so grateful to have worked with you. Thank you for your kindness and for not being a drill sergeant. I also thank the production staff at Manning, who helped shape this book into its final form.

To all the reviewers—Mariano Junge, Renato Sinohara, Dieter Späth, Oliver Korten, Kiran Anantha, Arun Kumar, Stuart Schmukler, Alex Lucas, Maureen Metzger, Raghav, Domenico Vistocco, James Tyo, Tobias Kilian, Maxim Volgin, Giampiero Granatella, Giri Swaminathan, George Carter, Fabian Barulli, Jonathan Camara, Flavio Lombardo, John Guthrie, and Marvin Schwarze. Your suggestions helped make this a better book.

about this book

Everyday Data Visualization is written as an approachable and tool-agnostic guide to designing beautiful and useful charts and graphs. It introduces some key foundational concepts and then dives deeply into several core areas that make up data visualization as a whole. Then we zoom back out and tackle visualization projects end to end.

Who should read this book

First and foremost, anytime you are learning something new, it will go best for you and be most memorable if you apply your new learnings as you go. Thus, I would strongly recommend that you come up with a project to work on by the time you start chapter 4, if you don't already have one in mind when you start reading.

This book is written assuming the reader has some kind of technical or analytical background and at least some exposure to data or data analysis. You could be a business analyst, a scientist, a software engineer, or anywhere in between, and you most of all will likely find this useful. If you're a designer or other creative type, you'll probably already be familiar with a lot of the design concepts found herein, but you would likely benefit from the discussions of how to apply those to visualizing quantitative information.

Or perhaps you're none of the above, and you just want to learn something new! That is most welcome, too, and I've put great effort into writing this book so that anyone can understand (and hopefully enjoy) its concepts and content, regardless of their background.

How this book is organized: A road map

This book is organized into three parts, with nine chapters in total. Part 1 introduces data visualization and some key concepts that will be used throughout the book. Don't skip this part!

- *Chapter 1*—An introduction to data visualization and the tools typically used to visualize data for a digital medium.
- *Chapter 2*—A discussion of the key concepts of gestalt principles and preattentive attributes, which are fundamental to understanding how we as humans ingest information that is laid out in front of us.
- *Chapter 3*—A brief primer about data and quantitative information, including some key data types and structures, mainly for those with little to no exposure to data thus far.

Part 2 delves deeply into the various facets of designing with, and for, data:

- *Chapter 4*—An in-depth discussion of all things related to color, starting with the science of light and how our eyes perceive color. We then take what we've learned about color science and learn how to create palettes of color, which allows us to encode data and information in a way that users can quickly and easily understand.
- *Chapter 5*—An in-depth discussion of typography and fonts and how we can use these to help set the tone of a project as well as establish a hierarchy of importance, thus subliminally guiding our users through a visualization.
- *Chapter 6*—Beginning with an in-depth discussion of what makes a good chart, we then examine some oft-used types of charts and how to maximize their effectiveness.
- *Chapter 7*—An in-depth discussion of interaction design and how we can best use it to deepen our users' experiences with our visualizations, including when not to use interactivity.

Part 3 helps you navigate real-world situations and scenarios you'll encounter in data visualization projects:

- *Chapter 8*—We walk through a case study to understand the full process of planning, designing, and building a visualization.
- *Chapter 9*—A brief discussion of some of the most common hurdles and obstacles you might face when creating visualizations for others and how to overcome them.

You do not need to read this book in order from cover to cover to make use of its contents, though I do strongly recommend that you first read chapters 1 to 3 in order, and then you can skip around the rest of the book as much as your heart desires.

liveBook discussion forum

Purchase of *Everyday Data Visualization* includes free access to liveBook, Manning's online reading platform. Using liveBook's exclusive discussion features, you can attach comments to the book globally or to specific sections or paragraphs. It's a snap to make notes for yourself, ask and answer technical questions, and receive help from the author and other users. To access the forum, go to https://livebook.manning.com/book/everyday-data-visualization/discussion. You can also learn more about Manning's forums and the rules of conduct at https://livebook.manning.com/discussion.

Manning's commitment to our readers is to provide a venue where a meaningful dialogue between individual readers and between readers and the author can take place. It is not a commitment to any specific amount of participation on the part of the author, whose contribution to the forum remains voluntary (and unpaid). We suggest you try asking the author some challenging questions lest her interest stray! The forum and the archives of previous discussions will be accessible from the publisher's website as long as the book is in print.

about the author

DESIREÉ ABBOTT has been a data visualization professional since 2016. Hailing from a very well-rounded background running the gamut from a wee bit of art and business to science and analytics, she is at ease communicating with a myriad of different types of people. She holds a bachelor's degree in Physics from Purdue University and a master's degree in Physics from the University of California in Davis.

From a very young age, Desireé has nurtured a love for making pretty things, so she finds data visualization to be the perfect marriage of the mathematical and technical with the creative and beautiful. Since fleeing a PhD program with a master's degree, she held positions in various product analytics teams, business intelligence teams, and software engineering teams before becoming a consultant in 2022 and setting out as a freelancer in 2023. She is also the instructor for a successful and highly rated course on Coursera, the first in an introductory five-course specialization about learning data visualization with Tableau, produced at the University of California in Davis. She has run various data viz workshops, including one for the Water Resource Control Board at the State of California.

Desireé currently resides in the East Bay outside San Francisco, California, with her husband and their fur babies. When she's not working, she likes to crochet and play piano, tries not to kill her plants, and plays Dungeons & Dragons weekly with her husband and a close group of friends.

about the cover illustration

The figure on the cover of *Everyday Data Visualization* is "Femme de Calamota," or "Woman of Calamota," taken from a collection by Jacques Grasset de Saint-Sauveur, published in 1788. The illustration is finely drawn and colored by hand.

In those days, it was easy to identify where people lived and what their trade or station in life was just by their dress. Manning celebrates the inventiveness and initiative of the computer business with book covers based on the rich diversity of regional culture centuries ago, brought back to life by pictures from collections such as this one.

Part 1

There's something almost quite magical about visual information.

—David McCandless

In the opening chapter of this book, we'll look at some examples of visualization throughout time and then we'll talk about some of the different tools you might want to use to make visualizations. In chapter 2, we're going to lay the foundation for the design concepts in this book by discussing how our brains perceive and organize information without our even realizing it. Finally in chapter 3, we'll lay the foundation for the data-related concepts in this book by going over different data types and data structures you'll encounter along your visualization journey.

Hello, data viz!

This chapter covers

- An introduction to data visualization (data viz)
- What this book is and what it isn't
- Knowing your audience
- Exploring examples of data viz throughout time
- Popular tools used to create visualizations today

Data visualization is all around you. Sometimes, it sneaks up on you in the most unlikely places. Have you played any video games lately? I bet there was some kind of viz to show your character's remaining health, your progress toward a goal, or a map to show you the lay of the land and maybe all the places you'd been.

Not only is it fun, but visualization can be incredibly important for the success of an individual, an organization, or even a society as a whole. In 19th-century England, Florence Nightingale turned the medical world upside down with visualizations of data she'd collected over decades of working in military hospitals. When she would present ideas to the "Powers That Be" and they would answer with, "That's just not how we do it," she managed to change minds only when she showed a visualization of her data.

3

Well-designed visualizations save lives and can turn entire industries around, but at the same time, they can also tell you how many lives you have left with your little red plumber guy before you have to restart the game all over again. ;)

In this first chapter, you'll get a brief introduction to data visualization as a whole, followed by a brief introduction to this book, which will include the first of many reminders that knowing your audience is the most important thing to remember as you design and build any viz. From there, we'll look at a handful of data visualization examples throughout time, and then, we'll talk about some of the most popular tools used to create data visualization today.

1.1   *What is data visualization?*

If you picked up this book voluntarily, chances are pretty good that you already have an idea of what data visualization is. Or perhaps you're stuck in a doctor's office somewhere, and this is the only thing available to you in the waiting room (I'd love to meet that doctor!), so you've picked up the book as a matter of self-preservation to save yourself from boredom. Either way, I'm still going to tell you: data visualization, or data viz as most of us in the biz usually call it, is how we communicate numerical or quantitative information in a visual manner. When I'm telling people what I do, and they get that quizzical look on their faces at the mention of data visualization (it is rather a mouthful, after all), I normally tell them that I make charts and graphs for a living, and then the penny drops. In data viz, we use things such as charts, graphs, maps, and sometimes even pictures and iconography to translate numbers into visual information—they do say a picture is worth a thousand words, right? The medium can be anything you want: print, an interactive web page, a static infographic, crayons on paper, or even three-dimensional objects such as modeling clay, among many, many other things. I'm sure you could even do an interpretive dance if you felt so moved. There are various principles about what makes one viz more effective than another, but in the end, they're still both visualizations. There are no absolute stipulations on how you do it, so the sky is the limit, and if you always keep your audience at the forefront of your mind and the center of your development process, you'll be set up for success.

1.2   *What can you expect from this book?*

It is my greatest hope that you will find this book to be a practical, approachable, and fun guide to making beautiful and useful data visualizations that power and inform our everyday lives. However, before I tell you more about what this book is, I would like to say that this book is not a technical manual about implementing a tool or learning a coding language. We will not be walking through any coded examples, and there won't be exercises at the end of each chapter or section: step-by-step tutorials are not the main attraction here. This book is meant to be a tool-agnostic guide about the principles of good design as they apply to visualizing data. You will be able to apply the concepts to any stage of any data visualization project on which you work, regardless of tool, size, or medium.

All that being said, you will find this book most useful if you are already working on a viz project, be it a personal gig that's just for fun (the data viz community is teeming with like-minded nerds who gleefully spend their free time making charts and graphs) or something you're making for work, which really can be just as fun. The first part of the book (chapters 1–3) serves as a foundation on which the other two parts will build, so I recommend you read that first (it is, after all, at the beginning). In the second part, chapters 4–7 each delve deeply into some aspect of viz, so we can understand the context of how it works and why it's important, and then each wraps up on the more practical side, applying those design principles to our actual work of visualization. In the last part, chapters 8 and 9 detail the entire process of building a data visualization from start to finish and then present some tips for troubleshooting and how to handle projects that go sideways. I've tried to write this book in a way that lets you get a lot out of it no matter where you are on your viz journey, to the point that you could skip around and not read it in order, but it would still behoove you to read chapters 1–3 first.

1.3 Data storytelling: Know your audience

The single most important thing you need to keep in mind when making a visualization is to know your audience. It's all about them, and don't ever forget it! You could make the most beautiful visualization that makes use of all the latest tricks and the trendiest charts, obeying all the best practices, but if it doesn't meet the needs of your audience, then you have completely wasted your time. Part of meeting those needs is that the audience truly understands the work, the message, and the story you're trying to tell. I can't stress it enough: no matter how much blood, sweat, and tears you pour into your work, none of it matters if your audience doesn't understand. Save yourself a ton of grief and talk to them early and often to find out what they need. Check in with them throughout your development process to make sure you're addressing their questions and that you're not making features that are too complex for them to grasp quickly.

To put a finer point on it, there's knowing who your audience is and knowing who your audience isn't. Have you ever tried to go out to eat with your entire family? If so, you probably shudder to remember how difficult it is to decide which restaurant or bar to bless with your patronage. Mom wants Italian, Dad wants "good ol' meat and potatoes," your siblings want something interesting like Ethiopian or Thai, and you just want to eat, for crying out loud. Whatever you wind up choosing is not going to please everyone—even if you wind up finding a unicorn of a restaurant that serves every cuisine under the Sun, they probably don't do any of those dishes extremely well, so everyone is still disappointed. If you try to please everyone, you will wind up pleasing no one.

Even as I write this book, toiling away during my free time—honestly, much of which would otherwise have been spent bingeing TV shows on my favorite streaming services—the need to know one's audience is still inescapable. My vision of who you are is that you're an analyst or someone in an analytics-adjacent field who finds that they need to create visualizations but don't have the design know-how to do so. No matter how hard or long I work, how eloquent my prose, how beautiful my examples, or how many people I pester to let me reproduce their gorgeous visualizations, none of it matters if that hypothetical analyst doesn't learn anything. Always put the needs of the audience above your own.

Now, with that in the back of our minds, we're going to take a quick trip through time to see examples of how data visualization evolved, and then we'll dive into some of the most popular tools used today to create vizzes.

1.4   Some examples of data viz throughout time

To spare you a full history lesson, we're going to instead flip through a metaphorical photo album of some ground-breaking visualizations throughout history. Being familiar with the history of a discipline gives us context for the developments and advances we have or haven't made by now, and many often find it inspiring in their current work.

1.4.1   Data viz in prehistory

Although it doesn't quite predate human language the way art does, surprisingly, data visualization has about as lengthy a history as astronomy. In fact, the Lascaux Cave paintings in southern France are some very early cave drawings that date all the way back to the Paleolithic era. According to Martin Sweatman and Alistair Coombs in their 2018 article about ancient knowledge of the precession of the equinoxes in the *Athens Journal of History*, some of the paintings just might use constellations to encode the date of an "encounter with the Taurid meteor stream." Figure 1.1 shows part of the Shaft Scene that depicts a rhinoceros on the left, followed by a man with a bird head. There is a bird above, which could be a duck or a goose. To the right, there is a bison or aurochs, and on an opposite wall (unpictured), there is a horse. Sweatman and Coombs contend that these are not just pictures of animals but are in fact constellations. The rhinoceros is thought to represent what is today known as the Taurus constellation, the bison/aurochs is thought to represent what is now Capricorn, the duck/goose is thought to represent Libra, and the horse is thought to represent what is now known as Leo.

Fast-forwarding a bit, we can also see the visualization of quantitative information in the *quipu*, or talking knots, like those shown in figure 1.2 which were used by the Inca people in what is now Peru, starting around 2600 BCE. Talking knots were used to keep records about everything, from census data to taxes.

Figure 1.1 The Shaft Scene from the cave walls at Lascaux depicting a rhinoceros on the left, a bird that could be a duck or a goose in the middle, a bison on the right, and a horse on another wall (unpictured). Coombs and Sweatman contend that these could represent constellations and are intended to reference certain dates. (Alistair Coombs. Used with permission)

Figure 1.2 Quipu knots of the Inca people were used to record numerical information (everything from census data to taxes). (Pi3.124, CC BY-SA 4.0 https://creativecommons.org/licenses/by-sa/4.0, via Wikimedia Commons)

1.4.2   Maps

The earliest *documented* visualizations undoubtedly are maps, such as the Turin Papyrus Map dating back to the 1150s BCE in Egypt (see figure 1.3). The nearly 9-foot-long map, drawn by the artist Amennakhte, accurately depicts the location of gold and stone needed to build statues of King Ramesses the 4th.

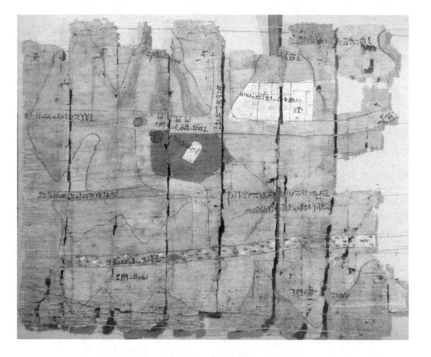

Figure 1.3   The Turin Papyrus Map drawn by Amennakhte dates from somewhere between 1156 and 1150 BCE, and it depicts roads through the eastern part of the Egyptian desert, in Hammamat. (Public domain, via Wikimedia Commons)

For the next couple thousand years, the most notable advances in data visualization were made in the world of cartography. However, around the 10th or 11th century, we start seeing evidence again of people recording astronomical information about planetary movement across the sky. By the 1500s, cartographers, navigators, and astronomers (among others) throughout the Eastern and Western worlds were regularly using instruments and tools to precisely measure geographical and astronomical locations, as well as other physical quantities.

1.4.3   *The early modern era*

By the 1600s, we start getting into the realm of "iconic infographics," according to RJ Andrews' "Interactive Timeline of the Most Iconic Infographics," which can be found

at http://history.infowetrust.com. It is a wonderfully delightful viz, and I highly
encourage you to take a look on your own.

One of my personal favorites from RJ's timeline is Napoleon's march during his
Russian campaign of 1812, shown in figure 1.4. This map expertly depicts six dimensions of data using only a single page: it shows the number of troops, distance they
traveled, temperatures they endured, latitude and longitude of their travels, direction
of their travel, and time. As you grow in your data viz skills, you will start to increas-
ingly appreciate this impressive feat of visualization!

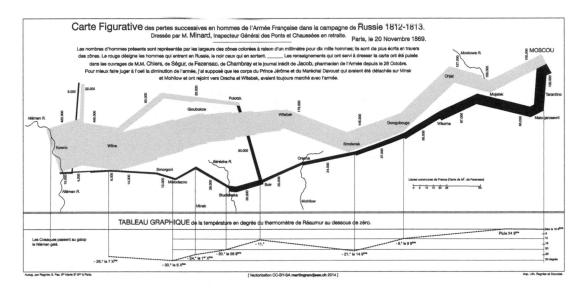

**Figure 1.4   Charles Minard's most famous work, a map of Napoleon's Russian campaign of 1812, depicting six
dimensions of data using only a single page (Martin Grandjean, CC BY-SA 3.0, via Wikimedia Commons)**

1.4.4   Florence Nightingale

Perhaps you have heard of the woman, the legend that is Florence Nightingale? As the
founding mother of modern nursing, this gentry-born Englishwoman collected and
recorded data from her own experiences as a combat nurse during the Crimean War,
from 1854 to 1856. Using this data about the conditions in the Barrack Hospital at
Scutari, she created visualizations upon visualizations to lobby for better conditions in
military hospitals. Pictured in figure 1.5 is one of her most famous pairs of compara-
tive polar-area diagrams, a new chart type that she invented and is known today as a
"Nightingale rose." In these roses, she demonstrated that the leading cause of death
in soldiers was not battle wounds (shown in red) but preventable diseases (shown in
blue). Radial visualizations such as these can be a bit controversial these days because,
as we'll learn later, the human eye doesn't interpret angles well. However, love them
or leave them, these drove some big change.

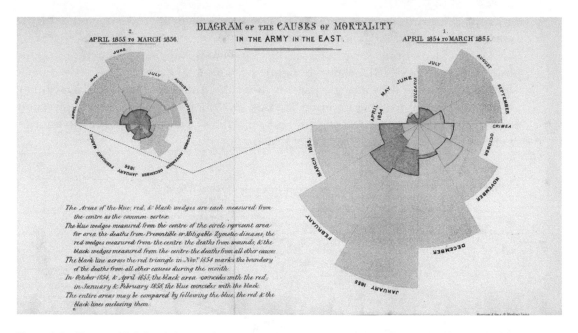

Figure 1.5   Florence Nightingale's most famous pair of roses, depicting the causes of death in soldiers during the Crimean War: preventable diseases in blue and battle wounds in red (Florence Nightingale, Public domain, via Wikimedia Commons)

Armed with her data and visualizations, Nightingale was an early champion of hand-washing and sanitation in hospitals, long before germ theory emerged. She lobbied all the powers that be of her time, sending self-published works to doctors, war offices, members of the House of Commons and the House of Lords, and even Queen Victoria herself. She drove massive change, the effects of which we still feel today.

1.4.5   *The later modern era*

Time marches onward, and so do we, into the 20th and 21st centuries. As one whose living is mainly made by the construction of interactive web-based data visualizations, it really blows my mind that up until the 1980s, you were going to be busting out (at best) a pen and paper if you wanted to make a data visualization. Spreadsheets didn't come on the scene until VisiCalc was introduced to the public, first in 1979 on the Apple II, and then in 1981 on the IBM PC (yes, the great divide really goes back that far). Even today, this is the very favorite way for anyone to turn data into insights: you still can't separate a finance person from a good old spreadsheet unless you pry it from their cold, dead fingers.

While we're on the topic of spreadsheets, let's talk a bit about tools for making data visualizations.

1.5 Data viz tools

As we mentioned in section 1.1, the medium, or tools, used for a data visualization can be just about anything that results in something visual. While modeling clay and interpretive dance are totally valid media for data visualizations, in this book, we're going to focus more on the two-dimensional and usually computational media.

Each year, the Data Visualization Society (DVS) conducts its State of the Industry Survey, and one of the questions they always ask is about the tools people use to create visualizations. Figure 1.6 shows the percentage of respondents each year stating they use a particular tool, where each tool is represented by a circle, and the percentage of respondents is represented by both the left–right position and the circle's size. It's important to note here that a tool's change in rank from one year to the next may not only be due to its popularity rising or falling but also due to the types of respondents taking the survey that year or the tool's presence in the multi-select list of options.

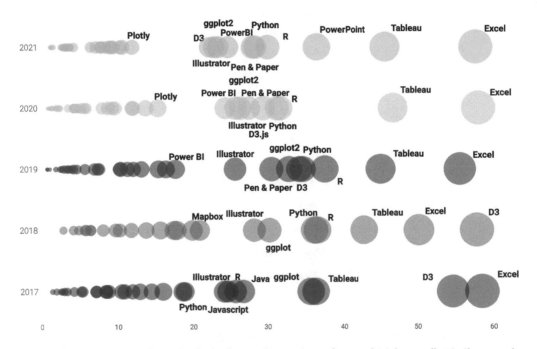

Figure 1.6 The most popular technologies by year (percentage of respondents) according to the annual State of the Industry Survey by the Data Visualization Society (DVS). Note that the emergence and increase in popularity of some tools may be due to the tool being added to the multi-select list of options for survey takers rather than a true increase in use. (Data Visualization Society. Used with permission)

It's okay if you are not familiar with the tools labeled in figure 1.6. We'll be going over a handful of them in this section, but just so you can at least get a decent idea of what the list entails, I've broken down the labeled tools by type in table 1.1 for you.

Table 1.1   A breakdown of the types of tools labeled in figure 1.6

Type of tool	Popular tools in figure 1.6
Spreadsheet	Excel
BI tools	Tableau, Power BI
Code	D3 (aka D3.js or d3 or d3.js), Python, R, ggplot, ggplot2, Plotly, Java
Design software	Illustrator
Other	Pen & Paper, Mapbox, PowerPoint

1.5.1   *Spreadsheets*

As shown in figure 1.6, Microsoft's Excel is the most popular tool for visualizing data (except for 2018, but it only dropped one place to #2 that year). Excel's popularity is completely understandable: as a program to which nearly all data viz practitioners have some level of access, its barrier for entry is remarkably low. It takes nearly nothing to paste or type in some data, and within two clicks, you can make a chart. The resulting chart, shown in figure 1.7, might not be beautiful, but it's a chart, nonetheless.

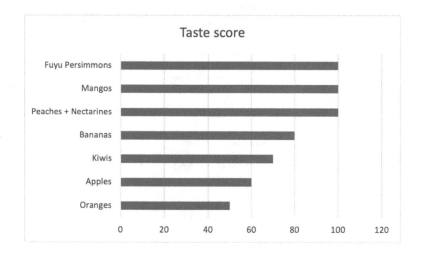

Figure 1.7   A bar chart I created in Excel using its defaults

Do you want to get more involved in your chart-making endeavors? Spreadsheet programs, even those not made by Microsoft, have you covered. You can create complex calculations to include in your chart, you can change titles and axes and formatting and legends, you can use tall data, you can use wide data, you can use big(-ish) data, and can use small data. There's a reason those finance people have such a tight grip: they're MacGyver, and spreadsheets are the Swiss Army knife of data analysis.

1.5.2 Business intelligence tools

I like to call business intelligence (BI) tools "spreadsheets on steroids" because, in many ways, they take what spreadsheets can do and greatly enhance it. As we saw in figure 1.6, Tableau was the most popular BI tool and in the top three tools overall for five years of the DVS survey. Power BI, which is Microsoft's data viz tool and the biggest competitor for Tableau, is gaining in popularity due to its lower barrier for entry, oftentimes in the public sector. There are also competing products such as Looker (owned by Google), Domo, and Qlik, among others.

Figure 1.8 shows my sample fruit data in a chart I created in Tableau with a handful of clicks and a couple of drag-and-drops. Again, it won't win me any awards, but it's a bit nicer than the Excel one in figure 1.7, as I find the size of the bars relative to the white space between them to be less jarring to my eyes, and the gridlines are much lighter and thus pushed to the background.

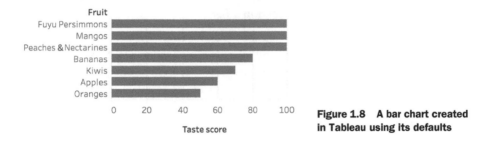

Figure 1.8 A bar chart created in Tableau using its defaults

BI tools might be your weapon of choice if you are making an internal-facing visualization for an organization. Many BI tools have an enterprise version that allows for some kind of publishing and sharing capabilities, as well as automatic updates of the data sources. This is great for regular reporting because it saves analysts and viz practitioners tons of time that they can use for better things than refreshing queries and emailing charts around. Oftentimes, there are options for stakeholders to subscribe to a report so that they automatically get updates and computer-generated screenshots sent to their inboxes or other communications platforms on a schedule. As a bonus, BI tools can often handle much more data than even the biggest spreadsheets.

Finally, depending on your technical prowess, many BI tools can handle various levels of coding, although you should keep in mind that the more you code, the more customized you can make your end product. The no-code GUIs usually don't have a lot of flexibility in their formatting, while products that allow more customization will often require more coding and complex calculations.

1.5.3 Code

If you're already a software developer or engineer, spreadsheets and BI tools probably aren't your cup of tea. In that case, you know well that writing code gives you the utmost control over exactly how your visualizations will look and behave. The good news is that even within the umbrella of coding, there are gradients of difficulty and control: you can use existing libraries tailored to the functionality you seek, or you can write your own functions, classes, and objects completely from scratch. When I'm coding, and I'm certainly not alone in this, I will often try to go the library route first—after all, why reinvent the wheel? Then, if I can't find what I need, that's when I'll resort to writing something myself, and while my code sometimes turns out kind of like some of those "Pinterest fails" you've seen online, the resulting visualizations are exactly what I was trying to accomplish.

This section will go over two types of visualization development using code: front-end web libraries and statistical packages. I apologize to those with very little experience in the coding world because this section is about to get more technical than pretty much any of the rest of this book will. Teaching the basics of coding is well outside my purview, and you wouldn't want to learn it from me anyway. Rest assured, we will not be doing any coding in this book, so if this is way outside your comfort zone, then you are welcome to skip to section 1.5.4.

FRONT-END WEB LIBRARIES

Front-end web development is pretty much synonymous with JavaScript these days. If you are okay with not fully understanding when the different pieces of your code are going to run, then you should be quite successful with JavaScript's asynchronous nature.

One of the most popular and powerful data visualization libraries for JavaScript is the free and open-source d3.js, also known as D3 or d3, which stands for "Data-Driven Documents." Created by Michael Bostock, Vadim Ogievetsky, and Jeffrey Heer of Stanford University's Stanford Visualization Group, it was released in 2011. As of this writing, Bostock is still by far the most active contributor to the d3 repository on GitHub, at https://github.com/d3/d3. It uses Scalable Vector Graphics (SVG), HTML5, and CSS standards and can be seen in action all over the web, such as in visualizations by *The New York Times*.

Figure 1.9 shows my fruit data again, but this time in as simple a bar chart as I could manage to make in d3. Creating the chart itself only took about 50 lines of code, which sounds like a lot, but d3 can be a bit wordy.

Earlier versions of d3 were rather monolithic in nature, where you had to import the entire library even if you only wanted to use a few pieces of it. When I first started using it, I would create entire web pages just using the d3 syntax (except for the barebones needed to create a blank HTML object). It was my gateway into JavaScript, and any front-end developer will tell you that this is an incredibly weird way to learn the language.

Nowadays, developers can use d3 in a piecemeal fashion, choosing only the components they need or want to use to create their visualizations. This makes it much easier to work within web frameworks such as React or Angular because, otherwise, there is a power struggle for control of the page once the code is running in a browser.

Fuyu Persimmons

Mangos

Peaches & Nectarines

Bananas

Kiwis

Apples

Oranges

Figure 1.9   A basic bar chart created in d3.js

Personally, I love using d3, which is why I chose it to make many of the graphics for this book. It has a rather steep learning curve, but when you finally internalize its patterns and ways of doing things, as a developer, you feel like the entire world is at your fingertips, and there's nothing you can't do or can't make.

STATISTICAL PACKAGES

If JavaScript and its asynchrony aren't your jam, perhaps you'd prefer Python or R. While Python is an entire programming language, and R is a software environment specifically made for statistical analysis, both are free and open source, have a cult-like following among coders, and are great for data viz practitioners. I'm in Camp Python myself, as that's what I started using in my undergraduate physics courses a hundred years ago, even though I've dabbled a little bit with R in the interim. Both R and Python have very friendly and approachable syntax, hence their considerable popularity. If you're a statistician or data scientist, you probably already know R, and if you're not, I'd wager you'd prefer Python. As for libraries to use in each, R users adore their ggplot/ggplot2 (which you may have noticed in figure 1.6 about data viz tools) and Shiny, while Python users have many other options, including Seaborn, Plotly, and Matplotlib.

Figure 1.10 shows my fruit data but this time brought to you by Python's Matplotlib library and only about 18 lines of code, including 9 lines of my fruit data. I should note here, however, that these bars are not horizontal because the example I found for that was tremendously more complicated. Such complexity would have defeated the purpose of this exercise, so I opted against it.

One thing I really enjoy about Python is the massive homage to the British comedy troupe Monty Python. While I am generally more of a Mel Brooks fan, I do appreciate all the little Easter eggs found throughout the Python language and documentation. One such example is the built-in IDE (Integrated Development Environment) called IDLE, which they say stands for Integrated Development and Learning Environment, but coincidentally, Eric Idle was one of the troupe members. Wink, wink! I think I might be one of the only people left on Earth who still knows about IDLE due to the hugely popular Jupyter and IPython Notebooks.

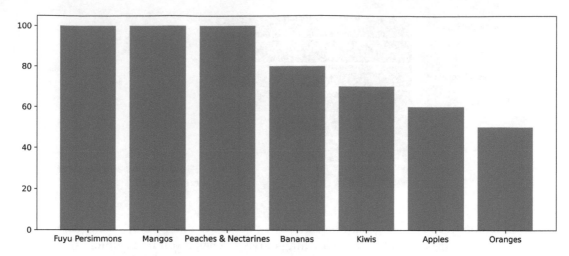

Figure 1.10   A bar chart created in Python's Matplotlib library, using its defaults

If you made it to the end of this section, give yourself a nice pat on the back because you made it through what is easily the most technical part of this book. Well done, you! And just to reiterate, this book will not be forcing any coding on you, so if you want to use code to create visualizations, then more power to you. If you'd rather use something else, there are plenty of other options.

1.5.4   *Design software*

Moving on from coding, we come to the final and least computational way of creating visualizations on a computer: design software. Before we get into the details of which software does what, this is as good a place as any to introduce the idea of raster versus vector images.

Under the hood, *raster images* are just a bunch of colored pixels, tiny squares that contain only one color. When you zoom way out, you see them as a coherent picture, much like the pointillist painting in figure 1.11. If a raster image's resolution is low, that means it contains few pixels in 1 square inch, while if the resolution is high, it contains many more pixels in 1 square inch. Some typical file formats for raster images include JPEG, PNG, GIF, and BMP.

In contrast, *vector images* are basically a set of instructions for where an imaginary pen should touch the page and the locations to where it should move until the pen is instructed where it should lift off the page. It's a set of *paths* that may or may not be filled with color, as well as instructions about the breadth and color of the stroke the pen makes, if any at all. Some typical file formats for vector images include SVG, EPS, and PDF.

The greatest thing about vector graphics is that resolution means very little to them—they can be scaled up or down ad nauseam and still maintain their fidelity because it's all about the pen's relative location on the page as it is drawing. As you

Figure 1.11 *A Sunday on La Grande Jatte*, Georges Seurat, 1884. The inset shows how the individual points of paint are similar to the pixels of a raster image. (Georges Seurat, Public domain, via Wikimedia Commons)

might imagine, a filled-in shape with no stroke will scale differently than a pen stroke because the width of the pen stroke is still specified in a constant number of pixels, as demonstrated in figure 1.12.

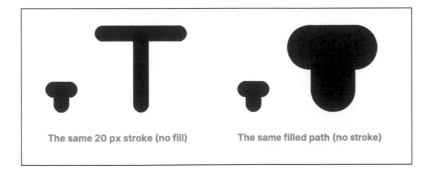

Figure 1.12 The difference between scaling a stroke (on the left) and scaling a path (on the right)

The takeaway here is not that one image type is better than the other but simply that they are different. I said all that to point out that the different design software applications out there typically specialize in manipulating either raster or vector images, not both. Adobe Photoshop is the go-to solution for creating and editing raster images, while Adobe Illustrator is a classic solution for creating and editing vector images. At an enterprise level, while many design departments will have Adobe licenses, Adobe hasn't done an amazing job at making it easy for designers to collaborate with each other or with stakeholders. Figma is thus my favorite solution for creating and editing vector images, including exporting them as raster images when necessary.

Figma can be used in a web browser on any device, or a desktop app is available to paid license holders. It has a freemium payment model, meaning that without paying, you can use nearly all the full features of the software in a browser, but you are limited in how many design files you can create and how you collaborate with others.

I adore using Figma for its intuitive interface and its cross-platform availability, but when I do collaborate on a file, that's when it really shines. You and any number of users can be in the same file simultaneously, making edits and seeing each other's changes (and even cursors) in real time! There is also a robust commenting feature where other collaborators can be tagged and notified, and then, they are taken directly to the place on the (infinite) canvas where the comment was left.

Not only does Figma excel at vector images and collaboration, but it's also a great prototyping tool, so it's perfect for the entire design process, from wireframing all the way through to high-fidelity, interactive prototypes. When you make something in Figma, you can click on any element and see the appropriate CSS (Cascading Style Sheets, which is the main way that the web is styled, including colors, animation, text alignment, and fonts, among many other things) tags to style final web elements exactly as shown in the mockup. It's a dream for front-end web development.

Finally, many of the professional data viz practitioners, like those who make amazingly bespoke one-time visualizations for major news outlets, choose to create their visualizations in d3 for its handling of data. Then, they import the resulting SVG into Adobe Illustrator or Figma where they can do any fine-tuning that was too difficult or they chose not to do using code.

Figure 1.13 is the result of taking the d3 bar chart from figure 1.9 and doing some Very Bad Things to it in a matter of minutes in Figma:

- Made the fruit names bold and colored them purple
- Right-justified the fruit names
- Added drop shadow and rounded corners to the bars
- Filled the bars with a tri-color angular gradient (don't try this at home, kids!)

Could I have accomplished all that craziness in d3? For sure, but I wanted to prove that you can do amazing things very quickly and easily in Figma.

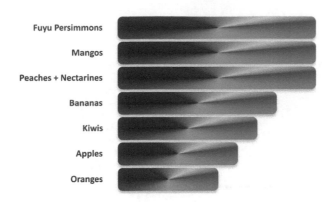

Figure 1.13   The bar chart created in d3 and updated in Figma

Summary

- Data visualization, which is how we communicate information in a visual manner, is everywhere!
- *Knowing your audience* is the most important thing to remember throughout the entire process of making a visualization.
- Data viz has nearly always been around, from charting the locations of stars on cave walls and hand-drawing graphs that drive massive change to using computers to put the power to create and understand data visualization in the hands of everyone who wants it.
- When it comes to tools, there is generally a pretty direct tradeoff between ease of use and degree of control over the final product:
  - Spreadsheets are widely available and easy to use, but you have the least amount of control over what your viz output is like.
  - However, coding gives you complete control, but it has a much higher barrier for entry.
- A powerful and easy way to get even more control over a viz output in the form of a vector image, or SVG, is to import the SVG into a program such as Adobe Illustrator or Figma and make design changes there. However, this only works for one-time visualizations and not something recreated each time a web page is loaded.
- With so many tool options out there for digitally creating data visualizations, there should certainly be at least one that would suit you well. Remember, though, just because a tool is wildly popular doesn't mean it's the right one for the job or the right one for you.

How we perceive information

This chapter covers

- Preattentive attributes of color, form, spatial positioning, and movement
- Gestalt principles of enclosure, proximity, similarity, symmetry, connection, closure, and continuity

Your brain is truly a wonder. How it works together with your eyes to decode patterns of light into actual information and data is, of course, well beyond the scope of this book. What we will talk about in this chapter is how your brain prioritizes and categorizes those patterns of light passed in through the eyes. We'll learn about preattentive attributes, which are the things our brains notice first about what our eyes see (e.g., color, form, spatial position, and movement). Then, we'll talk about the gestalt principles, which you might be surprised to learn were not named after a Mr. Gestalt but are instead ways that we see many parts come together as something more than their sum: enclosure, proximity, similarity, symmetry, connection, closure, and continuity.

2.1 Preattentive attributes

If I had a dollar for every time I had a stakeholder or a client tell me, "Just give me a table because I just want to see the numbers" or "Just show me the data, and that's all I need," I'd probably be able to retire early and become a stay-at-home pet mom.

Okay, maybe it hasn't been that many times, but as a lover of data visualization, it makes my soul shrivel up and die a little bit each time I hear it. So, your first lesson in data visualization is that your stakeholders and clients don't always know how to verbalize exactly what they want you, as the data viz expert, to do for them. If you immediately give them what they ask for without any kind of probing questions or discovery, chances are good that your viz won't really answer their underlying questions. Case in point, if you just blindly comply and give your stakeholder that plain data table, they're likely to get a little bit overwhelmed when their brain sees that uniform wall of numbers. If you instead make a visualization of it, what you're really doing there is using the preattentive attributes of color, form, spatial position, and movement. These attributes lend a helping hand to your stakeholder's brain as it goes about decoding and ingesting the information that you're presenting to them.

2.1.1 Color

For example, let's say you are working with a major bicycle rental company in London, and they want to look back at how popular their bike rentals were in 2017. They are very particular and ask you to make the crosstab shown in figure 2.1 about the

hour	Sunday	Monday	Tuesday	Wednesday	Thursday	Friday	Saturday
0	27	28	23	27	27	23	24
1	28	31	27	32	30	27	27
2	29	41	31	35	43	34	27
3	28	30	30	32	25	28	29
4	32	25	22	23	22	32	34
5	29	18	16	16	17	19	25
6	26	14	13	13	13	13	22
7	20	15	14	14	14	14	19
8	22	15	15	15	15	14	18
9	24	17	15	16	15	15	21
10	27	22	19	19	19	20	24
11	29	25	21	20	21	22	25
12	29	23	19	19	19	20	26
13	30	23	19	18	19	20	28
14	30	24	21	22	21	22	28
15	29	24	20	21	22	22	29
16	27	20	18	19	19	20	28
17	27	17	16	17	18	18	26
18	26	18	16	17	18	19	25
19	24	18	16	17	18	20	23
20	23	17	15	17	17	19	23
21	22	18	15	19	18	20	23
22	21	18	15	18	18	22	23
23	23	20	15	19	19	22	24

Figure 2.1   Crosstab showing the average duration of bike rentals in minutes by hour of the day and day of the week. Powered by Transport for London (TfL) Open Data. Contains OS data © Crown copyright and database rights 2016 and Geomni UK Map data © and database rights (2019)

average duration of their bike rentals by hour of the day in the rows and day of the week in the columns. They want to know when people are taking short trips, about 16 minutes or less. Skeptic that you are, you look at the table you've just created before handing it off to the client and wonder if you can even tell how many time slots are 16 minutes or less.

Not a super fun exercise, right? Then you remember reading about preattentive attributes and decide to throw a little color in there to show which time slots had durations less than or equal to 16 minutes, as shown in figure 2.2.

hour	Sunday	Monday	Tuesday	Wednesday	Thursday	Friday	Saturday
0	27	28	23	27	27	23	24
1	28	31	27	32	30	27	27
2	29	41	31	35	43	34	27
3	28	30	30	32	25	28	29
4	32	25	22	23	22	32	34
5	29	18	16	16	17	19	25
6	26	14	13	13	13	13	22
7	20	15	14	14	14	14	19
8	22	15	15	15	15	14	18
9	24	17	15	16	15	15	21
10	27	22	19	19	19	20	24
11	29	25	21	20	21	22	25
12	29	23	19	19	19	20	26
13	30	23	19	18	19	20	28
14	30	24	21	22	21	22	28
15	29	24	20	21	22	22	29
16	27	20	18	19	19	20	28
17	27	17	16	17	18	18	26
18	26	18	16	17	18	19	25
19	24	18	16	17	18	20	23
20	23	17	15	17	17	19	23
21	22	18	15	19	18	20	23
22	21	18	15	18	18	22	23
23	23	20	15	19	19	22	24

Figure 2.2   The same crosstab as in figure 2.1, but with the values less than or equal to 16 marked in red

That's so much better! When we use color judiciously, a story immediately emerges because your brain sees and recognizes the color before you even realize it: the bike rides tended to be the shortest during the morning commute hours on weekdays and, for some reason, also on Tuesday evenings. If you'd just given the client the plain old table of numbers they'd requested and hadn't gone to the (very small) trouble of adding color, they would have been hard-pressed to see that story so easily. Using color like this is great for representing categorical or qualitative information, such as denoting sales regions and whether a number is larger or smaller than a threshold. I should note here, however, that using only color as an indicator is not a great practice because some people have difficulty distinguishing colors. In this example, the color could be paired with something else (e.g., font size) to help draw attention. In any case, such changes can make clients eternally grateful to you and vow to involve you earlier in the design process for the next piece of the project.

2.1.2   Form

Now that you've impressed the client with your design knowledge, they want to see what you can do to help them find more patterns in their weekday rental data. Instead of looking at rental duration, they now want you to look at the number of rentals on all weekdays put together.

To start, you filter out Saturday and Sunday and show the total number of rentals by hour, which you can find in figure 2.3. The 8 am hour jumps out at you pretty quickly as the most popular time of day for weekday rentals, purely because it's nearly 100 times larger than the least popular time, with seven digits instead of five. Because the numbers are all aligned to one side and in the same units (e.g., we're not comparing 1 million to 529,000), you can mostly tell just from their length (form) that the morning commute picks up quite quickly in comparison to the rest of the day. But how can you further home in on the real underlying patterns here?

0	51,196
1	29,290
2	17,992
3	11,705
4	12,255
5	32,437
6	167,861
7	525,615
8	1,006,436
9	529,435
10	264,990
11	257,442
12	326,321
13	336,133
14	324,030
15	353,452
16	482,249
17	863,976
18	789,263
19	460,393
20	287,209
21	198,057
22	152,234
23	101,425

Figure 2.3   Crosstab showing the total number of weekday (not including Saturday and Sunday) rentals by hour of the day

You could try the color trick again, and that might work, but using color alone isn't the best way to tell such a story. Instead, you decide to turn them into bars (figure 2.4).

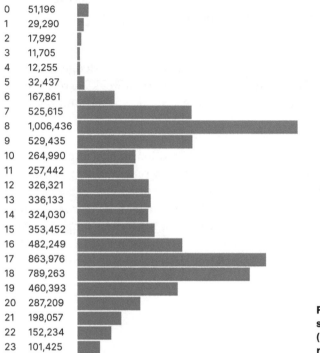

0	51,196
1	29,290
2	17,992
3	11,705
4	12,255
5	32,437
6	167,861
7	525,615
8	1,006,436
9	529,435
10	264,990
11	257,442
12	326,321
13	336,133
14	324,030
15	353,452
16	482,249
17	863,976
18	789,263
19	460,393
20	287,209
21	198,057
22	152,234
23	101,425

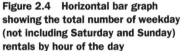

Figure 2.4   Horizontal bar graph showing the total number of weekday (not including Saturday and Sunday) rentals by hour of the day

It's easy to see that the morning rentals ramp up quickly from nearly nothing, while evening rides taper off more gradually as the days wane and Londoners ride home from the pub or a late night at work. Using form like this (i.e., using the size of an element) is a great way to represent quantitative information, especially when using a linear scale (as opposed to a non-linear scale like a logarithmic scale).

2.1.3   *Spatial positioning*

The next question the bike rental company is asking may be obvious to you by now because you probably have it yourself (I know I do). To confirm our commute hypothesis, we need to know where these weekday bike rentals start and end.

Lo and behold, we do have starting and ending latitudes and longitudes in the dataset. Presented with geographic data like this, the first thing a data vizzer usually thinks is to make a map, and who doesn't love a great map? After all, it makes sense because, as we learned in chapter 1, data visualization has deep roots in cartography. So, let's define commute hour rides as those beginning between 7 and 9 am, as well as between 4 and 7 pm because we can see in figure 2.4 that these are the most popular times. Then, we can make a bubble map, situating the bubbles at the locations of the starting and ending rental stations, sizing them by the percentage of all "commute hour" rides that started or ended at that station, respectively. The resulting map is in figure 2.5, with starting stations on the left and ending stations on the right, morning rides on the top, and evening rides on the bottom. All told, rides starting in the morning are in the upper left, and ending in the evening are in the lower right, with the other two permutations in between.

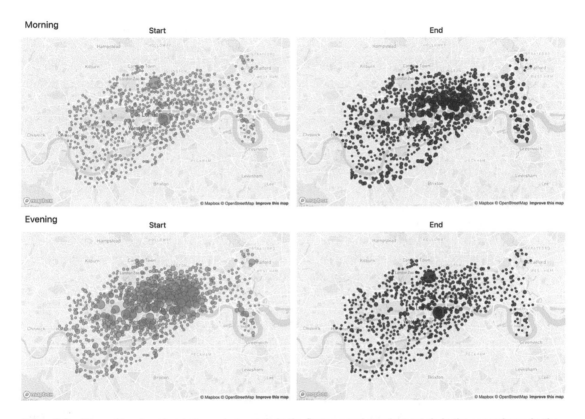

Figure 2.5 Maps of London showing morning rentals in the first row and evening rentals in the second row. In the columns, we have the locations of the starting and ending rental stations on the left and right, respectively. Thus, the starting locations for morning rentals are in the upper left, the ending stations for the evening rentals are in the lower right. The other two permutations are at their respective locations in between. (Base map © Mapbox © OpenStreetMap. See https://www.mapbox.com/about/maps/ and https://www.openstreetmap.org/copyright.)

In the top-left corner where the morning rentals begin, we see a mostly even distribution of circle sizes throughout London, but in the top right, where the morning rentals end, we see that larger circles are more concentrated in Central London. On the bottom, we see pretty much the opposite trend as people return home: a higher portion of rentals begins toward the center of the city, and they end rather evenly distributed in the outskirts.

The use of spatial position can best represent quantitative information such as a latitude and longitude, or an *x* and *y* value in the case of a scatter plot, but it can also be used to separate categories, as we'll see later when we cover gestalt principles.

2.1.4   *Movement*

Let's say, just for the sake of a good and well-rounded data visualization education, that the London bicycle rental company really wants to grab people's attention. They love the work you've done with color, form, and spatial positioning, so for this final piece of their project, they want you to pull out all the stops. Go nuts. Throw all the spaghetti at the wall to see what sticks. You can do no wrong in their eyes, and so you decide that this is a great chance to use that final preattentive attribute: movement. (I have never had a client or stakeholder ask me for an animated visualization, but please be a good sport and play along.)

One rather controversial example of the use of motion in data visualization is the racing bar chart phenomenon that took the data viz world by storm in 2019 and 2020. If you want to see a neat example, check out the one created by Mike Bostock of d3 fame at https://observablehq.com/@d3/bar-chart-race. Sure, racing bar charts aren't great for analysis, but they definitely get people's attention, and in my book (because that's what you're reading right now), something that so thoroughly grips the attention of so many is worth giving a chance. But I don't want to make any enemies here, so before we get back to the client, let's look at another, less controversial, example of using movement—Gapminder's World Health Chart, made famous by Swedish physician Hans Rosling (https://www.gapminder.org/fw/world-health-chart/). It's a bubble chart that depicts for each year between 1799 and (as of this writing; it's updated periodically) 2022 a country's average income per person on the *x*-axis and life expectancy on the *y*-axis, with a bubble for each of 200 countries. The bubbles are sized by the country's population and colored by their region of the world. Pressing the play button below the chart, you as the viewer quickly become transfixed, watching bubbles rise and fall, swaying this way and that as the years tick by. You watch with bated breath as life expectancy all over the world dips dramatically in the late 1910s and again in the early 1940s as the Spanish Flu and World Wars I and II go by. It makes one wonder what this plot will look like in another 10, 20, or 50 years.

With this inspiration fresh in our minds, let's take a big cue from the World Health Chart and add some animation to our bubble map. You can see the resulting viz on my GitHub site: https://callmedeeray.github.io/animated-map/. Because the original dataset is so very massive, I've limited it to just the morning commute hours on a single day in 2017.

As you can see, movement isn't great for detailed analysis, but it is captivating. With great power comes great responsibility, so use it wisely. All of that said (and done), though, outright animation like this isn't the only way to incorporate movement into your visualizations. Some tools, such as Tableau and d3, have a built-in feature that lets you animate transitions when the data changes, such as when a filter is selected or deselected. In some cases, this can be distracting, but in others, it's quite useful, so use your best judgment and when all else fails, ask your users whether they find such animations to be beneficial.

Now that we've finished our client project and have exhausted our list of preattentive attributes, we'll move on to discussing gestalt principles of design, which will help us understand how to organize elements to help convey a message.

2.2 Gestalt principles

You might be surprised, like I was, to learn that gestalt principles are not named for a Mr. Gestalt. Instead, *gestalt* is a German word meaning, "shape or form," or "unified whole," but it is one of those words that doesn't translate very well or directly into English. Gestalt is better defined by the *Merriam–Webster Dictionary* as, "something that is made of many parts and yet is somehow more than or different from the combination of its parts" (e.g., seeing a cloud in the sky that looks like an animal). In the realm of design, we use gestalt principles to describe how the brain recognizes patterns and simplifies complexity as we perceive the world around us.

I do not claim that this is an exhaustive list. Indeed, when one types into their favorite search engine, "What are the gestalt principles?" the search results can't even agree on their number (figure 2.6).

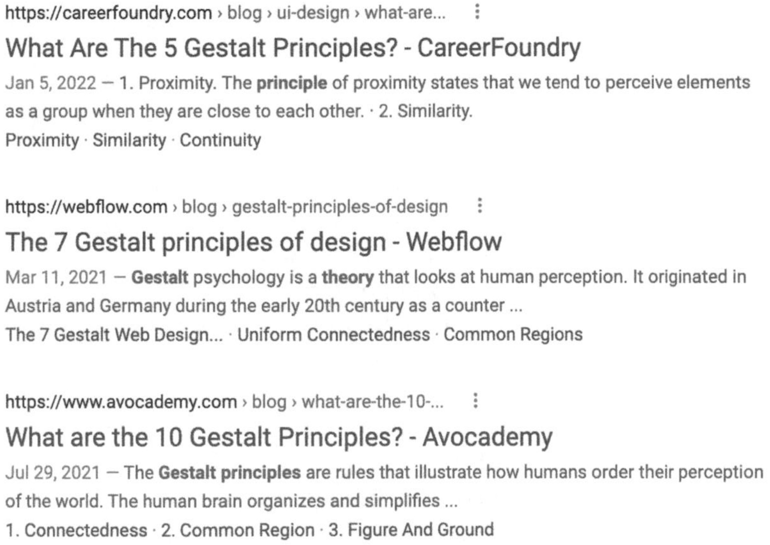

https://careerfoundry.com › blog › ui-design › what-are... ⋮

What Are The 5 Gestalt Principles? - CareerFoundry

Jan 5, 2022 — 1. Proximity. The **principle** of proximity states that we tend to perceive elements as a group when they are close to each other. · 2. Similarity.
Proximity · Similarity · Continuity

https://webflow.com › blog › gestalt-principles-of-design ⋮

The 7 Gestalt principles of design - Webflow

Mar 11, 2021 — **Gestalt** psychology is a **theory** that looks at human perception. It originated in Austria and Germany during the early 20th century as a counter ...
The 7 Gestalt Web Design... · Uniform Connectedness · Common Regions

https://www.avocademy.com › blog › what-are-the-10-... ⋮

What are the 10 Gestalt Principles? - Avocademy

Jul 29, 2021 — The **Gestalt principles** are rules that illustrate how humans order their perception of the world. The human brain organizes and simplifies ...
1. Connectedness · 2. Common Region · 3. Figure And Ground

Figure 2.6 Search results for the query "What are the gestalt principles?"

2.2.1   *Enclosure*

Elements tend to be grouped together when they are in the same enclosed space. If there's anything an organizer likes to do, it's putting things in boxes. I confess, I adore watching those home-organizing shows on my favorite streaming service where they come into a person's house, get rid of their old junk, and then put the remaining things in clear containers on shelves, thus making it easy to see everything that's available. And voilà, people are *so* happy! There is something so pleasing about enclosure because it helps our brains understand that these things go together. Like goes with like, as demonstrated by figure 2.7, with them all being in a box, living in harmony.

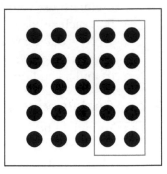

Figure 2.7   Principle of enclosure

The same goes with data visualization. As soon as you put a box around something, you are saying, "These things are more related to each other than to all that other stuff that's outside the box."

2.2.2   *Proximity*

Elements tend to be grouped together when they are near each other. Even if objects are just close together, regardless of whether they're enclosed in a box, they are seen to be related or part of the same group (figure 2.8). Think about the last time you counted the change in your piggy bank. First, you dumped all the change out on the table, and then you separated it into groups by how much each coin is worth. By putting all the quarters close to each other on your left, the dimes together in front of you, the nickels off to the right, and so on, you got the job done. You didn't need boxes because your brain knew that groups of coins that were closer together were more related than those far apart.

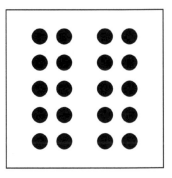

Figure 2.8   Principle of proximity

It is the same when you're putting together a visualization, such as when you have a chart, and you want to pair it with explanatory text or annotations. You would, of course, place the text close to the corresponding chart (or the labels by the corresponding data points) because, that way, your audience will naturally pair the text with the correct visualization.

2.2.3 Similarity

Elements tend to be grouped together when they have a similar appearance. Similarly (see what I did there?), when things appear alike, we naturally see them as being related or part of the same group. This works really well in things like scatter plots, where you might have several categories (or dimensions, as we'll discuss when we learn about the anatomy of data) that you want to plot on the same set of axes to see how they are correlated. If you represent each category with a different shape, your audience will immediately recognize that all the circles are one category, the triangles another, the squares are yet another, and so forth. They don't have to be near each other or even be the same size

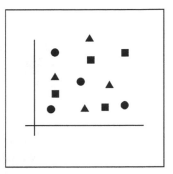

Figure 2.9 Principle of similarity

because as long as the shapes are the same, the brain will group them together as one category (figure 2.9).

2.2.4 Symmetry

Elements tend to be grouped together when they are symmetrical with one another. When you think of symmetry, you might only think of mirror images, but there are three different types of symmetry: reflection, rotation, and translation.

REFLECTION

Reflectional symmetry is the mirror image kind: when thing B is a mirror image of thing A, your brain naturally sees the two as related. This kind of symmetry is in play when you make a butterfly chart, one of my personal favorites. If you have two categories of data—for example, two age groups such as Millennials and Gen Z—and you wanted to show a (fictitious) histogram of how many avocados each group purchases in a single month, you might make something similar to figure 2.10.

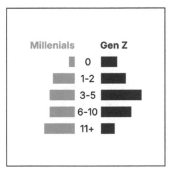

Figure 2.10 Principle of symmetry: reflection

ROTATION

Rotational symmetry is where things B, C, D, and E result from rotating thing A around a common axis at regular intervals. This is the symmetry used in radial charts, which use a polar coordinate system (radius, angle) instead of Cartesian (x, y). This is well-suited for cyclic data, such as months and seasons of the year, or hours of the day. In our London bicycle rental example, we could have made a radial bar chart with the hours of the day going around in a circle like the one in figure 2.11, which also looks like one of Florence Nightingale's rose charts. (However, just because you can, doesn't mean you should.)

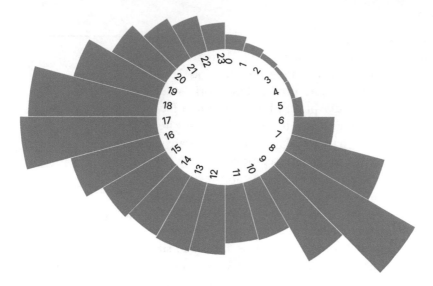

Figure 2.11   Principle of symmetry: rotation

TRANSLATION

Translational symmetry is where things B, C, D, and E result from basically stamping thing A throughout the page at regular intervals, while maintaining the same orientation. This is the kind of symmetry used in small-multiples graphs, which are great when you need to show a simple graph (line charts work great for this) for many categories of data, such as countries of the world or companies in a particular industry. It works best when the individual values are not as important as the relative differences between the categories because it's difficult to see the detail, but your brain inherently likes to look for patterns in the sea of charts.

One of my favorite examples of translational symmetry is Ivett Kovacs' viz about gender and ethnic disparities in tech companies (figure 2.12). There is a lot of information packed into a relatively small space here, so even though it is complex and takes some time to understand, that is all made possible by the consistency of the translational symmetry. This one is not an "everyday" visualization at which you'd want to have a quick glance. It's a more artistic and bespoke viz that begs you to spend some time examining and internalizing its details. I really encourage you to do just that with the interactive version online.

2.2.5   *The 3 Cs: Connection, closure, and continuity*

I've chosen to group these three together, not just because they are so nicely alliterative, but because when you come right down to it, they're very closely related.

CONNECTION

Elements tend to be grouped together when their forms are connected to one another. When elements are connected, your brain doesn't have to make a far leap to guess that the

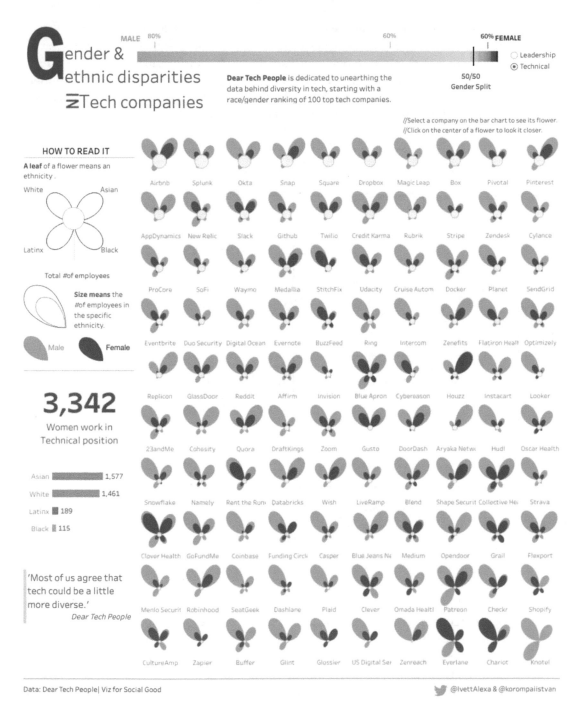

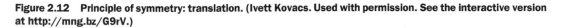

Figure 2.12 Principle of symmetry: translation. (Ivett Kovacs. Used with permission. See the interactive version at http://mng.bz/G9rV.)

elements are correlated and belong to the same group. This is most easily demonstrated in one of the simplest types of data visualizations—the humble line chart—which is created by plotting points of data and then connecting them with a line. If you have two categories of data that you are plotting, of course, you wouldn't connect the different categories to each other! You'd connect the dots of one category with one line, and the other category would get another line, keeping the related elements together (figure 2.13).

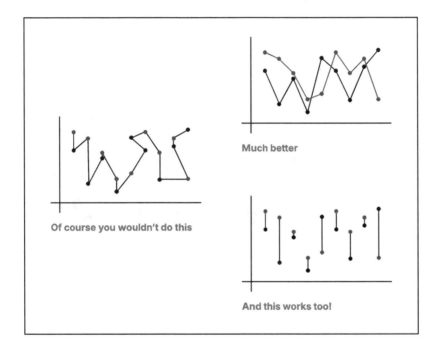

Figure 2.13   Principle of connection

CLOSURE

Our brains unconsciously complete incomplete elements. Your brain prefers to see complete shapes, so it fills in gaps between elements to make a whole picture. You might not realize it, but you've encountered this quite a bit in everyday life, for example, in the form of logo design. Ever seen the logos for IBM, WWF, Adobe, or the USA Network? (While we don't have permission to reproduce those mega-corporation logos here, just find them with your favorite search engine if you want to see what I'm talking about.) Notice how even though there are no outlines, you can easily read the letters in IBM, and see the panda in the WWF logo, the A in Adobe's logo, and the S in the USA Network logo. In data viz, this principle is illustrated best with a donut chart that's showing the percentage of completion, such as in figure 2.14. Although there's a chunk missing, you know it's a part of a full circle.

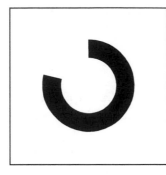

Figure 2.14   Principle of closure

CONTINUITY

Elements tend to be grouped together when their forms are aligned along a line or curve. This principle has so many practical uses in design and data viz! For instance, even the very text in this book follows the same principle: there are no lines drawn under the words, but because the letters all have the same implied baseline, you're able to read them just fine. One application in data visualization is that if you're presented with a bar chart, regardless of whether the bars extend horizontally or vertically, it's much easier to look at and understand if the bars are sorted in descending order of their length, as long as the order of the categories is not actually meaningful. (You wouldn't want to sort a time series bar chart by length because the times would be all mixed up then!) The principle of continuity works both at the base of the bars in a straight line and at the ends of the bars in a diagonal line.

A small note here: you could technically sort the bars in ascending order as well; however, typically, the biggest bar is the most important, so do your users a favor and put the most important stuff in the sweetest spot of your visualization, which is the top if the bars extend horizontally, or the left if the bars extend vertically (figure 2.15). More about that sweet spot in later chapters.

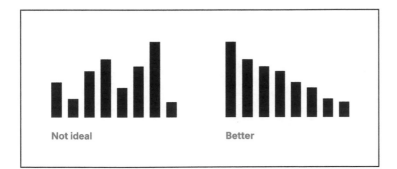

Figure 2.15   Principle of continuity

And no, you're not imagining things: this is indeed very similar to the principle of closure. You could think of them such that continuity applies to open paths, and closure applies to closed paths.

Summary

- The preattentive attribute of color can help you draw a user's attention to important values in a sea of otherwise similar data points or help distinguish qualitative categories of information.
- You can use the attribute of form, such as an element's length or size, to easily represent quantitative information. Similarly, spatial position is typically great for representing geographic location or the numerical value of a metric in a scatter plot.
- Movement is a tricky preattentive attribute to use well in data viz, so it should be used sparingly for maximum effect.
- The gestalt principles of enclosure and proximity are literal ways of grouping objects or elements to help your users see that the elements are correlated.
- Similar objects, such as those with the same shape, are naturally seen as members of the same group. This would be especially powerful when combined with reflectional, rotational, and translational symmetry, which help your users quickly wrap their brains around the information in your visualization by establishing repetitive patterns.
- The gestalt principle of connection tells us that our brains naturally see connections as indications that a group of elements is correlated. This stems from the principles of closure and continuity to the point that we unknowingly fill in gaps found in both closed and open paths to complete the objects.

It's all about the data

3

This chapter covers

- Where and how to acquire data
- Understanding data at a fundamental level
- Describing data values (discrete vs. continuous, sequential vs. categorical)
- Storing data in rows and columns
- Nesting data in key–value pairs

In chapter 2, we learned all about some basic design principles and concepts we'll be using throughout this book, but this chapter is all about the data. To ensure everyone has the same basic understanding of data fundamentals, we'll first touch on where you might find data out in the wild. Next, we'll answer the question "What is data?" and talk about several basic data types. After that, we'll learn how to describe the values of data and whether they are discrete or continuous and sequential or categorical. Finally, we'll cover the two main types of data structures you'll encounter in your visualization journey: tables and nested data.

3.1   *Where you get data*

Somehow, you've got some free time outside of work, where you don't typically have access to data managed by IT and then handed to you on a platter. With that time, you want to make a visualization, and I say, good for you, my fellow nerd! Now what?

The initial step when making a visualization could go one of two ways:

1 You have an awesome idea, a story you want to tell, but you need some data.
2 You have some awesome data, but you'll need to dig around to find a story.

Sometimes, the data comes first and sometimes the story, which is the classic chicken-and-egg problem. For now, we're going to focus on when you already have the story or idea, so the next hurdle is figuring out where you get the data you need.

3.1.1   *Find some open data*

Enter open data! If you've never heard of it before, open data is data that is out there on the internet, available for anyone to use, and it's basically the best thing ever for those of us who like to viz in our spare time. Sometimes, this data is only made available under certain terms and conditions, such as only being available for noncommercial use, and sometimes it's allowed to be used anywhere but requires attribution. Thus, if you find yourself in possession of some open data, be sure to check the terms and conditions before blasting it out to the world or charging others to see your super-awesome vizzes. For example, I have a few visualizations in my portfolio, some of my very favorite passion projects, but the subject of these visualizations is someone else's intellectual property, so I couldn't include those vizzes in this book despite the data being out there and available for anyone to see.

Open data might be a file to be downloaded, or it might come in the form of an API. An *application programming interface*, or API for short, is basically a website meant solely for computers, not people, to consume. When you write a program that interacts with or talks to an API, that is called "making an API call." In my experience, APIs are like people: each one is different, and each one has its own foibles, weirdness, and idiosyncrasies. Most programming languages have their own ways of programmatically making API calls, so whatever your preferred flavor of coding, there should be a straightforward way to make your code go and grab the data you want.

To find open data, simply query your preferred search engine for your topic plus "open data" at the end of the search string, and then go from there. I have listed a few of my favorite resources in the appendix.

I should note here that you might even be able to freely connect to an API to get your own data. There are many apps out there which make your data a part of their product, such as health and exercise apps, and some of them have open APIs that you can call to programmatically obtain large or small swaths of your own data from their servers.

3.1.2 Buy it

Perhaps you found a data set online, but it's not free. While it might seem strange to purchase data, these data sets are often very clean and well-maintained, with good data dictionaries meant to help you understand what each field in the data is all about. After all, you usually get what you pay for, right? In some cases, the license you purchase might even include updates in perpetuity, meaning your viz can stay up to date as long as you maintain the license.

One example of a for-purchase data set that might be *interesting* is points of interest (see what I did there?) like you might find at Carto (www.carto.com). This could include location information for restaurants, public parks, monuments, sight-seeing opportunities, or even collections of World's Largest stuff, such as the World's Largest Basket, which can be found in the Newark, Ohio, headquarters of the Longaberger Basket Company. The building is literally a basket, and I've seen it with my own two eyes. Mind you, I was just driving by and not going to see the World's Largest Basket on purpose. I swear!

3.1.3 Gather it yourself

Maybe your project is of such a personal nature or so very original that the data just isn't out there at all, neither for free nor for purchase, nor even in an API of your favorite app. In this case, you must gather it yourself. Once you figure out how to do so (be that writing a survey and collecting responses; web scraping, which is writing a bit of code that programmatically goes online and pulls information off a web page; writing down information by hand; or something else entirely), then, it's merely a matter of where and how to store it. My favorite place to store data that I'm collecting on my own is Google Sheets because it's available on all my devices, it has some sweet features that other cloud-based spreadsheets don't, and it's totally free.

When collecting data yourself in this way, you'll need to put some thought into your *data model* before you start collecting. The data model is the organizational structure of your data, including the types of data you want to store and how each data point is described.

Think back to chapter 1 and all those bar charts about different types of fruit. Let's take a step back in time to when I decided to collect and record data whenever I ate a piece of fruit so I could make a viz about it later. For the data model, past Desireé decided to note the type of fruit she was eating, the date she ate it, and a score between 1 and 100 denoting how tasty she thought it was, where 1 is absolutely wretched, and 100 is completely divine. And because I like to keep things organized, I probably also added an ID number to the mix to serve as a unique identifier later, should the need arise. In the rest of this chapter, we'll be delving deeply into that data, how we can store it, and how we can describe it. So, let's get started by answering the question, "What is that data, anyway?"

3.2   *Dimensions and measures*

A piece of data, when you get down to it, is a set of information about something. The bits of information I collected about each fruit—the type of fruit, the date I ate it, the taste score, and the ID number—are called the *dimensions* and *measures* of my data.

Dimensions are generally descriptive, telling us about the attributes of a data point, while measures are things one can quantify or easily aggregate, such as adding up or averaging. Knowing that, let's look at the fruity info I collected and decide whether each is a dimension or a measure:

- *Fruit type*—It would be a challenge to add up or average the names of fruits, and it is serving to name (describe) the fruit I ate, so this is surely a dimension.
- *Date eaten*—This one is a bit tricky because I could take the min and max to find the first and most recent dates, respectively, on which I had each type of fruit. However, I wouldn't really call that quantifiable, would you? Dates are typically descriptive, so they're best categorized as dimensions.
- *Taste score*—While one could argue that this is describing the fruit's taste, its purpose here is to be quantifiable. Even though I could technically add it up, that would be rather meaningless, but average (or mean), median, mode, min, max: all those statistics are totally reasonable things to do to a bunch of scores. Decidedly a measure.
- *ID*—It's a number here, but would we really want to aggregate it, such as adding it up or taking its average? No, that wouldn't really mean anything, so it's a dimension.

When making a visualization, you usually need at least one measure, something to quantify, and one dimension, something to describe the quantity that sets it apart from the other quantities. Looking at the fruit data model, you can see intuitively that there are different types of values there. Even though they're both dimensions, you wouldn't treat the fruit type field the same way you'd treat the date field. Once we know our dimensions and measures, it's also important to know exactly what kinds of values go into them because visualization tools, and we, ourselves, will treat them differently based on what data type the values are.

3.3   *A primer of data types*

I'm not going to delve into what's the difference between a float32 and a BigInt (I'll leave that to your own research, dear reader, should you be interested. Also, I didn't collect that much fruit data!), but let's discuss the differences between strings, numbers, dates, and Booleans because they're the building blocks used to make more complex data structures.

3.3.1 Strings

A string is just a bit of text, like a word or a letter. The "fruit type" field in the fruit data is decidedly a string, but all the rest of the fields can be treated as strings, too, usually by enclosing it in quotation marks. The following are some examples of strings:

```
"Athena"
"Fuyu Persimmons"
"L"
"42"
"October 25, 2022"
```

Note that it would *not* be particularly useful to treat the other fields, besides the fruit type, as strings, because strings are always sorted alphabetically, and you usually wouldn't want to sort numbers or dates alphabetically. If you've ever tried to prepend a file name with a number and then sort your files, you'll know that it works great until you get past 9 because you'll get something like this: 1, 10, 11, 2, 3, 4, 5, 6, 7, 8, 9. Knowing that, I'm sure you can imagine the disaster that would ensue from sorting dates alphabetically! So yes, while anything can be treated as a string, you probably want to be careful when doing so, unless it actually has some letters in it.

3.3.2 Numbers

We all know what a number is. Numbers, of course, get special treatment because we can do math to them. For our data visualization purposes, we can separate numbers into integers and decimals—any further categorization, such as BigInt or float32, is basically describing how big the number is or how many decimal places it has.

Just in case you slept through math classes from middle school onwards, integers are whole numbers, that is, numbers that are exactly that value, no more and no less. A decimal, however, has a value in between two whole numbers and can have any level of specificity we want by adding or removing decimal places. When rounding a decimal, any decimal place greater than or equal to 5 is rounded up, and anything less than 5 is rounded down.

In the fruit data, the ID number is an integer (although you wouldn't want to make any calculations with it because it's an identifier). For the taste score, even though I didn't include any decimal places, that can be treated as a decimal, which would be useful if you want to find its average.

3.3.3 Dates

Dates are a little funny, meaning that they can be very tricky, because not all tools or coding languages treat dates as having their own data type. SQL and BI tools do have a data type reserved for dates and datetimes (which are dates paired with times and sometimes time zones). JavaScript on its own, however, does not (dates are just strings there), so you must use either the built-in date *class* or an external library to treat dates correctly. This is because, as we touched on when we talked about strings, dates and date-like things need to be sorted and formatted and converted differently from strings or numbers. You wouldn't want to sort the months of the year in alphabetical order, because that just wouldn't make any sense. Instead, January as a month is its own thing, completely separate from `"January"` as a string.

Beyond sorting, dates and datetimes can be formatted in a myriad of ways, depending on personal or cultural preferences. Here are some examples of the same date in different date formats:

```
January 1, 2022
01 Jan 2022
2022-01-01
01/01/2022
Saturday, January 1, 2022 12:00AM
Fri Dec 31 2021 16:00:00 GMT-0800 (Pacific Standard Time)
2022-01-01T00:00:00.000Z
```

3.3.4   *Booleans*

We don't have any of these in the fruit data, but a Boolean (pronounced like "BOO-lee-uhn") is a humble yet mighty data type. It can have one of two values: true or false. Yes, that's it! Booleans are highly efficient when it comes to data storage and computing, and they're the basis of logical "if" statements such as, "If I see that something is true, then I'm going to do this thing; otherwise, I'm going to do that thing." The importance of this kind of logic in data viz cannot be understated. Need to treat one piece of data like a special little snowflake? Make an if statement. Need to make a really weird filter? Make a really weird if statement. Need to loop through a data set? Even that can be written as an if statement.

Understanding the different data types is vitally important, because within a dimension or measure, all the values must have the same data type, no matter what visualization tool you're using. If you have a dimension with a million numbers, and a single string sneaks in there, then every value in the whole dimension must be treated as a string, which will throw errors in the tool and/or break the viz.

Regardless of whether a bit of information is a dimension or a measure and what data type it is, how we *describe* its values affects how we *visualize* those values, so let's talk about that next.

3.4   *Describing data values*

Beyond knowing something's data type and whether it is a dimension or a measure, it's also important to think more holistically about what values that data might have because that will help steer you toward choosing the best way to visualize it. The two guard rails on the road to visualizing data are whether that data is *discrete* or *continuous* and whether the order of its categories is important, that is, whether it's *sequential* or *categorical.* First let's look at continuity.

3.4.1   Discrete vs. continuous

The differentiation between discrete and continuous information is important, because in data visualization, we tend to gravitate more toward using certain types of charts for discrete information and other types of charts for continuous. (Note: when I talk about discreteness here, I'm talking about information with separate and distinct values, not information that is purposefully subtle, which would be discreet info, and I'm pretty sure that's not a thing.) The opposite of discrete is continuous, meaning information that could have any value anywhere along a spectrum. In the case of the fruit data, the ID numbers are discrete integer values, while the taste score is continuous because it can be either a whole number or a decimal.

Numbers aren't really the only things that can go either way, discrete or continuous. This is also true for dates, times, and datetimes. On a scale of centuries, data that is at a daily level is basically continuous. On a scale of months or even weeks, data that is by the hour or minute is essentially continuous. I'm sure you can think of other examples, even in everyday life, of things that might at first appear discrete but are continuous if you give them more thought, as well as the other way around: things that appear continuous but are discrete.

Remember all the bar charts I made of the fruit data set in chapter 1 and how I didn't make any line charts of it? Also harken back to chapter 2, when we talked about the gestalt principle of connection, that elements tend to be grouped together when their forms are interconnected. That's why line charts are so great for continuous dimensions. If I'd desperately wanted to make a line chart of the fruit data, then it would have been a better choice to plot taste scores over time, which could be a good way to show when certain fruits are at the peak of their season, if I had enough data.

On the other side of the same coin, bar charts are extremely well-suited for discrete dimensions. For pretty much any set of discrete dimensions, like the fruity data set, a bar chart is nearly always a great choice. The golden child of data viz work, bar charts are inordinately versatile and usually very easy to read and make. If I tried to make a line chart by fruit type, as shown in figure 3.1, see how wrong that looks on the left, and how much better it looks as a bar chart on the right.

If you're not sure whether a particular dimension is discrete or continuous, consider how much it would matter if you omitted some labels from the middle of the axis. If the chart still works just fine with only the first and last values labeled, chances are you're dealing with a continuous dimension because gestalt principles tell us that our brains will fill in the missing values. If, however, that missing information is critical for knowing what that data point is, then odds are good that you've got a discrete dimension on your hands. If I'd left off the kiwis (K) label in the bar chart on the right of figure 3.1, there would be no way for you to extrapolate from bananas (B) and apples (A) that the missing label should be kiwis, so the fruit type dimension is definitely discrete.

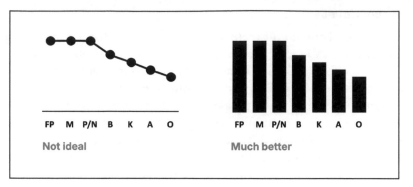

Figure 3.1   The fruit data shown as a line on the left just doesn't work because the fruits aren't continuous, nor could one approximate them as such. On the right, the viz works much better as a bar chart.

3.4.2   *Sequential vs. categorical*

Another way to look at information that is typically in a dimension rather than a measure is whether it is sequential or categorical (i.e., whether the order of its values is important). If a dimension is sequential, the order of the values is so important that it would be weird at best or nonsense at worst to display them out of order, which is why continuous dimensions would only be sequential (but discrete could go either way). The ID numbers of my fruits and the dates I ate each one are sequential examples in the fruit data set, but the birth order of siblings, steps in a sales funnel, levels on a pain scale, and generations are also all examples of sequential data, as well as responses to some survey questions.

Stepping back from fruits for a minute, you have certainly encountered these sequential survey questions, like the one where you are asked how likely you are to recommend a product to a friend or colleague, and you must answer on a scale from 0 to 10. When displaying the number of people choosing each response, that's not the best time to sort your bar graph in descending order of bar length because then you can't see which way people's opinions skew, whether toward the great or the not-so-great.

Net Promoter Score surveys

For the record, that kind of question measures what's called a "Net Promoter Score" or NPS® for short. If you choose 9 or 10, you're a "promoter." If you choose 7 or 8, you're neutral, and if you choose 0–6, you're considered a "detractor." To calculate the overall NPS, the percentage of respondents who were promoters is taken, and then the percentage of those who were detractors is subtracted from it. The remaining percentage is the score, which can go anywhere from 100 (everyone loves the product!) to –100 (everyone hates it!).

A nonnumerical example would be another popular type of survey response called a *Likert scale* (pronounced "LICK-ert"), where you select from five responses that vary in how much you agree with a statement, like the survey question shown in figure 3.2. It was invented by American psychologist Rensis Likert in the 1930s.

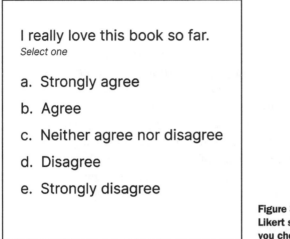

I really love this book so far.
Select one

a. Strongly agree

b. Agree

c. Neither agree nor disagree

d. Disagree

e. Strongly disagree

Figure 3.2 A survey question with Likert scale responses (Also, I hope you chose A.)

We'll cover some interesting ways to visualize this type of survey data in a later chapter, but for now, it's sufficient to say that order matters with these kinds of survey responses. Hence, the response values would be *sequential data.*

If, however, a dimension in our data is not sequential because the order of its values doesn't matter, then it is likely *categorical.* Categorical data is, I'm sure you guessed it, made of *categories.* The type of fruit in the fruit data set is categorical, but also hair or eye color, country, what your coworkers studied in college, whether someone says soda or pop (and from what region they hail), types of restaurants available in your area, and source of traffic to a website are all categories whose sort order doesn't really matter. Categorical data is great to pair with color or shape when you're making a visualization, as long as there aren't more than seven categories (but I try to cut it off at five to be on the safe side). More than that, and not only does the viz get busy and overwhelming, but you'll be hard-pressed to find a palette of colors (or shapes) distinct enough to be accessible; besides, our brains just can't hold that much information in our short-term memory bank. Next time you see a viz with more than seven colors denoting categories, pay attention to how difficult it is to understand what the viz is trying to tell you. In a later chapter, we'll cover how you can handle this situation when you face it, but let's move now to how data is most frequently structured or stored when it's bound for a visualization.

3.5   *Data structures*

While any data engineer will tell you there are plenty more data structures than this, we're just going to cover the two most common formats you'll encounter when making visualizations: *tabular* and *nested*. In my years of viz experience, these two structures matter the most for viz practitioners by a massively wide margin, to the point that it's just not worth covering others here.

3.5.1   *Tabular data*

Far and away, the most common type of data you will encounter as a viz practitioner is *tabular data*, that is, data stored in tables consisting of columns and rows. "Thinking in tables" is something I learned to do early on in my career, when I first became an analyst, and it has helped me tremendously in my visualization work, especially when using BI tools. Learning SQL (which stands for Structured Query Language and is generally pronounced like "sequel," except in the case of the SQLite system, which is pronounced like "ess-cue-light" instead of "sequelite") was instrumental because it forced me to think in terms of rows, columns, joins, and aggregations. So, if you're really looking to do this viz thing, and you'll be using a BI tool, I'd strongly encourage you to take a quick crash course in SQL. It's usually straightforward to find a free course online, and SQL is pretty much the easiest language you'll ever learn.

When storing data in a table, the names of the columns are the names of your dimensions and measures, and the rows contain each data point. Taking our fruit data set and putting it into a table like the one I described in section 3.1.3 results in table 3.1.

Table 3.1   A table of data I hypothetically collected about how tasty individual fruits have been recently

Fruit ID	Fruit type	Taste score	Date eaten
1	Apples	60	Jun 2, 2022
2	Kiwis	70	Jul 9, 2022
3	Mangos	100	Aug 15, 2022
4	Oranges	50	Aug 30, 2022
5	Fuyu Persimmons	50	Sep 17, 2022
6	Peaches + Nectarines	100	Sep 20, 2022
7	Peaches + Nectarines	95	Sep 23, 2022
8	Bananas	80	Sep 24, 2022
9	Bananas	75	Sep 25, 2022
10	Mangos	100	Sep 25, 2022
11	Fuyu Persimmons	100	Oct 3, 2022

When dealing with a data table, the first thing you ought to find out is what is the *grain* or *granularity* of the table, that is, what one row in the table represents. For example, when you open your online banking app and look at all the transactions, each row represents a single transaction. Elsewhere in your banking app, you might have a table with a grain of one row for every day, where each row has details about how many transactions you made and how much money you spent that day (this is *aggregated* data, i.e., data that has been summed up or summarized in some way). On the home-page, you might have a summary or snapshot table that has a grain of one row for each account, showing how much money each has in it today, and perhaps the date and amount of the most recent transaction. It's important to know the grain of these tables because tables with a different granularity are treated differently. In addition, if something goes sideways, and a row of one of these tables is accidentally duplicated, you can imagine the kind of havoc that could wreak on your account totals!

The grain of table 3.1 is one row per fruit because each row is an individual fruit that I ate, an observation of a single fruit, with columns housing the dimensions and measures that describe and quantify that fruit. However, if you remember all the bar charts from chapter 1, none of them had anything about an ID or a date. Instead, they were all based on an aggregated view of the data in table 3.1. If I were to make a table just for the aggregate data, it would look something like table 3.2.

Table 3.2 The aggregated table of data that powers all the bar charts in chapter 1

Fruit	Taste score
Fuyu Persimmons	100
Mangos	100
Peaches + Nectarines	100
Bananas	80
Kiwis	70
Apples	60
Oranges	50

The grain of table 3.2 is one row per type of fruit. When telling someone about this table, I would probably say that this is an aggregate or roll-up table, because it's the result of aggregating or rolling up the rows of table 3.1. To get from table 3.1 to table 3.2, I would make one row for each fruit type, note its maximum taste score, and then sort it in descending order of taste and ascending alphabetical order.

Tables 3.1 and 3.2 are decidedly *small data*. Conversely, any data set that is too large for a human to grok all its rows (like if I had a table similar to table 3.1 but for literally every single fruit I've ever eaten—and that's a lot of fruit) is known as *big data*. Many big-data tables are made of observations of some kind like this, with a grain of one row per observation, such as one row per visit, user, or click on an ad. In such tables, the columns exist to house information describing each observation, like the table with individual transactions in your online banking. This is when it's vitally important to have a *primary key*, a column whose sole purpose is to be a unique identifier for each row. Computationally, it's better for it to be an integer, but it can also be an alphanumeric string. Some examples of things that could serve as primary keys out in the wild would be a Social Security number (although this is not exactly best practice due to major privacy concerns), your driver's license number, your car's license plate, your car's Vehicle Identification Number (VIN), and so forth. Those IDs are tied uniquely to you (or your car) and could easily be primary keys in tables managed by the local motor vehicle governing body.

The other common way you will see data stored in your data viz life is called *nested data.*

3.5.2   *Nested data*

Nested data, or data not stored in rows and columns, is like one of those nesting dolls with layers (like onions, or parfaits, or even some ogres) you may have played with as a child. Nested data is a bit less commonplace when you operate in a SQL-dominated world because it doesn't play too nicely with the rigidity of rows and columns. Whether you dip a toe or dive headfirst into the coding world, you'll soon come face-to-face with nested data, and when you do, it will likely be in the form of JSON (pronounced "JAY-sahn"), which stands for JavaScript Object Notation.

Recall the fundamental data types we discussed earlier: numbers, strings, Booleans, and sometimes dates. Oftentimes when coding, we may want to group some of these data elements together so we can apply various operations to the entire group at once and/or refer to them more easily by using a single variable (or name) instead of many. How do we accomplish that? Arrays!

ARRAYS

Think of an array as one of those daily pill containers, but instead of storing a bunch of pills, you store one value of data in each little bucket. A one-dimensional array would have only one bucket for each of the seven days or maybe four buckets for a single day:

```
["Sunday", "Monday", "Tuesday", "Wednesday", "Thursday", "Friday", "Saturday"]
["Morning", "Noon", "Evening", "Night"]
```

In arrays found in JSON data, the elements are always surrounded by square brackets and separated by commas. Furthermore, all of the elements must be of the same data type (e.g., if one element is a string, each element in the array must be a string).

A two-dimensional array, however, would have more than one bucket for each day in the pill container. Let's say our two-dimensional pill container has four buckets for each of seven days—essentially, our big array is made of seven smaller arrays:

```
[
    ["Morning", "Noon", "Evening", "Night"],
    ["Morning", "Noon", "Evening", "Night"],
    ["Morning", "Noon", "Evening", "Night"],
    ["Morning", "Noon", "Evening", "Night"],
    ["Morning", "Noon", "Evening", "Night"],
    ["Morning", "Noon", "Evening", "Night"],
    ["Morning", "Noon", "Evening", "Night"]
]
```

To increase the number of dimensions, just keep burying containers inside of each bucket or arrays inside of array elements.

OBJECTS

As you might imagine, burying arrays in this way can get unwieldy and confusing. Without context, one might look at the previous two-dimensional example and wonder why there are seven copies of the same four-element array. However, if we place these inside an *object*, we can assign names to our arrays, and then the duplication makes all the sense in the world:

```
{
"Sunday": ["Morning", "Noon", "Evening", "Night"],
"Monday": ["Morning", "Noon", "Evening", "Night"],
"Tuesday": ["Morning", "Noon", "Evening", "Night"],
"Wednesday": ["Morning", "Noon", "Evening", "Night"],
"Thursday": ["Morning", "Noon", "Evening", "Night"],
"Friday": ["Morning", "Noon", "Evening", "Night"],
"Saturday": ["Morning", "Noon", "Evening", "Night"]
}
```

An object must be surrounded by curly braces, with each pair of a thing and its name separated by a comma. You can also include a comma after the last pair if you like, but it isn't necessary.

This name–thing pair is the beating heart of nested data and is called a *key–value pair*. You have the key on the left side, followed by a colon, and then the value on the right side. The *keys* of an object in JSON data must always be strings and be surrounded by double quotation marks ("). The *values* can be strings, numbers, Booleans, arrays, or objects. A value can also be *null*, which is just nothing, unassigned, empty.

One crazy thing about JSON is that the same data set can be organized in many different and equally valid ways. In this very simple example, the aggregated version of our beloved fruit data is shown as an object with seven key–value pairs of a name and a taste score:

```
{
    "Fuyu Persimmons": 100,
    "Mangos": 100,
    "Peaches + Nectarines": 100,
    "Bananas": 80,
```

```
    "Kiwis": 70,
    "Apples": 60,
    "Oranges": 50
}
```

You might see it in this format as part of a code-block example because it's very easy to key in by hand, and it just has the barebones of what's necessary to create a bar graph with one bar for each fruit with the bar's length based on the taste score.

In a slightly more complex world, it could look like this instead:

```
{
    "1": { "Fruit": "Fuyu Persimmons", "Taste_Score": 100 },
    "2": { "Fruit": "Mangos", "Taste_Score": 100 },
    "3": { "Fruit": "Peaches + Nectarines", "Taste_Score": 100 },
    "4": { ""Fruit": "Bananas", "Taste_Score": 80 },
    "5": { "Fruit": "Kiwis", "Taste_Score": 70 },
    "6": { "Fruit": "Apples", "Taste_Score": 60 },
    "7": { "Fruit": "Oranges", "Taste_Score": 50 }
}
```

In this second example, each of the object's seven key–value pairs is an index (like an ID number but not to be confused with the ID number from the disaggregated data) as a key paired with an object that has two more key–value pairs nested inside it. The first pair indicates the fruit's name, and the second indicates the taste score. While this was relatively easy to key in by hand, it's not as efficient as it was with the first example. Instead, you might see an object like this if it was generated programmatically by looping through some other data. In such a case, this would not be the end state of the object, but it would likely be a stepping stone on the way to adding more information later in the code, like adding information to be included in a *tooltip* (something that appears when you hover over an element).

In a still more complex third example, this is what the fruit object might look like if you download it from the internet somewhere:

```
{
    "title": "Fruits",
    "version": 1.1,
    "data": [
        {
            "fruit_name": "Fuyu Persimmons",
            "taste_score": 100
        },
        {
            "fruit_name": "Mangos",
            "taste_score": 100
        },
        {
            "fruit_name": "Peaches + Nectarines",
            "taste_score": 100
        },
        {
```

```
            "fruit_name": "Bananas",
            "taste_score": 80
        },
        {

            "fruit_name": "Kiwis",
            "taste_score": 70
        },
        {

            "fruit_name": "Apples",
            "taste_score": 60
        },
        {

            "fruit_name": "Oranges",
            "taste_score": 50
        }
    ]
}
```

At the top level, there are three key–value pairs: the title and its string value, the version and its number value, and the data with its array value. In the data array, each element is another object containing two key–value pairs: the fruit name and its string value, and the taste score with its number value.

As you may have noticed, all of these nested fruit examples are using our aggregated fruit data. If we wanted to change the grain from each type of fruit to each fruit eaten, these nested structures would get more complex as there would be more observations and additional fields, like the date field. In fact, the simplest example with the seven key–value pairs of name and taste score wouldn't work at all with our observational data, which is why it's important to think through and plan ahead when you're going to be recording and storing data on your own. Remember that it's always easier to start more granular and aggregate it up than to go the other way!

Summary

- In this age of technology, there is no shortage of data available for free or purchase, and if you can't find what you need, you can collect it yourself.
- Dimensions are descriptive, and measures are things you can quantify or aggregate. Numbers can go either way.
- At a fundamental level, data values can be strings, numbers, Booleans, null (nothing at all), or dates (depending on the environment where you're working). More complex data structures such as arrays and objects are built by assembling multiple values of the more basic types.
- Within a dimension or a measure, all the values must have the same data type.
- Usually, a visualization consists of at least one measure (a quantity you want to visualize) and a dimension (something to describe that quantity and set it apart from the rest).
- When confronted with data in a table, the first thing you need to determine is the table's grain (i.e., what a single row represents in the context of the data).

- Line charts lend themselves very well to continuous data, while bar charts truly shine when paired with discrete data; however, that doesn't mean you have to stay within these boundaries, as long as you know what you're doing and that your audience will understand the story your viz is telling.
- Data that you find in the wild will generally come in one of two formats: tabular or nested (and if nested, it is typically JSON).
- When choosing how to store data, remember that it's always easier to start with more granular data and aggregate it later than to start with aggregated data and try to get back to the details.

Part 2

As you'll learn in chapter 7, when I was about two years into my career as a product analyst, my boss sat me down in front of Tableau and said, "Make me a dashboard." As I fumbled my way through the task, the idea of putting any effort into the design of the resulting group of charts didn't once cross my mind. Even as I went on to make more reports for this boss and my stakeholders, I never gave any thought to my users' needs beyond the data they wanted to see until about a year later when I attended my first Tableau conference. It was only then that I began to understand the need for good design, but I didn't have the first clue about how to begin learning about this new world without going back to school, and there were extremely few resources at the time that were focused on designing with, and for, data. You, dear reader, are in luck: part 2 of this book is meant to be exactly that resource for you.

Chapter 4 delves deeply into the science of light and color as it applies to visualizing data, and then chapter 5 teaches you all about typography and how to style the text on the page to help guide your users' eyes through your visualizations. Then in chapter 6, we examine the humblest of viz building blocks—the chart—as we learn what sets good charts apart from their less effective counterparts. Finally, you'll get a crash course in interaction design in chapter 7, where you'll learn how and when to use interactivity in your designs.

Choosing colors

I don't know about you, but I cannot intuitively match colors to save my life. I kid you not, I legitimately keep a little color wheel in my closet that I use when picking out my clothes on those rare days when I leave my house to do something besides grocery shopping. So, while I can't promise that this chapter will tell you a secret that will magically demystify how to create a nice color palette (i.e., a group of colors that go nicely together for use in a design), I do promise to help you understand color better, so you can use it effectively to make some really awesome visualizations (and maybe help you pick out your clothes, too!).

In this chapter, we're going to discuss in detail all things color, starting with color theory's two models of color (how colors interact with each other) and the primary colors for each. Then, we'll delve into a few common color spaces (ways to quantify and encode color) that you're likely to encounter as you create visualizations, followed by different kinds of color palettes to pair with our different kinds of data, as well as where to find some ready-made palettes or how you can make color palettes yourself. From there, we'll learn about how to choose colors so that the maximum possible audience can appreciate them, from using accessibility guidelines for color blindness and other vision impairments to being mindful of what colors mean across different cultures.

4.1 A little (or maybe big) bit of color theory

The term *color theory* might sound intimidating, especially if you haven't had much exposure to the world of design before, but I want you to know that it's nothing to fear. Color theory is the set of fundamentals that helps us choose colors that play nicely with each other and convey the right message to our audience. It's not just a bunch of hand-wavy nonsense—color theory is rooted in science, specifically optics, which is the physics of light (and was one of the coolest physics lab courses I took in school, incidentally).

Ok, get ready, because I'm about to rock...your...world. Remember way back in your elementary school art classes as a kid, when you were taught that the three primary colors are red, blue, and yellow and that all other colors can be made by combining these colors? It was a lie! Yep, that's right: red, blue, and yellow are not the pure colors we were taught could be combined to make all other colors. The next question you have, though, is surely, "Then what are the three primary colors?"

Well, I hate to break it to you, but it's a bit more complicated than that. You see, there are two basic ways we talk about, interact with, or use color: as light (or on screens) and as paint (or on paper or some other substrate). Really, what this boils down to is two different models of color: an *additive model* in the case of light and a *subtractive model* in the case of paint.

4.1.1 The additive model of color

Let's set aside elementary school and primary colors for a little bit and advance instead to high school or maybe college science, specifically physics class. Light is a wave with energy proportional to its wavelength. (Yes, I know that light can also behave as a particle, a photon, but we're only going to deal with the wave behavior of light in this book.) There is no physical limit on how long or short light's wavelength can be, but only some wavelengths are visible to our eyes. That range of wavelengths is what we call the *visible spectrum.*

Different wavelengths of light interact differently with, well, everything. For instance, the various cone cells in our eyes absorb these different wavelengths in different amounts, which is what causes us to see the different colors. Perhaps you've heard of my old friend, ROY G. BIV? No, I'm not yelling his name, it's a pneumonic to help remember the seven classic colors in the visible spectrum: *r*ed, *o*range, *y*ellow, *g*reen, *b*lue, *i*ndigo, and *v*iolet.

Now, the reason that light's model of color is called additive is because when you *add* all those colors together, you get more light, and it's actually white! If you don't believe me, think about the last time you saw a rainbow after it rained. The Sun emits essentially white light, and when it hits the moisture in the air just right, the water droplets act like a prism. As a ray of sunlight enters a water droplet (or prism), it causes the light ray to bend so that it exits the droplet at a different angle. Remember, different wavelengths of light interact differently with everything, so the different colors (wavelengths) bend at different angles as they enter and exit the droplet, thus separating the white light into its constituent colors by their wavelengths (see figure 4.1). All that to say the result is a rainbow!

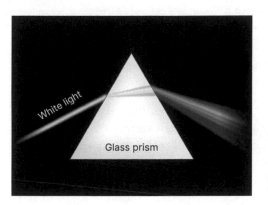

Figure 4.1   A ray of white sunlight enters a prism and exits as a rainbow because the prism causes the different wavelengths in the white light to separate. (Prism-rainbow.svg: Suidrootderivative work. Sceptre, CC BY-SA 3.0, via Wikimedia Commons. Labels added by me)

This is precisely what Sir Isaac Newton did with an actual prism and a beam of sunlight shining through a hole in the blind of his darkened room. He published the results of these and many other optical experiments in his 1704 treatise on light titled *Opticks*. In this experiment, Newton employed the help of a keen-eyed assistant while Newton himself held the prism and instructed the assistant to divide the rainbow into the distinct colors he could discern, as shown in figure 4.2.

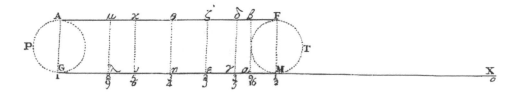

Figure 4.2   The spectrum recorded by Newton and his assistant, divided into color intervals, which Newton likened to a musical scale (Isaac Newton, Public domain, via Project Gutenberg)

Newton likened the resulting intervals to a musical scale, the cyclic nature of which led him to bend the spectrum around a circle, which resulted in the first color wheel ever (figure 4.3). Yes, you read that right: it was Sir Isaac Newton of apple-falling, gravity-theorizing, calculus-inventing fame who invented the color wheel. Seriously, is there anything he couldn't do?

Figure 4.3   Newton's color wheel, which communicates color relationships by relating them to music. The letters A through G on the outside represent the 7 + 1 (back to A) tones of the chromatic scale. (Isaac Newton, Public domain, via Project Gutenberg)

Later in *Opticks*, Newton goes on to demonstrate the power of his color wheel to combine colors in a mathematical way and predict the resulting color: "suppose a Colour is compounded of these homogeneal Colours, of violet one part, of indigo one part, of blue two parts, of green three parts, of yellow five parts, of orange six parts, and of red ten parts." This compounding he describes means drawing a circle at each of the points at the center of the arc corresponding to that color, as shown in figure 4.3 by the small circles just inside the edge of the big circle and labelled with x, v, t, s, r, q, and p, respectively. The size (area) of each small circle corresponds to the number of parts he indicated. He then found the center of mass of those circles (i.e., an average position, weighted by the areas of the circles) to be at the point labeled z and drew a line from the center of the big circle, through z, and out to the edge of the circle, thus showing "that the Colour compounded of these Ingredients will be an orange, verging a little more to red than to yellow."

In this way, Newton used his color wheel to predict what color would result from combining a bunch of other colors. The math is a little bit sketchy (he even says so himself in a later paragraph), but anecdotally, he was right. We'll come back to the color wheel in the next section when we discuss how to choose color palettes, but first we need to get the primary colors straight, so we can build a modern and more accurate version of the color wheel.

Taking a step back from Newton for a second, let's look with our own eyes at the visible spectrum of light as a continuous gradient instead of discrete bands (figure 4.4).

To say that there are only and exactly 7 colors in the spectrum shown in figure 4.4 doesn't feel quite right. There's a lot of fuzziness, making it difficult to say whether it's more like 5, or it could be 10, or even more. Instead of seeing how many there are, see if you can boil it down to as few colors or color groupings or dominant

Figure 4.4   An actual photograph of the visible spectrum, showing that the idea of counting the colors is pretty difficult (Maxim Bilovitskiy, CC BY-SA 4.0, via Wikimedia Commons)

regions as possible by holding the page far away from your face and letting your eyes blur. Come back and re-focus your eyes when you're ready.

4.1.2   *The primary colors of light*

If you said three regions, you win! Those three regions are categorized as red, green, and blue. Now guess what? These are the real primary colors of light, with the bells and whistles you know and love about primary colors from elementary school: combining all three gives you white light, and combining any two gives you a new color called a *secondary color*. This means that it turns out you don't have to add up every color in the spectrum to get white light. All you really need are the three primaries.

Wonderful man that he is, my husband was supportive of an almost $30 impulse purchase for the sake of science, so I could prove to myself as I was writing this chapter that red, green, and blue are truly the primary colors of light. Thus, armed with some white paper and a brand-new set of colored flashlights, including one each of red, blue, and green, I had a little photo shoot, presented in figure 4.5.

So, we've covered the additive model of color, which applies to light, and seen with our very own eyes in figure 4.5 that red light + green light = yellow light, red light + blue light = magenta light, and green light + blue light = cyan light. Hold that thought in the back of your mind while we switch gears a little bit and talk about the subtractive model of color, which applies to paints and ink and such. Pay close attention if you'll be making vizzes for print!

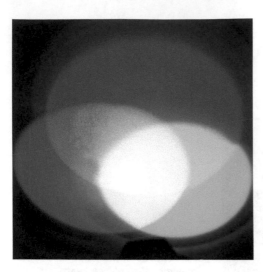

Figure 4.5   To prove to myself and to you that red, green, and blue are truly the primary colors of light, I had a little photo shoot with my new set of colored flashlights. Around the outside, you can see the primary colors, and then inside, where two overlap, you can see the secondary colors. Finally, in the center where all three lights overlap, you can see the white light. Nifty!

4.1.3   The subtractive model of color

Think back again to that physics class (Ha! And you thought we were done with physics!), where you learned about light and color. As you may or may not recall, light is generally a byproduct of a process that releases energy, so unless there's something going on inside an object to release energy, there will be no light emitted from it. The only way to see such inert objects is if there is light from some other source reflecting off those objects. This means that the color of an inert object stems from both the chemical makeup of the object and the color of the light being shone on it.

Yes, this is a bit of a brain twister. When you shine a white light on an object, and it appears red to your eyes, that means the object is absorbing all the blue and green light and reflecting the red back to you. Similarly, for an object that appears green, it's absorbing all the red and blue light and reflecting the green back to you. You get the idea. If not, then maybe figure 4.6 will help.

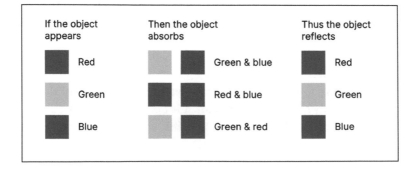

Figure 4.6   This illustration shows what colors of light are absorbed and reflected by objects of each additive primary color.

That's straightforward enough, but how do we get more than just three colors? If we mix red paint with green paint, then based on the way light mixes, we might expect to get yellow paint, but of course we don't. The red paint is absorbing the green light, and the green paint is absorbing the red light. So, when we mix them together, the resulting color is absorbing the red *and* the green *and* the blue. We'd have the same problem trying to make cyan or magenta with paint in this way. What gives?

It turns out that the colors we called secondary colors, which resulted from adding light of two different (additive) primary colors, are the *subtractive* primary colors: cyan (C), magenta (M), and yellow (Y). This is why printer ink is CMY or CMYK, where the K stands for black. Take a look at figure 4.7 for a more visual explanation of how the additive and subtractive models are correlated. This figure also shows how combining two additive primaries gives you more light, whereas combining two subtractive primaries yields less light (hence the name *the subtractive model*).

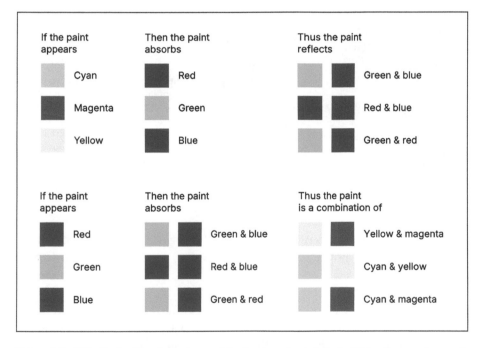

Figure 4.7   This illustration shows how paint primary colors relate to light primary colors and which light primary colors are absorbed and reflected by each paint primary color.

The CMYK system is generally only used in print, and because we're mainly going to concentrate on digital media here, we will focus our efforts on the additive model.

4.1.4   *Color vision deficiency*

What does this all mean in the context of color blindness? Approximately 1 in 12 males (8%) and 1 in 200 females (0.5%) live with some kind of color blindness. So, for every 100 men you know, about 8 of them probably have some kind of color vision deficiency. That's a lot of people! But what does it mean to be colorblind?

It all comes down to the cone cells in our eyes, of which there are three types. Each type absorbs light in a different part of the visible spectrum, so they are named for their regions: short, medium, and long (referring to the relative wavelengths of light they absorb), or blue, green, and red (for the colors that make up those regions). Check out figure 4.8 for a normalized graph of these sensitivities. The fact that our eyes rely on blending those three primary colors of light together to see color is called *trichromacy*, and people with all three cone types functioning are called *trichromats*.

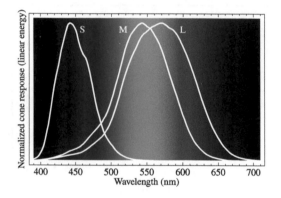

Figure 4.8   **This graph shows a normalized view of how much of each wavelength of visible light is absorbed by each type of cone in our eyes. S, M, and L refer to the short, medium, and long wavelengths of the light they absorb the most, also known as blue, green, and red, respectively, because that's where the most light is absorbed. (BenRG, Public domain, via Wikimedia Commons)**

When one type of cone is not functioning, this is called *dichromacy*; if two or all three types of cones are not functioning, this is called *monochromacy*. Furthermore, if all three types of cones are not functioning, resulting in the inability to see color at all, this is specifically called *achromatopsia*.

Dichromacy comes in three types: *protanopia* for those who rely on only blue and green light (red-blind), *deuteranopia* for those who rely only on blue and red light (green-blind), and *tritanopia* for those who rely only on red and green light (blue-blind). It is also possible that all three types of cones are still working, but one type of cone's sensitivity is shifted or weaker. In such cases, it is usually either the red cone that shifts toward the green peak, making reds look more green (called *protanomaly*), or the green cone that shifts toward the red, making greens look more red (called *deuteranomaly*). The third type (*tritanomaly*) makes it difficult to tell the difference between blue and green and between yellow and red.

That was a lot of new vocabulary, so let's see some of it in action in figure 4.9. What do color blind people see, approximately?

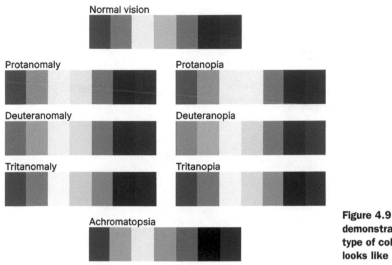

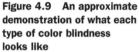

Figure 4.9 An approximate demonstration of what each type of color blindness looks like

The most common type of color blindness by a long shot is deuteranomaly, where the green cone's absorption is shifted toward the red causing greens to look more red. Tritanomaly and tritanopia are much rarer, and in fact, they appear to stem from a single genetic mutation that results in varying degrees of deficiency rather than two distinct deficiencies [1] (Went & Pronk, 1985). If you ever dig into the literature, you'll notice that the studies cataloging the prevalence of the different types of color blindness are generally Eurocentric, but that is likely because these deficiencies are generally pretty Eurocentric themselves. Total monochromacy is rarer still, making it nearly impossible to find information about its prevalence. See figure 4.10 for details about the prevalence of each other type of deficiency.

As you go about your merry way, making beautiful visuals for your clients, stakeholders, friends, family, and yourself, it is important to consider how the colors you choose are perceived by your users. We'll talk later in this chapter about how to ensure that as many people as possible can interpret and understand your visualizations based on the colors you choose.

Now that we've learned a bit about why and how we see the colors we do, let's start to apply our newfound knowledge, beginning with color spaces.

Prevalence of color vision deficiencies

among males and females (or overall).

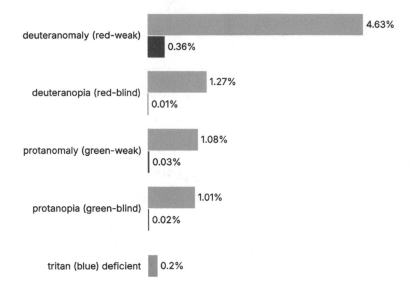

Figure 4.10   Illustration of the estimated prevalence of each type of color blindness. Protan and deuteran deficiency numbers are from Sharpe et al. [2], and tritan deficiency is from Went and Pronk [1]. (A million thanks to my eye doctor for helping me track down a source for the prevalence of tritan deficiency!)

4.2   *A few color spaces*

When it comes to color theory, there's the rainbow, the two sets of primary colors, the color wheel, and so forth, and that's all well and good. As with anything though, it's all an oversimplification—real life is always more complicated. If you try to make any color you want using only three primary colors, it's not going to work because there's more to color than just *hue*, which is essentially just the area of the color wheel or visible spectrum where that color falls, that is, its pure pigment. It's typically what we mean when we ask someone, "What is your favorite color?" Before we get into some different color spaces you'll encounter in your data viz travels, let's go over some other useful terms.

- *Hue*—As stated already, hue is basically just the name of a color (e.g., red, blue, purple, cyan). It's the thing that a five-year-old refers to as color.
- *Value or lightness or brightness*—Value describes how dark or light a color is. Thus, it is also referred to as lightness or brightness—a higher value means a lighter color, while a lower value means a darker color (see figure 4.11).

Figure 4.11   A color's value, brightness, or lightness extends from black at 0% to white at 100%.

- *Saturation or chroma*—Saturation describes the intensity or pureness of a color as opposed to gray. It's very closely related to a color's chroma, which is essentially the saturation normalized for different light sources. The saturation of a color extends from gray (no saturation) to the purest version of the color itself (highest saturation), as shown in figure 4.12.

Figure 4.12   A color's saturation or chroma extends from gray at 0% to pure color at 100%.

- *Color space*—Most *color spaces* are defined by three values, or axes, just like in mathematics' Euclidean space with the Cartesian coordinates of X, Y, and Z, and in fact, the really hard-core color scientists depict color spaces exactly like that. Modern color spaces are incredibly mathematical, and their diagrams often look like things I learned about in my advanced calculus classes back in college, with all kinds of weird shapes rotated around different axes. They're very difficult to visualize in your head without seeing it on the page. When I first started truly digging into color and color theory and heard about different color spaces, I thought it was totally crazy. How can an array of colors look different based on how you quantify it? Color is color, right? Spoiler: nope. If you wind up finding this section fascinating, I encourage you to dig into color science yourself. It's very interesting and mind-boggling, and there's a ton of it. There are also many more color spaces than the four we will cover in this section, and there are die-hard fans of each, which you'll find if you read up more on this subject.

4.2.1   *RGB space*

Unarguably, and with good reason, the most common color space you'll encounter as you embark on your data viz journey is the one based on the three primary colors of light, which you may recall is what a computer screen uses. A color in the RGB (red, green, and blue) space is generally represented by a triplet of numbers, each ranging between 0 and 255, such as (0,255,255), which happens to be cyan (remember, green + blue = cyan in the additive model), or (99,48,145) which is a very lovely purple (see figure 4.13). Quantifying colors in this way is very similar to Newton's thought experiment we talked about, where he added up different amounts of colors around his color wheel.

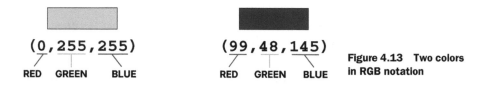

Figure 4.13   Two colors in RGB notation

But why 0 to 255? Excellent question!

This quantitative approach to color was born out of computation, because computer displays deal in the additive model of color where red, green, and blue are the primary colors of light. Each of these three primary color values represents 1 byte of information, which some of the nerds in the crowd may remember equals 8 bits. And as you may further recall, a bit of information is a single dimension: it can only be a thing or the absence of that thing (e.g., on or off, up or down, true or false, one or zero, although we'll go with 1 or 0 for our purposes here). If you have a collection of 8 bits that make up a single byte, then there are $2^8 = 256$ possible arrangements of 1s and 0s. If you start counting the arrangements at 0 (because that's just what you do in computing), then you can number your arrangements from 0 to 255.

Because 256 is the perfect square of 16 (i.e., 16 x 16 = 256), it is convenient and saves a few keystrokes to express these RGB values in base-16, or *hexadecimal*, as shown in figure 4.14.

Figure 4.14   The same two colors from the previous figure, written as hexadecimal or hex triplets

Hexadecimal vs decimal

Usually, we write numbers in decimal notation, using digits 0, 1, 2, 3, 4, 5, 6, 7, 8, and 9. When we get up to 10, we put a 1 in the "10s place" and a 0 in the "1s place," as we all grew up saying. This is called base-10. Ninety-nine, for example, is represented by a 9 in the 10s place and a 9 in the 1s place, because we take 9x10 (90) and then add another 9 to get 99. We find this by dividing 99 by 10 and getting 9 with a remainder of 9, so we put 9 in the 10s place and another 9 in the 1s place: 99.

If we change our base to 16 instead, that is called *hexadecimal*, base-16, or simply hex. Because we don't have 16 different numerals to work with, we use 0 through 9, and when we get to 10, we start with the alphabet so that 10 through 15 are expressed as A through F, respectively. Thus, the number 15 is represented by a single digit, F, and the number 16 in hex is 10: a 1 in the 16s place and a 0 in the 1s place. If we want to express 255 in hex, we divide it by 16 and get 15 with a remainder of 15, so we put an F in the 16s place, and another F in the 1s place to get FF (or ff, because hexadecimal is not case-sensitive).

With the three axes, each extending from 0 to 255, RGB space accounts for a total of $256^3 = 16,777,216$ colors. In practice, I haven't encountered a tool that doesn't accept either an RGB triplet (255,255,255) or a hex triplet (#FFFFFF) to specify a particular color.

4.2.2 HSB or HSV space

The HSB (hue, saturation, brightness, also known as HSV or hue, saturation, value) space is, as of 2024, available on Mac and Windows color pickers, but not in CSS. (So, if you're planning to do a lot of web development, maybe just skim this section and pay closer attention to the next. Otherwise, read on!)

HSB was invented in 1974 by electrical and computer engineer Alvy Ray Smith, who also went on to cofound Lucasfilm's Computer Division as well as Pixar, the animation giant. In the HSB system, hue is assigned a number between 0 and 360, corresponding to its position on a circle (the color wheel), where pure red is at 0° (and at 360° because 0° = 360°, as you might remember from math class). Check out figure 4.15 for a demo.

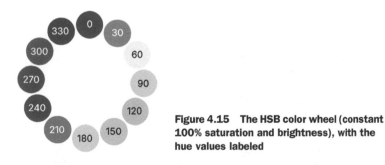

Figure 4.15 The HSB color wheel (constant 100% saturation and brightness), with the hue values labeled

What I find super cool about this system is that because hue corresponds to an angle on a circle, it's pretty easy to guess what will happen to a color as you dial the hue up or down. For example, if I start with a green of 120 (corresponding to RGB(0,255,0) or #00FF00 in hex) I can have a decent idea of what will happen if I tweak it up toward 150 or down toward 90. Up will edge it more toward blue, thus making it a bit of a cooler, more mellow green, and down will edge it toward yellow, thus making it a little bit warmer.

The saturation in the HSB system extends between 0% for gray and 100% for the fullest, most vibrant, and richest possible take on that color (also written as whole numbers 0 to 100). Figure 4.16 demonstrates this for four different hues and four different saturations.

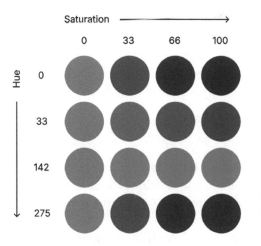

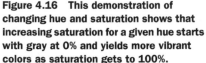

Figure 4.16   **This demonstration of changing hue and saturation shows that increasing saturation for a given hue starts with gray at 0% and yields more vibrant colors as saturation gets to 100%.**

This brings us to the final parameter in the HSB space, *brightness*, which also varies between 0% and 100% (it can also be written as whole numbers, 0 to 100). But before I explain, let me show you in figure 4.17 what happens when you take a single hue (in this case, hue = 0) and vary the saturation and brightness.

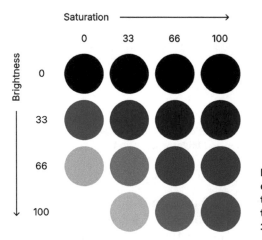

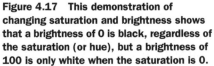

Figure 4.17   **This demonstration of changing saturation and brightness shows that a brightness of 0 is black, regardless of the saturation (or hue), but a brightness of 100 is only white when the saturation is 0.**

So, when brightness is 0, the resulting color is black, regardless of hue or saturation. It's like you're in a room with some red and white paint chips (from the lower left and right corners of figure 4.17), and you turned the light off. No matter how vivid the red or pure the white, they still look black when the brightness is completely removed. Similarly, if you turn the (white) light on full power and shine it on your paint chips, they'll appear as bright red and as pure white as possible.

You can think of it like adding food coloring to some white cake mix in your kitchen. One drop from the red bottle won't give you much color in the whole cake, but the more drops you add, the more saturated your cake's color becomes. And if you're doing it in the pitch dark, you're not going to see a darn thing, but if you put a white floodlight on a dimmer switch, you'll notice the brightness of the cake's color changes as you turn the switch all the way up. If you've got the whole bottle of red color in a single cupcake under the brightest setting of the floodlight, it will probably look something like the lower-right red circle in figure 4.17.

4.2.3 HSL space

If you'll be developing in the web more often than using BI tools or design software, you might want to know about the HSL space, which stands for hue, saturation, and lightness. As of this writing in 2024, it's available in CSS but not Mac and Windows color pickers. How convenient, right? (Yes, that's sarcasm.)

Happily for us, HSL is very similar to HSB, so we can skip right over the HS part and go straight to figuring out the difference between lightness and brightness, L and B. Again, before I explain the difference, let's take a look at figure 4.18, a recreated version of figure 4.17, where instead of varying brightness, we're going to vary lightness.

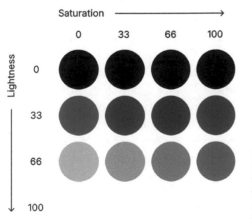

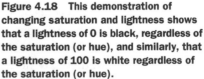

Figure 4.18 This demonstration of changing saturation and lightness shows that a lightness of 0 is black, regardless of the saturation (or hue), and similarly, that a lightness of 100 is white regardless of the saturation (or hue).

In figure 4.18, we can see that a lightness of 100 yields white for any hue or saturation, and similarly, a lightness of 0 always yields black. So, how do we get a true red? Let me update figure 4.18 by adding another row, for 50% brightness (see figure 4.19).

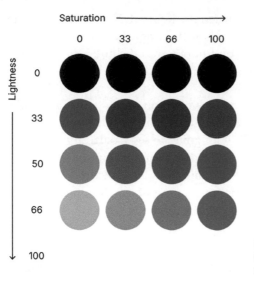

Figure 4.19   Aha, there's our true red! Center row all the way on the right, at 100% saturation and 50% lightness

From this figure, we can see that in the HSL system, black (0% lightness) and white (100% lightness) are opposites with the true color at 100% saturation living exactly at the center (50% lightness).

Okay, one more color space to cover, and then we'll move on to color palettes.

4.2.4   *The CIELAB or L*a*b* color space*

The CIELAB space, also known as L*a*b* (and don't leave out the asterisks, because that would refer to a different color space), is way more technical and mathematical, by leaps and bounds, than the rest that we've covered. Pronounced like "see-lab," this color space was created by the International Commission on Illumination (CIE for its French name, *Commission Internationale de l'Éclairage*) as a device-independent color space, meaning that its colors are defined the same, whether they are displayed on printed media, a computer monitor, or something else entirely. The CIELAB space is defined by three coordinates: L* (read as "ell star") or lightness, which is 0 at black and 100 at white, just like HSL. The a* and b* coordinates define the red–green and the blue–yellow axes, respectively. Both a* and b* extend out in both negative and positive directions from 0. Negative values of a* go toward green, while positive values go toward red. Negative values of b* go toward blue, while positive values go toward yellow. Technically, there are no bounds on how far negative or positive a* and b* can go, but usually, they range between –128 and 127. Figure 4.20 shows what a small section of the CIELAB space looks like at L* = 75, or a lightness of 75.

And just for completeness sake, let's have a look at what CIELAB looks like at L* = 25 in figure 4.21.

While CIELAB isn't available in a typical color picker, there are color converters out there that make it pretty easy to convert between CIELAB and the more mainstream

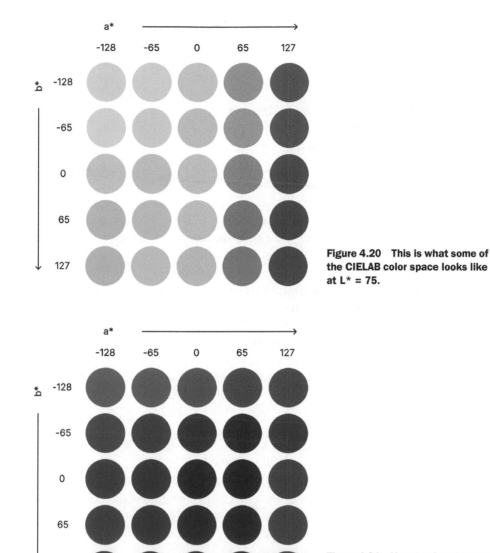

Figure 4.20 This is what some of the CIELAB color space looks like at L* = 75.

Figure 4.21 Here is what the same slice of CIELAB looks like if we shift it to L* = 25.

color spaces. To help make figures 4.20 and 4.21, I used a tool called Colorizer, which you can find in the appendix.

Having this knowledge of color spaces in your back pocket will make it so much easier to select and tweak sets of colors for use in your visualizations. As I made the graphics to illustrate my points, all throughout this chapter, I've been bouncing between color spaces in Figma. Sometimes, I'd start with hex because I like that I can set the levels of R, G, and B without having to tab into three different fields. Then, if I'd need to tweak the color at all, I'd jump into HSB because changing the hue just a smidge is as easy as spinning a dial around a circle, and changing the brightness and saturation feel so intuitive because I understand what they do. Armed with all this knowledge, let's put it into practice to choose colors for data visualization, also known as *creating color palettes.*

4.3   Different kinds of color palettes and how to make them

Before we dive into color palettes, I'll give you the most important advice you'll get about using color: get it right in black and white, and then you can add some color as you need it. This is the key to using color purposefully, and I will remind you again later, many times. Because you're now an expert in color science and spaces and can bend hues and saturations to your every whim, you will be very tempted to throw all the beautiful colors you find into your next visualization. Please resist that temptation! Color used poorly will completely ruin an otherwise great viz.

As you create a visualization, there are many different places you can use color: on the text, on the data itself, the literal background of your charts and visualization, any images or iconography, the non-data elements of your charts such as borders, axis lines, axis ticks, and so forth. Now, think back to chapter 3, when we talked about the different kinds of data and dimensions: we had discrete and continuous values and sequential and categorical values. Here, as we talk about color palettes, we'll look at them through just a slightly different lens: continuous palettes, which can be broken up into sequential and *diverging*, and categorical palettes. So, let's get colorful!

4.3.1   Continuous palettes

Best suited for continuous data values, continuous color palettes (also known as color ramps or color scales) are essentially what we get from drawing a single curve (it doesn't have to be a straight line) through a color space and using all the colors along that curve. When we map continuous colors onto continuous data in this way, the purpose is to simultaneously communicate both that order and the data's values. All the continuous palettes/gradients in this section were made using d3: you can find my source code repository in the appendix.

SEQUENTIAL PALETTES

As you may recall from chapter 3, having sequential data values means that the order of those values is important, and it basically always is in the case of continuous data. The most straightforward way to create such a color palette is by taking a single hue and varying either its saturation (from gray to full color) or its lightness (white or black to full color—white for light backgrounds and black for dark backgrounds), as shown in figure 4.22. The amount of color corresponds to the amount of the data: more color corresponds to larger data values, while less color (black or white) corresponds to smaller data values.

It can be tempting to vary just the saturation, but only when you vary the lightness as well as the saturation do these single-hue gradients make it easy to "get it right in

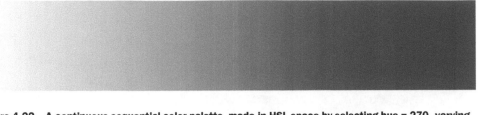

Figure 4.22   A continuous sequential color palette, made in HSL space by selecting hue = 270, varying the saturation from 0% (no color) to 100% (full color), and varying the lightness from 100% (white) to 50% (full color).

black and white." Furthermore, as long as the contrast with the background works (more on that later), it's also a good way to make a colorblind-friendly color palette. However, if you want to pump up the contrast even further and not risk losing the lower data points in the background, you can instead consider using multiple hues for your sequential gradient, as shown in figure 4.23.

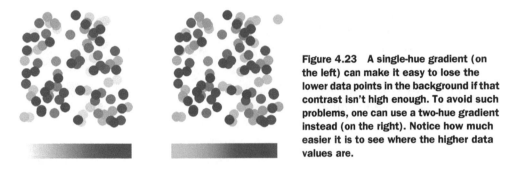

Figure 4.23   A single-hue gradient (on the left) can make it easy to lose the lower data points in the background if that contrast isn't high enough. To avoid such problems, one can use a two-hue gradient instead (on the right). Notice how much easier it is to see where the higher data values are.

Using two hues instead of one ensures that all values of data have a color—as opposed to just black, white, or gray—like in the palette on the right in figure 4.23. Again, make sure to vary the lightness/brightness, as well as the hue, because that will help your colors be more distinguishable from each other by folks with impaired color vision—remember, get it right in black and white! This will ensure that the colors are distinguishable in grayscale and make the scale more intuitive to interpret: the lighter color would correspond to smaller data values, and the darker would correspond to larger data values.

Essentially, as I mentioned earlier, a two-hue gradient means that you are taking two colors and drawing a line between them in a particular color space. Honestly, in my book (since that's what you're reading, and thanks for that, by the way!), this is the most interesting application of color spaces because a line between the same two hues in different color spaces will yield completely different sets of colors for each space. So cool! Figure 4.24 demonstrates this with two of the color spaces we learned about in section 4.2, at the top, and two new ones at the bottom (because these are what's currently available in d3).

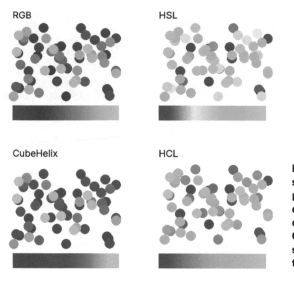

Figure 4.24   If we use different color spaces, we can generate four different palettes from the same two colors, a candy-apple-red on the left and a dark cyan on the right. Don't believe me? Check out the extreme left and right sides of each legend, and you'll see that they really are the same two colors!

There are times when using multiple hues might be too much for the story you're trying to tell with your visualization, such as when you're visualizing something more on the serious side. In these cases, your best bet is to stick with a single hue.

DIVERGING PALETTES

If you have continuous data that's about variation around a (meaningful) single value, it's a great time to employ a divergent color palette. Such a palette uses three hues: one hue for the lowest data values, one for the highest data values, and one (generally desaturated + brighter/lighter) for that meaningful midpoint.

A diverging color ramp is incredibly effective for applications such as showing variation around an average temperature, variation around a revenue target, the balance of power held by political parties, income above and below the poverty line, and so forth. Technically, you could use a sequential palette for these cases, but a diverging palette will help you show opposites more effectively by emphasizing the two extremes (figure 4.25).

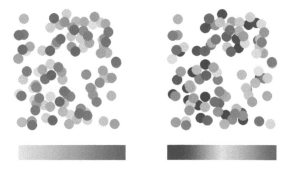

Figure 4.25   The sequential palette on the left is fine for highlighting the larger values, but the diverging palette on the right makes it easier to see both extremes (the low and the high) for the same data set.

Be careful with diverging palettes, though, because it's nigh impossible to pass the "get it right in black and white" test.

4.3.2   *Discrete palettes*

Discrete color palettes come in two flavors: stepped or discrete versions of the aforementioned continuous palettes, and categorical, which are meant for (you guessed it) categorical data.

STEPPED VERSIONS OF CONTINUOUS PALETTES

There are two cases where you might want to use a stepped version of a continuous palette. On the one hand, you might have continuous data but want to instead show the values in buckets or segments along a continuous spectrum. There are a variety of reasons to do this, such as you might want to simplify your use of color, or you might want to show how data is distributed, like into quartiles for example. Let's say we want to simplify our use of color in the case of the diverging palette on the right in figure 4.25. Instead of using a continuous gradient, we can divide that gradient into three segments to show something like low, medium, and high (see figure 4.26).

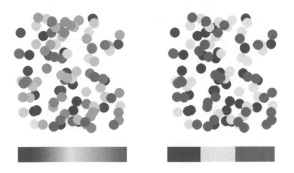

Figure 4.26   To simplify our use of color, we can divide the continuous diverging scale on the left into three bins (for low, medium, and high).

The second case for a stepped version of a continuous palette is also very straightforward: if your data is ordered but not continuous, you may still want to use a sequential or diverging palette (depending on the data's values and what you're trying to communicate). A stepped diverging palette is also fabulous for something like Likert scales—check out the chart in figure 4.27, which visualizes the results of the theoretical Likert question from chapter 3.

Did I need to add color in figure 4.27? Probably not, but it makes it easy for a user to see the sentiment of each response without having to read the words too closely. Adding color judiciously and purposefully in this way doesn't take away from the story. As a bonus, I chose a palette that looks great even for those with color blindness!

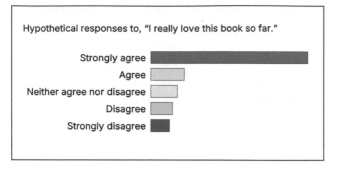

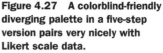

Figure 4.27   **A colorblind-friendly diverging palette in a five-step version pairs very nicely with Likert scale data.**

CATEGORICAL PALETTES

I saved categorical palettes for last because they're the trickiest to wrangle. If you thought there were a lot of dos and don'ts for ordered palettes, then it's time to put your seatbelt on because it's about to get bumpy.

If you decide to visualize data professionally, you will absolutely encounter stakeholders and clients who think they want a graph with a zillion categories, and each category must have its own color. It happens so frequently that it could probably be a drinking game: "Take a drink for every client you've ever had who wanted you to make a graph with more than a dozen colors." And they actually want it too, thinking that all those colors will magically not turn into rainbow spaghetti but instead make them able to see how each category is set apart from the others. Spoiler: *it doesn't work!* (Stay tuned because, in chapter 6, we'll talk about some alternatives that solve the rainbow spaghetti problem.)

The challenge even with small categorical palettes is that you must find colors that look nice together, convey the correct tone and emotions (which varies depending on culture— more on that a little later) without being controversial (well hello there, blue and pink!), and are distinct enough from each other so that they can easily be discerned by those with and without color vision deficiencies. It's a bonus if they can be named distinctly, too, which helps when people are referring to your graphs—unless your audience is full of designers or artists, they're not likely to be able to verbalize the difference between light burnt sienna and rust orange, let alone see the difference.

Okay, enough cautionary tales. Let's find some pretty colors!

4.3.3   *Coming up with categorical color palettes*

There are approximately 943,567,231 tools (of course I jest, but it's a lot, and more are released every day) out there on the web that generate a color palette in one way or another. I have included my favorites in the appendix, but I will go over a few different types of tools here, so you know how to query your favorite search engine next time the need arises and in case you don't find what you need in the appendix.

TOOLS THAT CHOOSE BASED ON COLOR THEORY

Yep, that's right! All that rigamarole we went through earlier in the chapter has practical applications! (I wouldn't dare leave you hanging after such a dive down a scientific rabbit hole.) Using a color wheel is probably one of the most common and familiar ways to generate a color palette based on theory. The idea is that you (or a tool) can choose a set of colors that are evenly spaced, or at least balanced around the wheel, and they will naturally be well suited, as shown in figure 4.28.

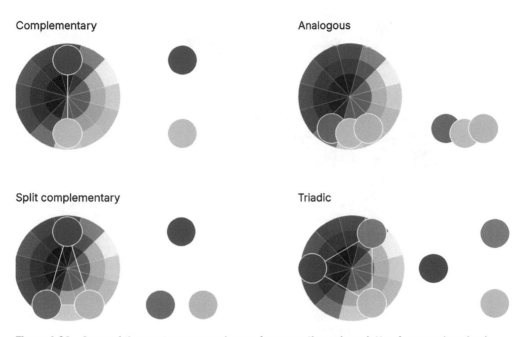

Figure 4.28 Some of the most common schemes for generating color palettes from a color wheel

Figure 4.28 has some terms that we haven't encountered yet, but they're good to know before you go out into the wild and start reading about using a color wheel to choose color schemes. *Complementary* colors are exactly opposite each other on the color wheel, as shown in the top left corner of figure 4.28. In the bottom left corner, we have *split complementary*, which means that you pick one color on one side of the wheel, then draw a straight line to the color on the opposite side, but instead of using that color, you pick the two colors that are immediately adjacent on each side of it. *Analogous* colors, in the upper right, are all adjacent to each other on the color wheel, and you don't have to limit yourself to three colors like I did in the figure. Finally, a *triadic* color scheme, in the lower right corner, is made by making an equilateral triangle, or a triangle with all sides of equal length, on the color wheel.

TOOLS THAT CHOOSE COLORS FROM A PHOTO OR AN EXISTING PIECE OF ARTWORK

Choosing colors from photos or artwork is probably one of the most interesting ways to come up with a categorical color palette, especially if you use a photo of nature—after all, there are some pretty darn gorgeous palettes around us in the natural world. Think about the last time you saw a stunning sunrise or sunset, a field of wildflowers against a bright blue sky, an underwater ecosystem in the tropics, or even a misty morning in the mountains. To be quite honest, I have underutilized this type of tool in my own work, but I believe it has tons of potential. Check out figure 4.29 to see a picture I took, which I then fed to a tool, and the resulting palette that tool created.

Figure 4.29   A photo of a sunset in Kihei, Hawaii, and a palette I generated from it

The tool I used for this was Google's Art Palette tool, and it really was as simple as uploading my photo and clicking a button to generate a palette. What's more, I wasn't very happy with the original colors the tool spit out because they weren't quite different enough for my liking, so I was able to drag the little dots around to find a more suitable set of colors that I could share with you.

TOOLS THAT CHOOSE FROM A BASE COLOR OR COLORS AND GENERATE RANDOM COLORS TO ACCOMPANY I think the tool type I've used the most is one that generates random colors based on a base color or colors, although it can be difficult to generate a particularly large palette or a colorblind-friendly palette. A tool like this is great when you might have to work with a single brand color and you want to create an entire palette around it or when you just really want to use your favorite colors in a viz and you need to build out from them. Some of these tools will even let you specify whether your palette needs to meet accessibility guidelines (more about those soon), which is very cool and helpful. In figure 4.30, I used a tool called Coolors, which you can find in the appendix. My husband and I are quite partial to purple and green, so I picked shades of those colors that I like, and I was able to use Coolors to randomly generate three more colors to go with my purple and green.

If I were to use the palette in figure 4.30 to do data viz, I'd probably tweak some of the colors, so nothing is accidentally emphasized (e.g., that green is pretty vibrant so I'd probably dial down the lightness a few notches) and make sure they are different

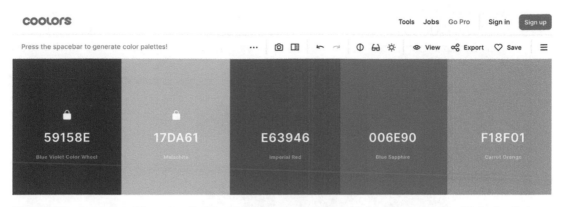

Figure 4.30   A palette of five colors that I randomly generated from two chosen colors using the tool called Coolors

enough, even for those with some sort of color blindness (the orange and the red might be a bit too similar for those with some kind of red blindness), but this provides a nice starting place.

SOME FINAL NOTES ON CATEGORICAL PALETTES

Finally, as I said before, these are the trickiest palettes to work with because there are so many moving pieces, so be patient with yourself. If you are working with the built-in color picker on your computer and you select a certain color space, you don't have to stick with that one color space to get your color just right! Let's say you choose a pre-made palette online and then use hex codes to put the colors into your data viz tool. After applying the colors to your data, you find that some of the colors are sticking out a bit more than others, causing some data to be emphasized that shouldn't be, like in figure 4.31. You can switch your color picker from hex to HSB, for example, and then dial down the saturation on the offending colors to make them stick out less.

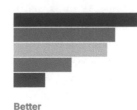

Not ideal   **Better**

Figure 4.31   Starting from the color palette on the left, the one generated from my sunset photo, I made a few simple tweaks to saturation and lightness (brightness) and no change to hues, and ended up with the palette on the right.

In figure 4.31 on the left, we see the color palette I generated from my sunset picture. The yellow sticks out a bit, and the nearly black bar on the bottom isn't quite different enough from the blue bar on the top when seen against a white background. Finally, the tan bar (second from the top) could also use a little help as it's just a smidge too close to the yellow for my liking. To get to the palette on the right, I first tackled the yellow by dialing down the saturation, which helped with the accidental emphasis problem. When I opened the color picker in Figma to tackle the almost-black bottom bar, I found that it wasn't blue at all, but it was a shade of magenta! If you don't believe me, check out figure 4.32.

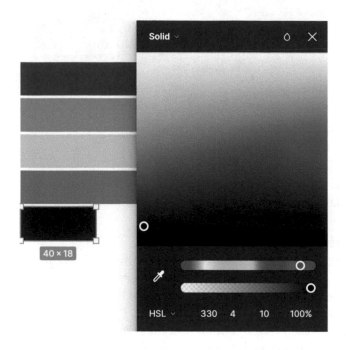

Figure 4.32   Lo and behold, that almost-black color is, in fact, a very dark and desaturated shade of magenta!

To lean into the magenta hue, I turned up the saturation and lightness, from 4 and 10 to 30 and 40, respectively. Finally, the tan color on the left became closer to brown on the right by upping the saturation and lightness again. And presto, we have a palette of colors that are still inspired by the sunset picture but are better balanced and still distinguishable from each other. As I was writing this section, I showed figure 4.31 to someone who is colorblind, and to my chagrin, they told me that they could more easily distinguish the bottom two bars on the left rather than on the right. Let this be a lesson in the competing priorities you will come up against as you choose color palettes for your visualizations. Sometimes, we have to pick our poison, so to speak: we must choose between accidental emphasis or an inclusive palette. While there is no absolute right or wrong choice, this does bring us nicely to the next section, where we'll get into the weeds of choosing colors in a way that maximizes the number of people who can appreciate (and distinguish) them, so do read on!

4.4   *Inclusive color palettes*

If you have ever rolled a wheeled object down a little curb-cut ramp outside the grocery store, whether it was a shopping cart, a baby stroller, a hand truck, a wheelchair, or something else entirely, then you have benefited from accessible, or inclusive, design. Designing inclusively in this way makes everyone's lives better! In this section, we'll talk about how to design for color blindness, for other types of vision impairment (whether permanent or temporary), and also how to be mindful of the meanings of colors in cultures other than your own.

4.4.1   Designing for color blindness

The single best thing you can do to make your designs inclusive is to have empathy for your users. Putting yourself in their shoes and trying to see the world (and your design) the way they see it is a huge step toward becoming a more inclusive designer. There are free desktop apps and browser plugins galore that apply a color filter over your work, so you can see it through a lens of each type of color vision deficiency. While these are always an approximation, it's still better than not trying at all.

If there was a contest among popular data visualization methods and features to find the most notorious offenders when it comes to color vision deficiencies, the winner would absolutely be the traffic light color palette of red, yellow, and green. As you are almost certainly aware, this palette is meant to communicate that the red is bad or needs attention, the yellow is medium or might eventually be cause for concern, and the green is good, or no action is needed. Still, as you may recall from our discussions of color blindness earlier in the chapter, those with deficiencies in their red or green cones have trouble telling the red and green apart if the shades aren't chosen well. If you don't believe me, check out the green-cone-deficient simulation in figure 4.33.

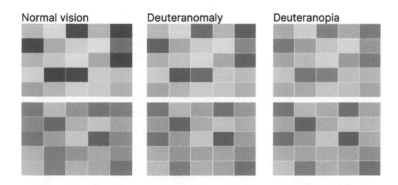

Figure 4.33   The top row shows a classic traffic light palette applied to a heatmap and what it looks like to someone with deuteranomaly (center) and deuteranopia (right). The bottom row shows a more colorblind-friendly palette of orange, gray, and blue instead of red, yellow, and green, respectively, under the same simulations. Remember, deuteranomaly is the most common type of color blindness, where the peak absorption of the green cone shifts toward the red end of the spectrum making greens appear more red. Deuteranopia is when the green cone isn't functional at all.

Employing a more colorblind-friendly palette of orange, gray, and blue makes it much easier for colorblind users to see the differences that a diverging palette is so good at showing, as shown at the bottom of figure 4.33. But sometimes, no matter how hard you try, you might have a client or stakeholder who insists on traffic light colors for a visual. In such cases, there are a few things you can do to make life easier for colorblind folks:

- Try to spatially separate the red components from the green components, either with a border or another color.
- Choose shades of red and green that have very different brightness or lightness.
- Limit the number of colors overall: as my colorblind reader told me, "A traffic light scheme with many shades of each color is much harder to interpret than one with only three colors."

Still, relying on using only a color filter to help make your designs accessible for color blindness is a little hand-wavy and subjective. After all, at that point, you're just relying on your own vision and interpretation in hopes that what you see and interpret will be applicable to a very wide audience. While it may work a lot of the time, it also may not, and you'll never really know how effective it is unless you follow well-established guidelines instead. Enter WCAG.

4.4.2   *The Web Content Accessibility Guidelines and color*

Pronounced like "wuh-KAG," the Web Content Accessibility Guidelines (WCAG) are a set of guidelines laid down by the World Wide Web Consortium (W3C), the closest thing the internet has to a governing body. These guidelines are meant to help developers and designers make the web accessible to as many people as possible, including those with physical and cognitive disabilities, but also those on very limiting devices such as screen readers and mobile devices. As of this writing, WCAG is still on its second major version, WCAG 2.1, but in late 2021, it was announced that WCAG 3.0 is under development and will eventually replace WCAG 2. As Version 3.0 has not yet been released, we'll stick to Version 2.1 here.

WCAG 2.1 consists of four guiding principles: the web must be *perceivable, operable, understandable,* and *robust.* Each of these principles is broken down into guidelines (12 total), and for each of those guidelines, there is a set of *success criteria* (61 total) by which a developer may know if they have met the guideline. For each of these success criteria, there is a specified *level of conformance:* A, AA, or AAA. These levels correspond to how strongly developers and designers are urged to comply with the guideline. For level A, it's a *must,* a bare minimum so that most people can see, operate, and understand the website. For level AA, it's that you *should* do this so that even more people can see, operate, and understand your website. Finally, level AAA is that you *may* conform to this guideline. Level AAA is very strict, and even WCAG itself states, "It is not recommended that Level AAA conformance be required as a general policy for entire sites because it is not possible to satisfy all Level AAA Success Criteria for some content." In all cases, if your website does not meet the specified standards, you can instead provide an alternative that does meet them. For example, if you have a color palette you really love or that you absolutely must use, but it doesn't meet WCAG's color guidelines, you can use that palette and also provide a toggle switch so that a user can change to an accessible palette if they need to, which would then make your site compliant with the color guideline.

On that note, how does this all apply to color, anyway? We'll look to the principle of perceivable for our answers. (The full text of WCAG 2.1 can be found at https://www.w3.org/TR/WCAG21/.)

Within the principle of perceivable, there are four guidelines: text alternatives, time-based media, adaptable, and distinguishable. Use of color falls squarely under guideline 1.4 Distinguishable, which states, "Make it easier for users to see and hear content including separating foreground from background." Within that guideline, there are 13 total success criteria, but we'll focus on the 5 which are relevant to color: use of color, contrast (minimum), contrast (enhanced), visual presentation, and non-text contrast.

Success criterion 1.4.1 (Level A), about use of color, states that as a bare minimum, we must not rely on color alone to convey information. This doesn't mean you can't ever use color to convey information, but if you do, you must (again, for level A conformance to WCAG) pair it with at least one other indicator or preattentive attribute (remember those?). In case you forgot, the preattentive attributes are color, form, spatial position, and movement. As mentioned in chapter 2, just be sure to use extra care when employing movement in your visualizations because it can easily cause more confusion and overwhelm the user. To be on the safe side, as you're starting out, stick to pairing color with either position or form (shape, length, etc.). When in doubt, also consider adding a label.

Success criterion 1.4.3 (AA) is about a minimum level of contrast, which is the next criterion we deal with a lot in data viz: text colors should have at least a 4.5:1 ratio of contrast with the background, except in the case of large-scale text and images (large scale means anything wider than 3 pixels, like most visualization elements such as bar graphs), which should have a contrast ratio of at least 3:1 with the background. If your font includes a border on the text, or you add a border to elements in your visualization (e.g., a fine black border around a blue bar on a gray background), that changes the contrast; therefore, the ratio would be calculated between the border color and the background color, instead of the viz element's color and the background color, like in figure 4.34.

So, how does one even calculate this contrast ratio, anyway? The formula is $(L1 + 0.05) / (L2 + 0.05)$, where $L1$ is the relative luminance of the lighter color, and $L2$ is the relative luminance of the darker color. Suffice it to say, there's a bunch of math under the hood of those relative luminance numbers. While it's not too complex as math goes, unless that's really your jam, you'll probably prefer to use a calculator that someone else has already made. My favorite is available in the appendix, or you can just go to www.accessible-colors.com.

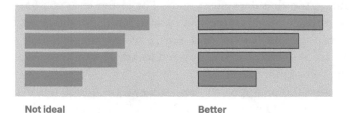

Not ideal   Better

Figure 4.34   On the left, the blue bars have no border, so the contrast is calculated between the blue and the light gray as 1.93:1, which is too low to pass WCAG's AA level of 3:1. However, if you add a dark-gray border, the contrast is then calculated using the border against the background, which shows up better than just the plain blue bars. The contrast between the darker gray border and the lighter gray background is a whopping 8.7:1, beating out the AA level by almost a factor of two.

Success criterion 1.4.6 (AAA) enhances 1.4.3 with higher thresholds: a contrast ratio of 7:1 for smaller-scale color against the background and 4.5:1 for larger-scale color (again, more than 3 pixels wide) against the background.

Success criterion 1.4.8 (AAA) is about visual presentation of blocks of text (paragraphs), which aren't usually present in data visualizations meant to report data on an ongoing basis (i.e., with new data flowing in periodically), but are often present in ad hoc analyses (i.e., static, resulting from a one-time data pull) and infographics. Most of its bullet points are about typography and are covered in chapter 5, but there is one bullet requiring that the text and background color can be chosen by the user to suit their own readability needs. This is aimed mostly at web and software developers rather than those using spreadsheets and BI tools.

The final color-related success criterion, 1.4.11 (AA), is the newest color-related success criterion in guideline 1.4 and is about the contrast of non-text elements. The first of its two bullet points essentially says that the colors of things such as buttons and navigation menus must have a contrast of at least 3:1 with the other colors that touch them, unless they are disabled, or if you have no control over the appearance because it's controlled by the app displaying the content. Its second bullet point specifically applies to data visualization (hey, that's us!) and says that the 3:1 contrast level with bordering colors is required for any portion of a visual a user needs to discern to correctly interpret that visual (e.g., bars in a bar chart, slices in a donut chart, or lines in a line chart).

Now that we've talked about being inclusive regarding disabilities, let's shift gears a bit and look at being inclusive regarding different cultures.

4.4.3   *Colors across cultures*

In art and anthropology, the idea that color has different meanings in different cultures is called color symbolism. With such diversity in the world and relatively few hues with which to work, you can probably imagine how a single color could evolve to have a vast array of meanings across cultures, in much the same way that different ancient cultures saw different constellations in the same sky.

I happened on David McCandless' *Information is Beautiful* (the originator of the annual data viz awards by the same name) website early in my data viz career. The first visualization that stuck out to me was his work about 84 different interpretations of about 10 colors across 10 cultures. The graphic is too large and detailed to reprint here, but it also serves as the cover illustration of the *Information is Beautiful* book, and you can easily find it by typing "colo(u)rs in culture information is beautiful" into your favorite search engine. (You'll find it with or without the "u" in colors. The author is British.) In this fascinating visualization, it becomes quickly apparent that the meaning of a color is not at all intuitive, so care should be taken before making assumptions that the reader will interpret a color the way you think. For example, let's look at the color of death. In Japanese, Native American, and Western / American cultures, black is generally considered the color of death, but, according to McCandless' sources, that role goes to the color white for Hindu and Chinese folks, silver for Arab folks, and green for those in (at least some) South American cultures. Interestingly, red is both the color of flamboyance and of heat, and black is the color of evil across *all* cultures in McCandless' visualization. Still, one thing I'd love to see someday is a more inclusive version of this graphic because it fails WCAG's contrast and color guidelines spectacularly.

Summary

- Color models come in two flavors: additive in the case of light (because combining colors reflects more light) and subtractive in the case of paint and the like (because combining colors reflects less light).
- Each model has its own set of primary colors: red, green, and blue in the case of additive, and cyan, magenta, and yellow in the case of subtractive.
- RGB space (the color space defined by using red, green, and blue as the primary colors) is the one used by computer monitors; thus, it is the most prevalent in data visualization. RGB colors can also be expressed as hexadecimal triplets.
- When choosing colors for your visualization, first, *get it right in black and white*, and then you can add some color as you need it.
- Using color purposefully and well requires careful thought and planning, but thankfully, there are tools out there that can guide you toward better choices.
- When it comes to making your designs more inclusive, if you're ever in doubt, consider adding a label to make it clear what you're trying to convey.
- A given color doesn't mean the same thing to everyone across all cultures.

Typography 5

This chapter covers
- Some basic vocabulary of typography
- Optimizing your type choices for readability
- Using typography to set the tone of your designs
- Establishing a hierarchy of importance using typography
- Choosing inclusive fonts

Back in the day when desktop publishing was a thing (and it happened to be a thing that I quite enjoyed at the time), I remember when Microsoft Publisher would suggest pairs of sometimes very different-looking fonts that went nicely together, with one to be used for headings and the other for body text. These font schemes, as they were called, felt as enigmatic to me as suggested color palettes did—where did they come from? How could someone know which fonts would pair well and which wouldn't? Font pairing, like wine pairing or chocolate pairing, is a skill that requires practice, and you have to start with a firm foundation in the basics.

In this chapter, we'll learn some basic vocabulary about typography, and then we'll learn how to make sure our text is as readable as possible. After that, we'll talk about how different fonts set different tones, how we can use type to subliminally communicate a hierarchy of importance, and finally, how we can be inclusive in our typographic choices. [*cracks knuckles*] Ok, let's go!

5.1 Some basic vocabulary of typography

The field of typography has a rich history, with movable type dating back to 11th-century China, and an unsurprisingly rich set of vocabulary to accompany it. I won't delve deeply into either, but I want to give you a teensy taste of the history because I just can't help myself. Did you know that the terms *uppercase* and *lowercase* that describe capital and noncapital letters, respectively, come from the fact that the lead letter blocks ("slugs") used in European movable-type printing presses were kept in separate boxes, or cases? The capital letters were kept in a case stored physically above the noncapital letters, hence *upper* versus *lower* cases. (See, just a teensy taste. And now, onward!)

As with color, there are some key terms that you should know before jumping into the rest of this chapter. This is not even close to an exhaustive list! If you want to find more terms, though, check out the glossary from FontShop at https://www.fontshop .com/glossary.

5.1.1 Character

A *character* is any individual bit or bauble included in a font, every little thing that would have had its own block to place in a printing press: letters, numerals, punctuation, currency symbols, etc.

5.1.2 Typeface vs. font

As with many things, the distinction between a typeface and a font has been all but completely eroded with the passage of time, leaving these two words to be used pretty much interchangeably today. However, if you want to be very technical about it, a *typeface* refers to the general design or artistic interpretation of the letters and characters (e.g., Arial, Times, Baskerville, Comic Sans), while a *font* refers to the typeface and any specific styles you apply to it, including the weight, size, and whether it is italicized (more on all those styles in a bit). Figure 5.1 should make it clearer.

Typeface		Font
	The quick brown fox	Roboto Thin
	The quick brown fox	Roboto Condensed Thin
	The quick brown fox	*Roboto Light Italic*
	The quick brown fox	Roboto Regular
Roboto	***The quick brown fox***	***Roboto Medium Italic***
	The quick brown fox	**Roboto Condensed SemiBold**
	The quick brown fox	Roboto Serif
	The quick brown fox	Roboto Mono
	The quick brown fox	***Roboto Condensed Black Italic***

Figure 5.1 Demonstrating what the same phrase looks like in the Roboto typeface, but in various fonts (all the same size)

5.1.3   *Serif vs. sans serif*

A *serif* is a small flourish, a small stroke or line at the end of open letters. Typefaces that have serifs on their letters are called *serif* typefaces, while those without serifs are called *sans serif*, where *sans* is literally the French word for "without." Figure 5.2 shows an example.

Serif   Sans-Serif

Figure 5.2   A demonstration of the same typeface, Roboto, in its serif style on the left, with the serifs in red, vs. its (usual) sans serif style on the right

5.1.4   *Weight*

A font's *weight* refers to the thickness of the strokes that comprise the characters. This can be expressed as words (e.g., light, regular, extra bold) or numbers (e.g., 300, 400, 800, respectively), as shown in figure 5.3.

The quick brown fox	Roboto Thin	100
The quick brown fox	Roboto ExtraLight	200
The quick brown fox	Roboto Light	300
The quick brown fox	Roboto Regular	400
The quick brown fox	Roboto Medium	500
The quick brown fox	Roboto SemiBold	600
The quick brown fox	Roboto Bold	700
The quick brown fox	Roboto ExtraBold	800
The quick brown fox	Roboto Black	900

Figure 5.3   All the font weights of Roboto

5.1.5   *Italics*

Unsurprisingly, *italics* originated in Italy, first designed during the 15th and 16th centuries. According to its Google Fonts entry, "Italic is a type style that's almost always slanted and is designed to create emphasis in text. Originally based on semi-cursive forms, italics are a direct contrast to the upright style" (https://fonts.google.com/knowledge/glossary/italic). True italics are drawn from scratch and have forms and features that don't appear in the upright form of the typeface, unlike *obliques*, which are merely tilted or slanted versions of the upright form (though usually with small corrections to ensure that proper balance and proportions are maintained). Check it out in figure 5.4.

Figure 5.4   A demonstration of the regular vs. italic forms of three different typefaces

5.1.6   *Font size*

I can hear you now: "Surely, Desireé, this one is self-explanatory." If only it was! How big or small a font appears may in general seem straightforward, but as with the very nature of typography, font size is quite nuanced. First, there's the issue of what units are used to measure font size. *Points*, abbreviated as pt, have been used in printing for hundreds of years and are still used today. Originally, a point was roughly 1/72.28 of an inch or 72.28 points per inch (though the exact size varied by year, country, and printer), but this was rounded and standardized to 72 points per inch (i.e., dots per inch or DPI) with the rise of desktop publishing in the 1990s. It is now known as the DeskTop Publishing point, or DTP.

> **A note concerning CSS and web development**
> So, points are great: comfortable, well-known, widely available, and now standardized in print. In front-end web development and CSS, however, there's an extra layer of complexity when it comes to measuring stuff, be that font sizes, widths and heights of elements, margins, padding, etc. In CSS, other units of measure besides a point include a pixel (abbreviated as px, of which there are 1.333 in 1 point) and a pica (abbreviated as pc, where 1 pica = 12 pt), both of which are absolute measurements, meaning that they are always the same size and can be related back to a physical quantity like an inch. There are also scalable or relative units such as an em (relative to the font size of the parent element) and a rem (relative to the font size of the HTML element), and many more. According to the MDN Web Docs (now an open source project, but initially stood for Mozilla Developer Network), "The benefit of using relative units is that with some careful planning you can make it so the size of text or other elements scales relative to everything else on the page." Remember criterion 1.4.8 from WCAG 2.1, which we talked about in chapter 4? It is an AAA criterion stating, "Text can be resized without assistive technology up to 200 percent in a way that does not require the user to scroll horizontally to read a line of text on a full-screen window." This is where relative units for font sizing come in very handy because they can scale or stretch based on the user's preferred font size, or the size of the screen.

Alright, we've got font size *units* in the bag, but what are they measuring, exactly? Back in the day when type was set using lead slugs, the size of a font was the height of the lead slugs, and even the largest letters had a tiny bit of space on at least the bottom, as shown in figure 5.5.

Figure 5.5   A lead type slug for the ligature of the letters i and a long s (now defunct in typography and can often be confused with a lowercase f when reading old texts) in 12 pt Garamond (Daniel Ullrich, Threedots, CC BY-SA 3.0, via Wikimedia Commons)

Today, the measurement of a font's size is actually a measurement of the height of the *bounding box*, the rectangle forming the boundaries of the character and the height of which is the same for all characters in a font. You have probably noticed that even when the font size is the same, oftentimes the same character will appear different sizes in different fonts (see figure 5.6).

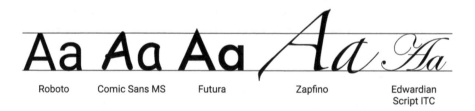

Roboto   Comic Sans MS   Futura   Zapfino   Edwardian
                                                              Script ITC

Figure 5.6   A demonstration of five different fonts and how their heights can be different even though the fonts are all the same point size and aligned on the same baseline

These differences in height across fonts, even at the same font size, contribute to the individual "feel" unique to each font. The way each font uses the space allotted to it almost personifies it in a way, much like how a person uses a space allotted to them, such as a room, office, desk, locker, car, patch of land, etc.

5.1.7   X-height

While a font's size is specified by you as the designer/developer, the *x-height* is a property inherent to the font itself, the height of lowercase letters as measured from the baseline, as shown by the space between the blue baseline and the red line for each font sample in figure 5.7.

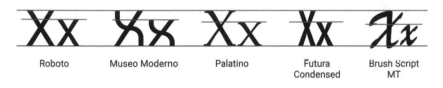

| Roboto | Museo Moderno | Palatino | Futura Condensed | Brush Script MT |

Figure 5.7   A demonstration of the different x-heights (baseline to red lines) for five fonts, sized so they all have the same *cap height*, which is the distance from the baseline to the top of the uppercase letters (marked by the top blue line)

The x-height of a font plays a very important role in readability, which is what the next section is all about.

5.2   Optimizing for readability

In a data visualization, the typography is not the star of the show, but it does help set the stage, not unlike a good stagehand during a theatre production. The stagehands don't have the fancy costumes or even any lines, but their job is of paramount importance for driving the story along because they make sure the pieces of the set are in the right place at the right time; a good stagehand fades into the background, not calling attention to themselves as they go about their work. It is the same for typography in a data viz. Good typography does not call attention to itself, and while it should be colored in such a way that it does stand out from the background enough to be legible, typography is doing its job to the very best if you don't notice it (unless of course you're a typographer). You have surely seen visualizations where the text is a bad color, too fine or too bold, too squished or too loosely spaced, too big or too small, or the font is just too fancy to be readable at all. To avoid all of those problems, you want to always optimize your font choices for readability.

5.2.1   Small font sizes

In everyday data visualization, we don't use a whole lot of large, loud typography because it would overshadow the data story we're trying to tell. Usually, most of the text on a visualization is pretty small, limited to axis and data labels, annotations, captions, and maybe a block of text here and there. Blocks of text don't tend to show up a whole lot on automated dashboards and reports (yet?). Perhaps AI will change this in the future, crafting readouts and key takeaways automatically, but as of this writing, that time has not arrived. Titles and headers are the larger-sized exceptions, which we'll get to in a bit. For now, we'll focus on sweating the small stuff like font weight, x-height, letter shape, and distinguishability.

FONT WEIGHT

The easiest qualitative test a font can pass for readability at small sizes is whether the weight is just right—not too light and not too heavy. Readability at small sizes depends heavily on a balance of ink and *white space*, or *negative space*, the unoccupied area around and all throughout your design. White space is your best friend when it comes to any aspect of design, so if you're someone who likes to use up every single pixel or millimeter of a page, it's time to start getting more comfortable with letting your designs have room to breathe. We'll ease into it by starting on the smallest scale with our font choices.

Have a look at figure 5.8, where we see the same paragraph in three fonts of the same size, but with three different weights.

Lato Thin Two households, both alike in dignity, in fair Verona, where we lay our scene, from ancient grudge break to new mutiny, where civil blood makes civil hands unclean. From forth the fatal loins of these two foes a pair of star-cross'd lovers take their life; whose misadventured piteous overthrows do with their death bury their parents' strife.

Roboto Regular Two households, both alike in dignity, in fair Verona, where we lay our scene, from ancient grudge break to new mutiny, where civil blood makes civil hands unclean. From forth the fatal loins of these two foes a pair of star-cross'd lovers take their life; whose misadventured piteous overthrows do with their death bury their parents' strife.

Archivo Black **Two households, both alike in dignity, in fair Verona, where we lay our scene, from ancient grudge break to new mutiny, where civil blood makes civil hands unclean. From forth the fatal loins of these two foes a pair of star-cross'd lovers take their life; whose misadventured piteous overthrows do with their death bury their parents' strife.**

Figure 5.8   Three fonts with different weights applied to a paragraph of text (the prologue of William Shakespeare's *Romeo and Juliet*, public domain)

Too much white space and not enough ink make the Lato Thin example at the top of figure 5.8 quite difficult to read or even see, but the opposite problem plagues the Archivo Black example at the bottom: too much ink and not enough white space makes me feel like it's assaulting my eyes. Do your users a favor and save the very thin and very thick fonts for larger headers and titles, and stick to a regular weight everywhere else except where you need to add emphasis, which is the only time you should need a heavier weight on a small font.

X-HEIGHT

While the actual x-height metric is the height of the lowercase letters, what matters more for readability at small font sizes is the distance between the x-height and the cap height, or the height of uppercase letters, shown previously in figure 5.7 by the top blue lines. The larger the x-height is relative to the cap height, the more readable the font generally is at smaller font sizes because that increases the white space inside the letters. Have a look at what each of our five fonts from figure 5.7 looks like with a paragraph of text in figure 5.9.

Roboto

Two households, both alike in dignity, in fair Verona, where we lay our scene, from ancient grudge break to new mutiny, where civil blood makes civil hands unclean. From forth the fatal loins of these two foes a pair of star-cross'd lovers take their life; whose misadventured piteous overthrows do with their death bury their parents' strife.

Museo Moderno

Two households, both alike in dignity, in fair Verona, where we lay our scene, from ancient grudge break to new mutiny, where civil blood makes civil hands unclean. From forth the fatal loins of these two foes a pair of star-cross'd lovers take their life; whose misadventured piteous overthrows do with their death bury their parents' strife.

Palatino

Two households, both alike in dignity, in fair Verona, where we lay our scene, from ancient grudge break to new mutiny, where civil blood makes civil hands unclean. From forth the fatal loins of these two foes a pair of star-cross'd lovers take their life; whose misadventured piteous overthrows do with their death bury their parents' strife.

Futura Condensed

Two households, both alike in dignity, in fair Verona, where we lay our scene, from ancient grudge break to new mutiny, where civil blood makes civil hands unclean. From forth the fatal loins of these two foes a pair of star-cross'd lovers take their life; whose misadventured piteous overthrows do with their death bury their parents' strife.

Brush Script MT

Two households, both alike in dignity, in fair Verona, where we lay our scene, from ancient grudge break to new mutiny, where civil blood makes civil hands unclean. From forth the fatal loins of these two foes a pair of star-cross'd lovers take their life; whose misadventured piteous overthrows do with their death bury their parents' strife.

Figure 5.9   A demonstration of the same five fonts as in figure 5.7, normalized to the same cap height, but this time with a few sentences of text

Which would you say, just based on eyeballing, are the most and least readable fonts in figure 5.9? I want you to hold that thought as we move on to letter shape.

LETTER SHAPE

Readability at small sizes also depends heavily on the shape of the letters, more specifically their *counters*, or the space inside closed or partially closed letters like a, o, and d. Usually, more round equals more readable, where the key word here is *usually*. Let's see what the counters look like for these same fonts in figure 5.10.

| Roboto | Museo Moderno | Palatino | Futura Condensed | Brush Script MT |

Figure 5.10   The shape of the *counter*, or the space inside closed or partially closed letters (colored red here), affects readability. Generally, more round = more readable.

So far, we have three yardsticks by which we can grade our five fonts for readability at small font sizes: font weight, x-height, and counter shape. By x-height, Roboto comes in first, with Museo Moderno in close second, while by roundness of counter, it's Museo Moderno by a mile, with Palatino in second and Roboto very close on its heels in third. What do you think about that when you look back at figure 5.9? I think Futura Condensed and Brush Script MT aren't even on the leaderboard due to the lack of white space. They might each be using a regular weight, but they have the smallest relative x-heights, and their counters are very squished, such that those of Brush Script MT are nearly nonexistent. Those two fonts and other fonts like them should never be used for blocks of text. Futura Condensed is a reasonable choice for a headline/title, but honestly, I'd just avoid Brush Script MT altogether, even though it's considered web safe, meaning that it's widely available and exists on pretty much every device already (though why it's so widely available is beyond me).

Of the other three fonts—Roboto, Museo Moderno, and Palatino— which do you think is the most readable? By our three yardsticks so far, Museo Moderno should probably be the winner, but by my eyeballs, I'd hand that victory to either Roboto or Palatino. Let's look to the last tenet: *distinguishability*.

HOW WELL CAN YOU DISTINGUISH DIFFICULT LETTERS?

Out of our four tenets of readability, I'd say this one is the least quantifiable. What I mean by distinguishability is that your user needs to be able to tell one letter from another and be able to determine what letter it is at all; this is where I think Museo Moderno finally tumbles from its little pedestal. Will you just *look* at Museo Moderno's w's in figure 5.9? My brain immediately hitches on them like I'm driving over a rumble strip on the highway, which is not the kind of reaction you want your users to have when trying to read text on your visualization. To be highly readable at small sizes, a font's letter forms need to look like we expect them to look.

Not only should the letters look as we expect, but it's important that you can tell the difference between a lowercase L, an uppercase i, and the number 1. Let's see how our top three fonts fare on this test, in figure 5.11.

Roboto   Museo Moderno   Palatino

Figure 5.11   **In our throo top contenders, how easy is it to distinguish these three oft-confused characters?**

Roboto, I'm so disappointed in you: making the capital I about 5% shorter and just a hair fatter than the lowercase L is not enough to make these two characters distinct from each other! Museo Moderno would take first place on this one again if we hadn't disqualified it based on those silly w's. This leaves Palatino as the de facto winner of this battle because that upper serif on the number one is pretty darn big, likely making it easy enough to tell whether you're looking at a lowercase L or a number 1.

So where does that leave us for a readable font at small sizes? Thankfully, there are more than five fonts out there in the world, but you can pretty easily do this exercise yourself with fonts that are available to you for your own projects. Just know that you might need to blow them up really big (like 200+ font size) to see differences in x-height and counter shape. You'll want to use a regular weight and check that the x-height is somewhere in the realm of about two-thirds the cap height, the counters are more round than squished, the letters look like real letters, and the oft-confused characters are distinguishable from each other (don't forget about the uppercase letter O and the number 0, as well as the I–l–1 problem we demonstrated). It sounds like a lot, but give yourself some grace as you're just learning to do this. It doesn't have to be perfect; as long as you try, even if you miss the perfection target by a little, it's better than not having tried at all. Remember, when all else fails, ask for some input from someone else, ideally one of your users-to-be!

5.2.2 *Lining, tabular, and uniwidth numbers*

Ok, this is a book about data, so let's talk numbers. Your choice of font can have a dramatic effect on how the numbers in your visuals are perceived, especially when you have no other choice but to show the data in a table (finance folks, pay close attention!). When numbers are densely packed as in a tabular structure, it's best if they align both horizontally and vertically. The horizontal alignment is called *lining numbers*, while the vertical alignment is called *tabular numbers*. As a bonus, there are even (a few) decent-looking fonts that align vertically at all weights—these are called *uniwidth* or *multiplexed* fonts.

LINING NUMBERS

The alternative to lining numbers is *old-style numbers*, which are cute and charming when you see them in old texts surrounded by prose, but they are dreadful for displaying numbers in a table. Have a look at figure 5.12, where the old-style numbers look a bit like a jumbled mess, while the lining numbers look neat and tidy.

Magra: Old style numbers   Roboto: Lining numbers

1,458,934   1,458,934

Apples	Oranges	Bananas
452	452	452
521	521	521
2,394	2,394	2,394
9,875,324	9,875,324	9,875,324
139,875	139,875	139,875
2,309	2,309	2,309
92,385	92,385	92,385

Apples	Oranges	Bananas
452	452	452
521	521	521
2,394	2,394	2,394
9,875,324	9,875,324	9,875,324
139,875	139,875	139,875
2,309	2,309	2,309
92,385	92,385	92,385

Not ideal   **Better**

Figure 5.12   On the left, we see old style numbers at work, and they look scattered, almost haphazard. On the right, we see a better way to display numbers, all of them sharing the same baseline and height, which makes for a much tidier and easier-to-read table.

Given that serif fonts for normal, everyday use tend to be a bit on the old-fashioned side, and sans serif fonts tend to be a bit more on the modern side, I would not have expected to see old style numbers without serifs. This is explicitly why I chose Magra for the demo in figure 5.12: it's sans serif and otherwise looks like quite a nice, unassuming, modern font. So don't be fooled!

TABULAR NUMBERS

The alternative to tabular numbers is proportional numbers, which again look great sprinkled throughout a run of prose because they make efficient use of their allotted space on the page. However, once again they're rather dreadful for use in a table. Figure 5.13 demonstrates this, where on the left side, we see proportional numbers, making it impossible to guess even the rough value of a number by how much space it takes up. Instead, on the right, tabular numbers mean that all numerals are the same width, which makes it very easy to estimate a number within an order of magnitude (factor of 10) at a quick glance.

Montserrat: Proportional numbers   Roboto: Tabular numbers

Apples	Oranges	Bananas
958	958	958
521	521	521
111	111	111
294,324	294,324	294,324
131,831	131,831	131,831
2,419	2,419	2,419
92,345	92,345	92,345

Apples	Oranges	Bananas
958	958	958
521	521	521
111	111	111
294,324	294,324	294,324
131,831	131,831	131,831
2,419	2,419	2,419
92,345	92,345	92,345

Not ideal   Better

Figure 5.13   On the left, we see how proportional numbers don't line up vertically, which means the user must work extra hard by looking closely at each individual number to understand even its rough value relative to those around it. On the right, we see a better way to display numbers, with each numeral taking up the same amount of space, which allows them to perfectly align vertically and make for a much tidier and easier-to-read table. A user can scan a table of tabular numbers and pick out the largest and smallest values within about an order of magnitude (factor of 10).

The importance of numbers aligning vertically in a table cannot be understated. If they don't align, the user is forced to closely examine each number, regardless of whether they want to know an order of magnitude (factor of 10) or the exact value. When they do align, users can easily pick out the largest and smallest numbers just by quickly skimming the table because the big numbers stick out a lot more than the smaller ones, as you saw in figure 5.13.

UNIWIDTH, OR MULTIPLEXED NUMBERS

Alright, by this point I hope I've likely sold you on the ideas of tabular and lining numbers and how much better they are for your users, especially when displayed in a table. If you want to stay there, that will likely be sufficient for at least 90% of your tabular font needs. However, if you do a lot of emphasizing in your tables by using bold weights mixed with regular weights, you might want to take things a step further by finding a font that has tabular and lining numbers and uniwidth characters. The idea behind *uni-width*, also known as *equal-width, duplexed,* or *multiplexed,* characters is that each character in the font (at a particular size) has the same width across all font weights. If you've ever heard of monospace fonts, which are normally used to display code and have a typewriter feel to them, you might be wondering how that is different from uniwidth: if a font is *monospaced*, it means that *every single character* in the font at a given font size has the same width—all letters, numbers, spaces, punctuation, the whole lot. The difference is subtle, but important: in a uniwidth font, *each individual character* has the same width across all weights, but that width may vary between characters, which is a long way of saying that a uniwidth font *can also be proportional* (see the previous section about tabular numbers for a demo of proportional characters). However, that, of course, doesn't help us much because we still want tabular numbers, not proportional numbers. There are very few fonts out there (as of this writing) that satisfy all of these criteria—that have tabular numbers *and* lining numbers *and* are uniwidth. There are even fewer free and widely available fonts that satisfy these criteria; thankfully, there is one available in Google Fonts, and that is Recursive (of the Sans Linear flavor, meaning it's sans serif, and the characters have a more linear look than the rest of the styles in the typeface). Have a look at figure 5.14 to see it in action on the right against Roboto on the left.

Roboto: Multiwidth tabular numbers   Recursive: Uniwidth tabular numbers

Apples	Oranges	Bananas		Apples	Oranges	Bananas
958	958	958		958	958	958
521	521	521		521	521	521
2,419	2,419	2,419		2,419	2,419	2,419
111	111	111		111	111	111
92,345	92,345	92,345		92,345	92,345	92,345
131,831	**131,831**	**131,831**		**131,831**	**131,831**	**131,831**
294,324	**294,324**	**294,324**		**294,324**	**294,324**	**294,324**

Not ideal   Better

Figure 5.14   On the left, we see that the characters of Roboto are not the same width across all weights, while those of Recursive Sans Linear are. At smaller sizes, the width difference in Roboto does not appear to be very great (even though I used the thinnest and thickest possible weights to contrast the regular weight, in the middle), so if you don't have a uniwidth font available to you, it's likely not the end of the world.

In figure 5.14, we see three different weights at work on each font—the lightest weight (thin for Roboto, light for Recursive), regular, and the boldest weight (black)—to demonstrate the multi-width nature of Roboto on the left and the uniwidth nature of Recursive on the right. At smaller font sizes, the differences for Roboto don't appear to be dramatic, so if you don't have Recursive or some other uniwidth font available for your project, it's probably not the end of the world. If you desperately need the effect of a uniwidth font but don't have one, you can use a monospace font instead. Turns out, Roboto has a monospace flavor called Roboto Mono, and it doesn't look half bad. Check out figure 5.15!

Roboto Mono

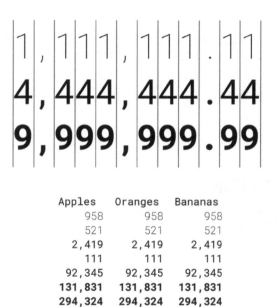

Apples	Oranges	Bananas
958	958	958
521	521	521
2,419	2,419	2,419
111	111	111
92,345	92,345	92,345
131,831	131,831	131,831
294,324	294,324	294,324

Figure 5.15 I added a few lines to prove that every character of Roboto Mono is truly the same width at all font weights. And monospace doesn't look half bad in the table example underneath!

One final note on uniwidth fonts: if you happen to be a Tableau user, you'll be delighted to know that all styles of the proprietary Tableau typeface are uniwidth! I had a coworker ask me very randomly one day what my favorite font is to use in Tableau, and my answer was an immediate and unequivocal: "The Tableau font!" (At the time, I didn't fully understand the difference between a typeface and a font. What I really meant was the Tableau *typeface*.) When Tableau created their typeface, they hired a prominent typographer and created a very solid typeface that is excellent for data visualizations, has many weights available, and looks great at large and small sizes. (And no, neither this book nor I have been sponsored by Tableau. I just like and recommend their typeface *that much*.)

Now that we've learned about the best ways to display numbers, let's move on to our last bit on optimizing for readability: limiting the number of fonts we use in a project.

5.2.3   *Limit the number of fonts*

Finally, when optimizing for readability, it's best to limit the number of fonts you use in your design—yes, that's fonts, not typefaces. Remember we're not designing pizza boxes here (I kid you not, my friends and I once tried to count the number of fonts used on a pizza box from a major chain, and we lost count at 20); we're designing data visualizations. In our designs, most of the type should play the ultimate supporting role of informing, helping the story along, and propping up the most important features, while still remaining largely unremarkable.

As with color, it helps to strip all formatting and styling from your text, so you are down to a single font at a single size in a single color for your entire design. Or better yet, start the project that way. Unlike color, where you will usually want to add back at least a little bit after you "get it right in black and white," you might not even need to add any extra styling to the type. Using a single font size across an entire project results in a very clean, uniform, and business-like look, making for a solidly minimalist aesthetic. White space used judiciously helps set elements apart. If text needs to be deemphasized, then a lighter font color can be applied, or if the header needs a bit more emphasis, then it can be bolded. Check out the example in figure 5.16.

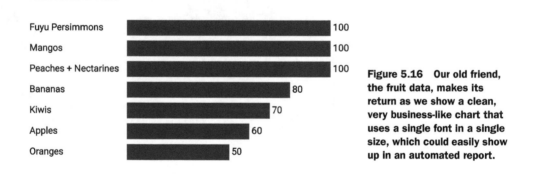

Figure 5.16   Our old friend, the fruit data, makes its return as we show a clean, very business-like chart that uses a single font in a single size, which could easily show up in an automated report.

If this simple look isn't right for your users, try adding just one style to the mix to add a bit of contrast, the spice of design that enhances interest and flavor (we'll talk more about that later in this chapter). If you're using a typeface that is part of a very large *family*, that is, there are many different styles under the same typeface umbrella, as we have seen with Roboto—be they different weights, spacing, italics, with and without serifs, and so forth—then your job is easy. The best place to try this first is to make the title or header a contrasting style to the rest of the text, for example, make the title font bolder, or larger and thinner, or if you're using a sans serif font, then try using a serif font on the title, or vice versa. See figure 5.17 for a slightly updated version of figure 5.16, where we use a bold weight on the title instead of regular weight.

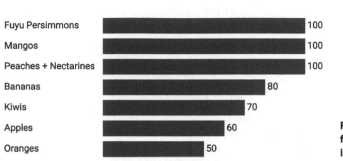

Taste Scores of Fruits

Figure 5.17 **Same idea as figure 5.16 but with a bold title instead of regular weight**

Let's see what changing the title to a serif font looks like and making it just a tad bigger in figure 5.18.

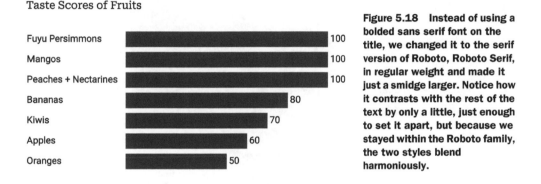

Taste Scores of Fruits

Figure 5.18 **Instead of using a bolded sans serif font on the title, we changed it to the serif version of Roboto, Roboto Serif, in regular weight and made it just a smidge larger. Notice how it contrasts with the rest of the text by only a little, just enough to set it apart, but because we stayed within the Roboto family, the two styles blend harmoniously.**

In figure 5.18, we have our first attempt at mixing serif and sans serif fonts, where the serif appears only in the title and at a slightly larger size (18 px instead of 16 px) than the rest of the text. By using Roboto Serif, we know it will blend nicely with the regular Roboto everywhere else because of the similar x-heights and counter shapes.

Serif or sans serif?

There is a great debate among the typography and design communities about which is easier to read: serif for large blocks of text and sans serif for smaller pieces, or the other way around. Some even say that the medium makes a difference, for example, whether the text is printed on a page or presented digitally.

It is likely the debate will continue to rage on in the years and decades to come, so in the meantime, we can listen to prominent data visualization designers Lisa Charlotte Muth and Tiffany France, who agree that for labels on a visualization, it's usually best to stick with sans serif fonts because they are less likely to become muddied by the extra ink (the serifs) at small sizes. If you are going to use a serif font, it generally fits best as a title or header.

Keeping the two styles you use in your design in the same typeface family will ensure that the two fonts will harmonize beautifully with each other without having to do any extra legwork.

If, once you've changed the style of the header to contrast with the rest of the text in your viz, you still find that you need more styling options to further set some other text, such as an annotation or callout, apart from the rest of the main text, you can try adding *one* more style. This time, keep it in the same typeface as the rest of the text, and choose whether to vary the weight *or* size *or* color; you only want to up the contrast with the rest of the text by a little so it will be *slightly* more noticeable than its surroundings. It's like the difference between driving over the reflectors on the highway rather than rumble strips or (science forbid!) speed bumps. Figure 5.19 shows the addition of an annotation with smaller text. Even though it's smaller, it still stands out as different, but it's not so different that it's overwhelming.

Taste Scores of Fruits

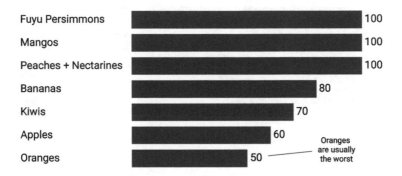

Figure 5.19   Here we've added an annotation in smaller text to the same graph in figure 5.18. Even though the text on the annotation is smaller than the rest, it still stands out just enough because it's different.

One thing about which there is no debate is that you should *never* use a fancy display font anywhere except a large title (where *display* means it doesn't fit either serif or sans serif, but instead has lots of ornamentation and/or creative flourishes, sometimes very elaborate and usually quite loud), and it really does have to be large so that it can be read despite the "typejunk," to adopt Tufte's lingo. However, the fancy title fonts generally aren't quite right for our everyday data vizzes—the charts, graphs, reports, dashboards, which are used to drive and track aspects of our everyday lives—because their fanciness and attention-grabbing are much more likely to detract from the story inside the data than a more straightforward serif or sans serif font. Remember, for these purposes, type and text are the stagehands, not the headliners of the show. As always, make sure readability and insight are of foremost importance: never let your design choices get in the way of communicating a message to your audience! When it comes to limiting the number of fonts you use, most designers say that you should never need more than three fonts in a design. As beginners, I encourage you to start small and simple, and only build out if you truly see the need.

5.3   *How type sets the tone*

When you learned to read and write, however long ago that was, you learned what different letters typically look like. You learned how to draw the simplest forms of capital and lowercase letters, and as you advanced, you learned that sometimes, the same letter, or even number, can be represented by a slightly different shape, like the single-versus double-story example in figure 5.20.

FUTURA   LATO

Figure 5.20   You learned at an early age that some letters can be drawn differently and yet still have the same meaning, like lowercase a and g. Futura uses the single-story variant, while Lato uses the double-story variant.

Part of learning to read and write is learning how to expect the characters of a written language to look. That's why you can read them—because (other than a few exceptions) the general shapes don't deviate from what you expect, so you can associate them with sounds and meanings, which is the *phonological* component of language.

When typographers create new typefaces and fonts, they keep your expectations in mind and then change the tiniest, most minute of details. They might add an extra little flick here, or round an edge there, or maybe taper another edge over there in multiple places on every single letter in every single bit of text. These tiny changes, these ever-so-slight departures from your expectations of how each letter should be shaped, then have subtle but far-reaching effects that add up to a big but usually subliminal effect on the tone or feeling of a design.

Early in this chapter, I touched on the idea that how a font uses the space allotted to it is almost like how a person uses a space allotted to them. Our perceptions of these uses of space affect our impression of the person or the font. You likely get the same sense about a teenager whose bedroom walls are covered in vibrantly colorful posters and whose bedspread is a giant radiating rainbow tie-dye pattern as you would from a font with large, rounded, handwritten-like script with big circles (or even hearts!) to dot every lowercase i and j. Similarly, you may liken a minimalist desk or office that shows only the barest of essentials with not even a pencil out of place to a crisp-edged sans serif font. Departures from our expectations and how a font's characters extend into, or retreat from, the space around them are what make typography come to life and communicate tone and feeling, even personality and emotions, completely decoupled from the meaning of the typed words.

In figure 5.21, we demonstrate three sans serif fonts (Roboto, Source Sans Pro, and Lato) and three serif fonts (Garamond, Goudy Old Style, and Times New Roman). After looking at the figure but before reading on, think about how you feel toward each font sample. How are they similar, and how are they different? What emotions, feelings, or impressions does each evoke? Can you attribute any of those emotions, feelings, or impressions to the differences you see in letterform or stroke?

SANS SERIF

SERIF

Cat

Let me not to the marriage of true minds
Admit impediments. Love is not love
Which alters when it alteration finds,
Or bends with the remover to remove.

ROBOTO

Cat

Let me not to the marriage of true minds
Admit impediments. Love is not love
Which alters when it alteration finds,
Or bends with the remover to remove.

GARAMOND

Cat

Let me not to the marriage of true minds
Admit impediments. Love is not love
Which alters when it alteration finds,
Or bends with the remover to remove.

SOURCE SANS PRO

Cat

Let me not to the marriage of true minds
Admit impediments. Love is not love
Which alters when it alteration finds,
Or bends with the remover to remove.

GOUDY OLD STYLE

Cat

Let me not to the marriage of true minds
Admit impediments. Love is not love
Which alters when it alteration finds,
Or bends with the remover to remove.

LATO

Cat

Let me not to the marriage of true minds
Admit impediments. Love is not love
Which alters when it alteration finds,
Or bends with the remover to remove.

TIMES NEW ROMAN

Figure 5.21   The subtle differences in each of six fonts can be seen plainly when zoomed way in on a single word. How these differences pan out on a block of text can be seen in the paragraph to the right of each enlarged sample. (From Shakespeare's Sonnet 116, public domain)

Serif fonts are generally felt to be more old-fashioned, so it should be no surprise that this excerpt from a Shakespearean sonnet feels more correct in a serif font on the right in figure 5.21 than in sans serif on the left. We who are not typographers would not have been able to put a finger on why Roboto gives the sonnet in figure 5.21 such a different feeling than, say, Goudy Old Style, if we had not seen the nuances in the letterforms blown up to 200+ font size. Roboto's heavy strokes with their squared and non-tapering edges, plus the fact that the nonvertical strokes are very nearly as wide as the heavy vertical strokes, yield a very solid, no-nonsense, impersonal, and almost robotic (therefore more modern) feel. Goudy Old Style, on the other hand, has a smaller x-height, and the graceful strokes on curves in letters such as a, n, and d are very fine at their smallest. Both give this font a daintier, warmer, and more diminutive feel, which put together usually skews more toward old-fashioned. Knowing this, we can see that a sans serif typeface with very rounded edges is going to evoke a different feeling in your users than a sans serif typeface with no rounded edges at all. Have a look at figure 5.22, which shows a rounded font compared to two that are nonrounded.

Let me not to the marriage of true minds
Admit impediments. Love is not love
Which alters when it alteration finds,
Or bends with the remover to remove.

.SF NS ROUNDED

Let me not to the marriage of true minds
Admit impediments. Love is not love
Which alters when it alteration finds,
Or bends with the remover to remove.

HELVETICA

Cat

Let me not to the marriage of true minds
Admit impediments. Love is not love
Which alters when it alteration finds,
Or bends with the remover to remove.

RECURSIVE SANS LINEAR

Figure 5.22   Here we can see the difference in tone across three different sans serif fonts. The rounded font at the top has a more open and friendly feel than the others, while Recursive Sans Linear has a rather cold and impersonal feel to it, almost slightly alien.

In figure 5.22, the first font has rounded edges, conjuring thoughts of balloons, which gives it a friendly and open tone. Helvetica, in the middle, has what I'd call an almost neoclassical feel to it because it is such a widely used font, but it's sans serif, which makes it not quite old-fashioned. Recursive Sans Linear at the bottom almost feels cold and impersonal with hints of a typewriter feel to it. This typewriter nature is probably why it feels a bit alien, but this feeling likely comes from how wide it must be to allow characters to take up the same space across all font weights, almost like the letters are holding each other at arms-length not to get too close.

If you are obligated to use certain brand- or company-approved typefaces in your projects, the task of choosing a font is a bit less difficult, but I would still encourage you to make sure those fonts are right for your needs and convey the right tone. Regardless of whether you are limited to certain typefaces, as you go about choosing a typeface for your project, try applying different fonts to very, very enlarged samples of text to see what the differences are. If you find that a font you are required to use is grossly out of line with your needs—whether that's in tone or readability—try having a chat with the person or team responsible for setting those guidelines, and keep an open mind because you may learn a thing or two from each other.

5.4   *Communicating a hierarchy with type*

Knowing what we know now about how typography allows us to set the tone of a project ever-so-subtly, it should be no surprise that another main job of typography is to communicate a hierarchy of importance. Conveying this structure is an essential part of enabling your users to intuitively navigate their way around your viz, because if you don't do it well, there are two consequences: first, the user will not know where to direct their eyes or attention to recognize the story that is unfolding before them; and second, they will have no way of knowing what parts of your viz are important or noteworthy. The key to establishing this hierarchy is creating visual interest, and the key to creating visual interest is *contrast*.

Stepping back from typography, visualization, and reports for a minute, think about what kinds of things you see out in the real world that catch your eye as being well designed. What was the last thing that captivated your attention? Perhaps it was a vibrant outfit someone was wearing, or a beautiful flower, a striking billboard, a really sleek car, or honestly maybe it was the shape of another human's body. What these things all have in common is contrast. Your favorite flower pops out to grab your attention because its bloom has a color that is very different from the greenery around it, and a top-tier sports car stands out from the rest on the road because of its unique, sleek silhouette and usually vibrant color (and maybe because it's passing you on the freeway like you're going backward). Contrast creates visual interest by grabbing our eyes and demanding we look at it.

To understand how to judiciously apply contrast so our typography establishes a hierarchy, we return to our old friends from chapter 2, *gestalt principles* and *preattentive attributes*, specifically color, form, spatial position, proximity, and symmetry. To demonstrate, have a look at figure 5.23, to which we'll be referring frequently throughout this section. When I made this viz in 2018, I kept things simple and consistent by sticking to one typeface throughout, the Tableau typeface, though I probably could have gotten by with fewer styles for even better simplicity and clarity.

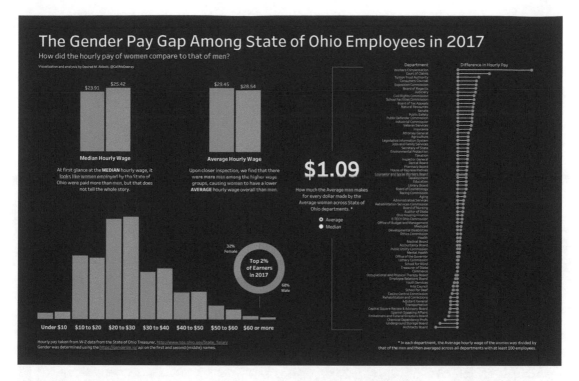

Figure 5.23   This is an interactive visualization I made in 2018 (direct link to viz: http://mng.bz/p1wE) using publicly available payroll data for employees of the State of Ohio. I used a single typeface, the Tableau typeface, throughout the visual to maintain consistency and simplicity, although I could have done a better job at keeping the number of fonts (styles) lower.

5.4.1   Color

When we first learned about how our brains perceive information, we started with the preattentive attribute of color. Using color is one of the two easiest ways to pump up the contrast on typography to show importance (or lack thereof, and we'll discuss the latter right after this). Color should be used sparingly on text, especially because it's challenging to choose colors with an accessible level of contrast for small, delicate elements like the letters of body text. For this purpose, it's best to use a dark, neutral color for your text if on a light background, or a light, neutral color on a dark background and then alter the brightness (or lightness) of the font color to *deemphasize* where needed by nudging that font color more toward the background color—lighter on a light background or darker on a dark background. This is what is meant by "pushing something to the background" to deemphasize it.

One dashboard style I really love is a monochromatic look, wherein you use only a neutral color (usually black, white, or gray) paired with a single nonneutral color in varying shades. Have a look at the gorgeous example of a monochromatic palette in figure 5.24. Built by Pradeep Kumar G for #ProjectHealthViz in January 2021, it was shortlisted for the 2022 Information Is Beautiful awards (he took third place in the Business Dashboard category for a different viz, but it wasn't monochromatic).

Figure 5.24   When going for a monochromatic look, it's vitally important to get the typographic color choices right. Here, there are three different colors for text in the main dashboard (not including the footer): white on the headers, bright green on the data elements, and a very light green on the axis labels. The interactive version is available at http://mng.bz/IV72 ("NHS Hospital Admitted Patient Care Activity" by Pradeep Kumar G is licensed under CC BY 4.0. Source data copyright 2020 NHS Digital. Publishing permissible under UK's Open Government License)

There are three different font colors in action in figure 5.24: white on the headers, bright green to match the data on the data labels and BANs (big-ass numbers, and yes that's the technical term), and a very light green on axis labels. By using color this way, Pradeep made the headers pop out as important because they have the maximum contrast with the background. Between that and the use of white/negative space, the headers give the dashboard structure so your eyes know where to look. Next, in the pecking order of importance, the BANs pop out because they are large and the same color as the bars and circles that make up the other data elements. The BANs can occupy the same level in the hierarchy as all the other data elements because they are data elements just like the bars and circles and even data labels; thus, it makes sense that they're all the same color (even if not quite the same shade of that color). In fact, in this dashboard, the data labels don't pop out at you because they're the same color as the data they're labeling, which shows us that they're the same level of importance. Finally, the axis labels are ever so slightly pushed to the background because they're a very light shade of that dark green background color. If, instead, all the text was the exact same color—either white or maybe the bright green to match the bans—and everything else stayed the same, the hierarchy of importance would not be as evident, and your eyes wouldn't know where to look.

5.4.2 *Form*

When we first learned about the preattentive attribute of form, it was in the context of the length (size) of numbers in a column or, similarly, bars in a bar chart. More broadly, though, form is about size *and shape*. In the context of typography, shape translates to typeface, weight, and case (upper vs. lower), and size is just the size of the font, as you'd expect.

Size is the second of the two easiest ways to add contrast to your text, to the point that I'd venture to say it's challenging to try to establish a solid visual hierarchy without using variations in size. It is possible, as we saw in the single-font chart in figure 5.16, but that was a very simple example and as we all know, real life is not usually quite so simple. If a single font or even just a single size was applied to an entire dashboard with many charts and a lot of text, the hierarchy would be easily lost. When an element is much bigger than the other elements surrounding it, it's absolutely going to attract your attention. In my gender pay gap viz in figure 5.23, you can see the hierarchy of sizes, and therefore importance, at work: the title and callout are very large, demanding that you look at them first, followed by the subtitle, then the axis and donut labels in the charts on the left side of the viz. Finally, the body text sizes are the smallest.

If you pair a contrasting size with another kind of form like a contrasting typeface, weight, or case, you're basically guaranteed to draw a user's attention to the element in question, as in the callout in the gender pay gap viz and seen close-up in figure 5.25. The "$1.09" is both larger *and* bolder than all the other text on the viz. This sort of emphasis should be used very sparingly! Remember, if you try to make everything important, you end up making nothing important.

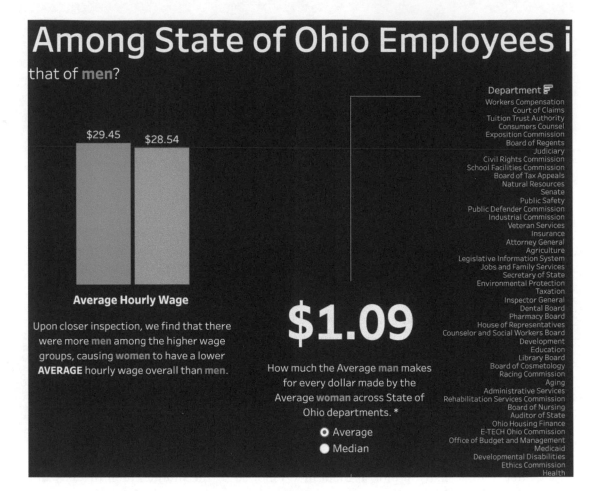

Figure 5.25 The callout on the gender pay gap viz is larger and bolder than all the rest of the text on the viz. Be very careful when using this type of emphasis because it is incredibly easy to overdo!

5.4.3   Spatial position

When we first learned about the preattentive attribute of spatial position, we were in the midst of an analysis about London bike rentals, so we made a map. However, again we can think more broadly than before: spatial position isn't just about conveying the geographic location of a data point; it's also about how and where an element is positioned on a page. Placement and alignment are both ways we can apply a spatial location to text. (Alignment could also be considered a type of form because for a paragraph, alignment affects the shape or outline of the text block; but for a single line of text, it's more about the location than the shape.) Have a look at figure 5.26.

In figure 5.26, the title and subtitle occupy the most important area on the page: the top left. In Western cultures, because we read from top to bottom and left to right, we tend to look for the most important things in that top left spot, while the less

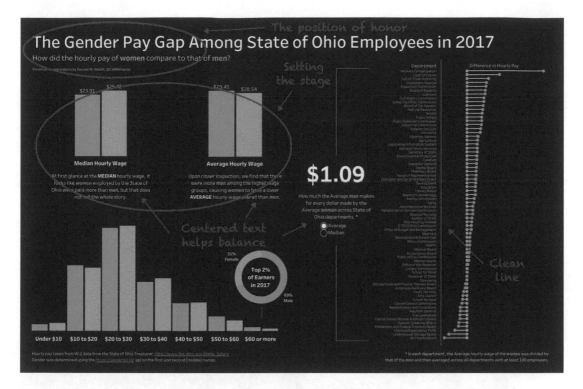

Figure 5.26   The position and alignment of text can be used to establish importance (header and subtitle position), as well as bring balance (centered text on the pair of bar graphs and the callout) and unification (the clean line of the right-justified axis labels on the right).

important things can be pushed down and/or to the right. Proceeding down from the title and subtitle, we reach the first set of graphs, which set the stage for the rest of the story. The text accompanying and describing each graph is aligned centrally to achieve some visual balance, and similarly with the body text of the callout. On the right, the y-axis labels are all aligned to the right to form a clean line that acts as a partial border for the barbell-like visual and unifies so the set of labels feels like a single element.

5.4.4   Proximity

When we learned about the gestalt principle of proximity, we learned that objects that are close to each other are seen as related or grouped together. On the flip side of that coin, objects that are farther apart tend not to be related or grouped together; herein lies the concept of white space, which is a crucial part of the contrast needed to communicate a hierarchy of importance using type. A bit of text with a lot of white (or negative) space surrounding it will pop out as overall important content, like the callout in the pay-gap viz, seen close-up in figure 5.27. Meanwhile, the bits of text that are much closer to other elements are relevant only to those elements, like the labels on top of the bar charts or on the donut chart slices (also in figure 5.27).

Figure 5.27   **The extra space around the callout dissociates it from the rest of the viz, while the close proximity of the donut chart labels makes it clear that those elements are associated.**

This is why it's important to include plenty of white space throughout your designs because if you use up every available morsel of the page and don't leave space, nothing will stand out, and the visual will feel like an overcrowded dance floor. Elements will just look like they're clumsily stepping on each other's toes and elbowing each other in the ribs, rather than waltzing gracefully with poise.

5.4.5   *Symmetry*

Finally, we come to symmetry. Remember the gestalt principle of symmetry, specifically the translational kind? That was where we talked about small multiples charts and that they work well because a user can understand what a pattern means in one place. When that pattern is repeated at regular intervals throughout the page, it's easy for them to see the relative differences between each instance.

In the case of typography, when we establish a set of styles we use consistently (and repetitively) throughout the design, it's easy for our users to see and understand the hierarchy of importance. As humans, we learn very well through repetition, and that's exactly what this translational symmetry in our typography uses. In the gender pay-gap viz, you can see this at work in the labels at the bases of the bar graphs—the median hourly wage, average hourly wage, and the wage histogram—as well as the label in the center of the donut chart, because they all have the same level of importance. See figure 5.28 for a zoomed-in view of the wage buckets bar chart/histogram and the accompanying donut chart.

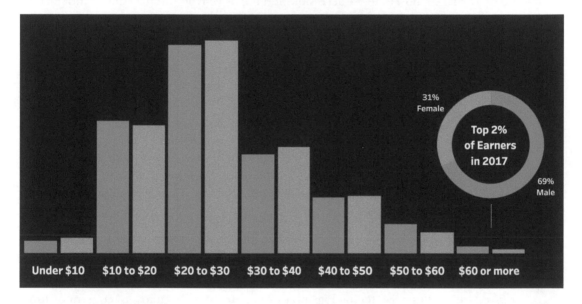

Figure 5.28 The main labels on the wage histogram and accompanying donut chart have translational symmetry with the labels on the pair of bar graphs above (not pictured) because they are all the same font, establishing the same level of importance.

Body text and data labels are also all the same size in the pay-gap viz. If this was an automated dashboard for ongoing use, each chart would likely have a title, using a consistent font in a consistent size and in a consistent location relative to the corresponding charts. Consistency is key!

In short, communicating a hierarchy of importance using typography in your designs is definitely not the most challenging part of making an effective data viz. Remember your preattentive attributes and your gestalt principles, and then use them consistently to establish contrast, and you'll be golden. And one more reminder for good measure: if you try to make *everything* important, then the real message the users will see is still that *nothing* is important.

5.5   *Accessibility and typography*

When I was in my 20s, I can remember trying to show my dad something, likely on my cell phone, and then teasing him as he held it farther away from his face, "Hey Dad, want me to hold that over here, across the room?" (Actually, for a while, I could just give him my glasses if his weren't on his face, and they worked for him too! But anyway. . .) The deterioration of one's eyesight as we age is something most of us will face as we get older, and as we all get there, we will have a profound appreciation for the designers and developers who make it easier for us to continue reading for as long as possible. (Am I speaking from experience? Yes, yes, I am.) So, pay it forward starting now by learning how to make accessible and inclusive typographic choices, not just for those whose eyesight has deteriorated beyond the length of their arms, but also for other vision and neurological impairments.

In this section, we'll talk about WCAG and how it applies to typography, and then we'll talk about dyslexia.

5.5.1   *WCAG and typography*

Typography mainly falls under the Principle of Perceivable, WCAG guideline 1.4, which states, "Distinguishable: Make it easier for users to see and hear content including separating foreground from background." We went over several success criteria in guideline 1.4 that are relevant to color in chapter 4; however, there are two more relevant to typography, as well as portions of 1.4.8, which we already covered in chapter 4, but I'll go over again here.

> **TIP**   If you need a reminder about what the WCAG is and why it has guidelines, jump back to section 4.4.2 to refresh your memory.

Success criterion 1.4.4 (AA) says, "Except for captions and images of text, text can be resized without assistive technology up to 200 percent without loss of content or functionality." There is a similar bullet in criterion 1.4.8 (AAA), and these are mainly aimed at those coding visualizations from scratch. If instead you are using a tool like a spreadsheet or a BI tool, the resizableness of the text is the responsibility of the developers of that tool and not you.

> **NOTE**   As a reminder, as long as you're not required to conform at a certain level to be in compliance with accessibility laws, then level A conformance means you *must* do these things so that more people can see, operate, and understand your website because they're a bare minimum. Level AA means you *should*, and level AAA means you *may*.

The rest of the text-related bullets in criterion 1.4.8 are about making it easier for readers with visual, cognitive, and reading disabilities to keep their place and navigate the flow of the text. Limiting the length of each line and including extra space between lines, with more space between paragraphs, helps readers see where their eyes should track next as they are reading. For the justification bullet, the uneven word spacing caused by forcing all lines of text to be the same exact width creates "rivers of white space" throughout the page due to stretching, but it can also compress words so that they're too close together, which impedes readability. All told, our choices around line length, spacing, and justification help us control the white space in a visualization, not only to engage and direct a user's attention as we saw in figure 5.26, but also to increase accessibility.

Criterion 1.4.12 (AA) says that, to the extent that it's within your control, you should use the measurements they give for line height (aka line spacing), paragraph spacing, letter spacing (aka tracking), and word spacing to allow plenty of white space around your text, which increases readability for all users. And if you choose not to use those measurements and then a user forces such styling on your site, it should still function properly and have all the same content and information without them having to change anything else.

5.5.2 Dyslexia

If you asked me about dyslexia even 24 hours before I spent an entire day reading academic journal papers about it so that I could write this section for you, I'd have said that it is a vision deficiency and that people with dyslexia often mistake some letters for their mirror image (like d/b and q/p) and/or transpose letters within words; I even once heard that sometimes the words on a page move or fly around. I'd heard from a friend and former coworker with dyslexia that there are specific fonts meant to help dyslexic folks, and we gasped together that the Very Large Tech Company that owned our company's communication platform of choice wouldn't allow a user to change the display font to my friend's preferred dyslexia-friendly font. As I've thought about and planned what I would write in this section, prior to reading all those papers, I had visions of telling you, my dear reader, that I'd even read that the nearly universally hated Comic Sans MS is actually a good font for those with dyslexia (spoiler: this may, or may not, be true—no need to go change all your fonts to Comic Sans!) and that you should consider giving your users the option to change the font in their web-based visualizations to one of the dyslexia-friendly fonts out there (namely, OpenDyslexia, a freely downloadable font available on all platforms, or Dyslexie, a paid option created by Dutch designer Christian Boer in 2008). But in my pouring over academic texts today, I've learned that as usual, it's not quite as simple as that.

According to Lyon et al. in their 2003 definition of dyslexia (the latest definition as of this writing), "Dyslexia is a specific learning disability that is neurobiological in origin. It is characterized by difficulties with accurate and/or fluent word recognition and by poor spelling and decoding abilities" [1]. Dyslexia is not a result of vision impairment, but it instead exists in the brain itself, resulting "from a deficit in the phonological component of language that is often unexpected in relation to other cognitive abilities and the provision of effective classroom instruction" [1]. To state it yet another way, dyslexia comes from a difficulty associating strings of letters with the sounds they make (hence "phonological").

Notice how this definition doesn't say anything about reversing or transposing letters? Turns out that reversing letters thing is a bit of a myth: studies show that most people with dyslexia do not reverse their letters. Sometimes children do, but even children without dyslexia reverse their letters periodically as they are learning to read and write.

Tons of studies exist on children with dyslexia, to the point that dyslexia is generally considered a well-understood neurological disability. However, when it comes to adults with dyslexia, it's another matter entirely. A 2021 study by Peter et al. was among the first to demonstrate that there is a statistically significant decrease in accuracy between adults with and without dyslexia when it comes to sequential (as in "two tow") and spatial (aka left/right, as in "cob cod") reversing of letters. However, they go on to say that "sequential and spatial letter reversals do not necessarily characterize all individuals with dyslexia," but that they might "characterize a severe dyslexia subtype" [2]. Thus, letter reversals happen in some adults with dyslexia, but not all.

So, how do we use this information to make inclusive typographic decisions in our visualizations? While there is currently not enough evidence for the case that there are special fonts out there that empirically, repeatably, and peer-reviewedly improve the reading experience for all folks with dyslexia, there is evidence that loose character [3] and line spacing, as well as shorter line lengths [4] do help. The best part is these measures don't only help folks with dyslexia, but also improve readability for everyone else, too, as we just saw in the WCAG guidelines!

Really, if you're optimizing your typography for readability, like we talked about at the beginning of the chapter, you will be at least 80% of the way toward accessible and inclusive typography, and probably even more if you're using a third-party tool like a spreadsheet or BI tool. If you're coding from scratch, you'll have a little extra work to do to meet any necessary WCAG guidelines, but if you were afraid of extra work, you wouldn't be coding from scratch in the first place. WCAG itself has tons of documentation on exactly what each guideline and success criterion mean, including examples of how to code for each correctly.

Summary

- Fonts that have a lot of white space, like large x-heights and well-rounded counters, tend to be much more readable than those that don't.
- For maximum readability by the most people possible, make sure that your selected fonts have easily distinguished letters (e.g., lowercase L, the number 1, and uppercase I should all look different).
- If you're going to be displaying numbers in a large table, choose at least tabular and lining numbers. Bonus points if you can also use a uniwidth font like Recursive in the Sans Linear flavor.
- To help determine a font's tone or feeling, blow up a sample to a very large font size, like 200, to see the small details that give the font its personality. Pay attention to any extra flicks and strokes, the shapes of the ends of strokes (tapered,

rounded, square), the shapes of the counters, and how the letters use the space allotted to them.

- We can apply the gestalt principles and preattentive attributes of color, form, spatial position, proximity, and symmetry to our text to create a hierarchy of importance.
- If everything is important, then nothing is important (and you've also likely overwhelmed your user).
- Being inclusive with typography generally means optimizing it for readability, keeping lines in a block of text relatively short, and leaving plenty of space between lines and paragraphs.

Creating a good chart 6

This chapter covers

- Making a "good" chart
- Bar chart alternatives that are a bit more interesting
- Map visualizations that don't secretly tell a different story without your consent

Let's look at the tools in our tool belt, the hammers and power drills of making a viz, if you will. We have the preattentive attributes of color, form, and spatial position (also movement, but we'll leave that one out for now). This means we can encode data using color, shape, size, and position, and then we can encode relationships between our data points using the gestalt principles of enclosure, proximity, similarity, symmetry, connection, closure, and continuity. We have all different types and categorizations of data, and we have the mighty tools of color and typography, which we've learned how to wield properly. You're ready to start thinking about charts now.

In this chapter, we'll take a deep dive into what makes a chart "good." Then, we'll talk about some ways we can make bar charts more interesting and engaging, sometimes without even using bars! Finally, we'll wrap up with a few tips to make map-based data visualizations in such a way that they aren't accidentally telling stories you hadn't intended to tell.

> **Choosing a good chart type: Use a visual vocabulary!**
>
> I have wrestled with this for months while working and reworking the outline of this book, but I'm ready to admit it: I desperately don't feel it would be valuable for me to regurgitate a laundry list of charts into these pages because there are some exceptional resources online, each of which can serve as a sort of data-chart dictionary, taking a data need and translating it into one or more particularly well-suited chart types, in much the same way as a French–English dictionary translates French words to English (or used to, before smartphones). Those online resources will be way easier for you to refer back to later than flipping through a book, which may or may not be within arm's reach when you need it. So, I invite you to check out and bookmark both the static Visual Vocabulary poster created by *Financial Times* at http://ft.com/vocabulary and the interactive version built in Tableau by Andy Kriebel, available on Tableau Public at http://mng.bz/BAJ1. (If that link dies someday, just type "Andy Kriebel Visual Vocabulary Tableau" without the quotes into your favorite search engine, and you should be golden.) For some other resources about chart types that I've found useful and inspiring, check the appendix.

6.1   What makes a good chart?

In both the color and typography chapters, we could draw on hundreds of years and millions of brains' worth of science and real-world experience on our trek to understand the here and now of both fields. When it comes to chart-making, though, we do not have the same luxury. I would argue that the computer did for visualization what the printing press did for typography: before these technological advances, the processes for creating charts and printed books were painstakingly manual, with each finished work being something to cherish because of the hundreds and maybe thousands of hours of toil behind it.

Because we're still pretty close to the cutting edge here in the early 21st century, the idea of what makes a good chart is not only still being formed today, but it's also heavily dependent on the purpose of the chart. Even with these two confounding factors, I believe we can narrow it down to just four things: a good chart is simple, holds a user's attention, is truthful, and ultimately, it gets the point across.

6.1.1   A good chart is simple

Ok, before you skewer me and start pointing out all the beautiful, bespoke, and artistic visualizations you've ever seen, please remember that this book is not about how to make bespoke works of art. This book is about *everyday data visualization*, the stuff that gives insight into your business, your health, your little red plumber guy, that sort of thing. And those visualizations, nine times out of ten, need to be simple.

What does it mean for a chart to be simple, though? It could mean uncomplicated in the sense of not overcrowding or overcomplicating a visual, or it could mean clean, elegant, and free from extraneous decoration.

WHY'D YOU HAVE TO GO AND MAKE THINGS SO COMPLICATED?

Like the esteemed lyrics go, sung by one Avril Lavigne, "Why'd you have to go and make things so complicated?" Some of the most popular types of charts can get quite crazy when you have a lot of categories, so let's talk a little bit about how to tame the chaos.

One of the worst offenders when it comes to overcomplicated (and highly controversial) chart types is a pie chart. People *love* pie charts. Analysts like making them, and users often like seeing them. So, *when it's reasonable*, I think it's completely okay to indulge both sides if you're careful.

Pie charts and their cousin, the donut chart, are engaging to look at and, when used wisely, can be very effective at communicating parts of a whole. (Honestly, I don't love making pie charts when I can make a donut chart instead because I enjoy having that center section of a donut for a label.) Nevertheless, there is a very good reason that viz professionals everywhere avoid these tasty charts like the plague: the human eye is truly awful at estimating angles. As such, do your users a favor and keep the number of segments to a minimum when you do use a pie/donut chart. Many say that you should keep it to five or less, but I say keep it to only two or three. And if you've got slices that are similar in size, you're better off using a different chart type altogether because, again, *people are terrible at estimating angles.* Finally, one more strong word of caution when making pie/donut charts: try to avoid making users compare these charts to each other.

I love using donut charts to communicate something with only two segments, like "Did they, or didn't they?" or "passed versus didn't pass," or "something versus others." Have a look at figure 6.1, which shows Hass avocado sales for the fourth quarter of 2022 by Bagged versus Others. Look how simple and clean that is!

Figure 6.1   A nice, clean donut chart that shows the percentage of three months of avocado sales, which were bagged avocados, in green (Open data from https://hassavocadoboard.com/)

This is also a great place to talk about multiline charts and stacked bar charts that can go very quickly and easily off the rails. Let's say we want to see a trend over time showing the sales of each product category of avocado. In the full data set, which you can find in my code repo (link in the appendix), we are given three different PLU numbers (those are the codes you see on the little stickers when you buy produce in the store; e.g., conventional bananas are 4011, and yes, that was off the top of my head because I've bought quite a lot of bananas in my time), bulk GTIN, and bagged avocados. Table 6.1 shows a snippet of the data, and you can see that when we add up these numbers from the raw data set, we get the total number of avocados sold in a given week.

Table 6.1   A snippet of data from the Hass avocado data set

Week ending	Product category	Units sold
12/4/22	Bagged	9,943,202
12/4/22	Bulk GTIN	10,945,411
12/4/22	PLU 4046	9,707,868
12/4/22	PLU 4225	6,151,495
12/4/22	PLU 4770	329,482

DEFINITION   GTIN stands for Global Trade Item Number, a 14-digit number that normally accompanies a barcode. The bulk GTIN here represents unspecified PLU sales data meant to ensure better traceability back to the avocado growers. Neat! (And many, many thanks to the kind soul at the Hass Avocado Board who actually got back to me after I called asking about what that bulk GTIN means.)

We already know that we don't want to use a bunch of pie or donut charts because a) we'd be comparing them to each other, and b) there are five segments (the three PLUs + bagged + bulk GTIN), which is more than three. So, what's the story we'd want to tell with a time trend of avocado sales by category? Users would probably use this chart to answer the following three business questions:

1 Is any single product category experiencing particularly high or low sales volume?
2 Are certain categories more popular at certain times?
3 How is the share of sales divided among the product categories?

Since this is a time trend, we could use a line chart with five lines, one for each category, and that would be okay. Have a look at figure 6.2 to see what I mean.

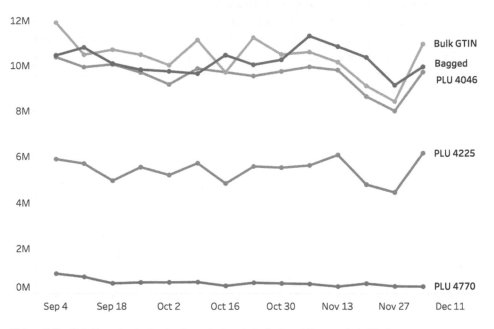

Figure 6.2   This line chart of sales by category is just okay. We can do better!

But we can do better than just "okay." So, why is figure 6.2 merely an "okay" line chart? For one, it's very busy when the categories are similar—notice how the three lines at the top crowd each other, intersecting and dipping above and below each other periodically. That's a good insight, but it's overwhelming and difficult to see. Also, I've used the Hass Avocado Board's brand colors (as closely as I could grab from their website with a color picker browser add-on), and it's not a very inclusive, accessible palette. If they can even tell the difference between colors at all, a user might wonder why one line is orange and another gray, yet three other lines are different shades of green. This is not a great example of using color purposefully but, instead, is a classic example of what some of us in the biz like to call a "spaghetti graph" because it looks like someone threw a bunch of spaghetti on the page and called it a day. (Dunno about you, but rather than in a chart, I prefer my spaghetti on a plate, doused in my mom's homemade sauce that was cooking for two days and generously dusted with pecorino Romano cheese.)

How can we un-spaghetti figure 6.2? We have a couple of options: separate the lines so they no longer share a *y*-axis (figure 6.3 top) or turn it into small multiples (figure 6.3 bottom), which works especially (and surprisingly) well when you have a very large number of categories.

Option 1: Separate y-axes *(but same scale)*

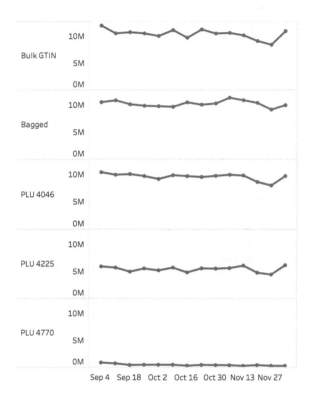

Option 2: Small multiples

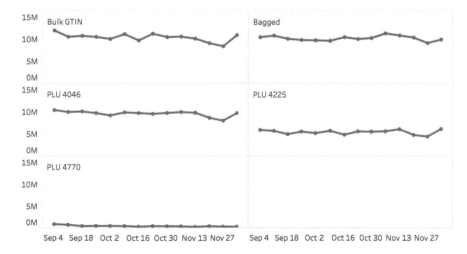

Figure 6.3   Two separate options for un-spaghetti-ing figure 6.2

The un-spaghetti-ing options in figure 6.3 work quite well for stacked bars, too. Along with many others, I severely dislike stacked bars. Check out figure 6.4, which shows the same exact data as 6.2, but in the form of stacked bars instead of lines.

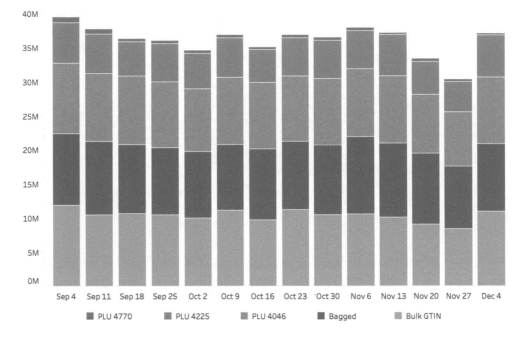

Weekly Avocado Sales by Product Category, Latest 3 Months

Figure 6.4   Same data as figure 6.2, but this time as stacked bars. I would argue that the only thing this chart has going for it is that you can see the total sales each week.

The only good thing I can see about figure 6.4 (stacked bars) over figure 6.2 (spaghetti lines) or figure 6.3 (un-spaghetti-ed lines) is that you can see the total unit sales by week. However, that is an easy fix: simply add a line for the total to either figure 6.2 or figure 6.3, and that solves the problem.

Keeping it simple also means not making your users tilt their heads to read anything, including axis labels. As you might have noticed, when I'm making a bar chart with categorical data, you will basically never see the bars extending vertically from the *x*-axis, but instead, they will extend horizontally from the *y*-axis. This allows the labels to be as long or as short and as numerous or as few as the data requires. Throwing it back to the fruit data for just a second, have a look at figure 6.5 to see what I mean.

One final note about keeping things simple: when there's an obvious convention regarding the data, go with it. For example, put a time series in ascending order (from

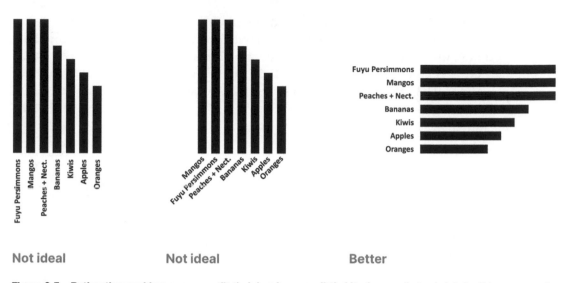

Not ideal   Not ideal   Better

Figure 6.5   Rather than making your users tilt their heads even a little bit when reading axis labels, I'd recommend just flipping the axes entirely and making the labels and data extend out horizontally from the y-axis instead of vertically from the x-axis.

left to right), not descending. People will not think you are avant-garde or "thinking outside the box" if you sort your months from December to January (or worse, alphabetically). Instead, they will think you are crazy and stop paying attention to you.

DECORATION OR LACK THEREOF

According to Edward Tufte's works, namely, *Envisioning Information* and *The Visual Display of Quantitative Information*, "chartjunk," which is what he calls *any* kind of extraneous decoration, degrades the credibility of a chart and distracts the user from the data, the message, the very intent of the chart. While I do not take quite such a hard stance against decoration, I admit it's true that everything you throw onto a chart that isn't data means that a user's attention is that much more diluted.

Whenever I'm teaching folks about how to up-level their data viz skills quickly and easily, one of the first things I recommend they do when making a chart in their chosen viz tool is to completely strip away everything the tool adds by default. This means removing gridlines, removing color down to a basic medium gray (get it right in black and white!), and then removing data point labels and everything to do with the axes: lines, ticks, labels, titles, all of it. I tell them to give their chart the Marie Kondo treatment, that is, to thank each element for its service and then chuck it in the bin (except the data—keep that!). Then, once they have a clean slate, they are free to start adding elements back as necessary.

Let's see an example. Even though your high school chemistry teacher would completely disagree, you usually don't need to add titles to both of your axes if you give your chart a decent title. If you decide you want to label every data point, then you can do without the corresponding axis entirely. (One notable exception to this is a scatter plot, for which you need both axes, and they definitely need axis labels.) On the left in figure 6.6 is a chart made with Tableau's defaults, except that I've already removed the gridlines, while on the right, I added an informative title, removed the axes, and then labeled the end of each bar directly with the labels outside and not inside, for better readability. The data again comes from the Hass Avocado Board, so I used their main green (snagged from their website using a color picker browser add-on) instead of the default Tableau blue, or even a medium gray.

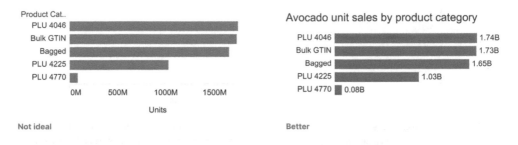

Figure 6.6   Even though the chart on the left is already pretty simple, we simplified it even further by removing the axes and axis titles, instead opting to give the chart a good title and labeling the bars directly. The user's eyes are already on the right, looking at the end of the bar, so placing a label there makes sense.

As I said, I don't take as hard a stance against decoration as Tufte, but I do caution you to first learn how to make simple and clear vizzes before you go and try to add any whimsy to them, and then consider *why* you're adding whimsy before doing so. But, if you've heard the warnings, you know the cautionary tales, and you're sure it will land well with your users, then you're ready to take the plunge and add a little pizzazz to a viz you're making. Just make sure it doesn't detract from the message and isn't distracting for the user! This brings us to our next point: a good chart holds the user's attention.

6.1.2   *A good chart holds the user's attention*

To again quote Tufte in *Envisioning Information*, "If the numbers are boring, then you've got the wrong numbers." If you're trying to jazz up a viz simply because people are disinterested in it, you might want to go back to the drawing board. Remember, you're creating visualizations to answer questions, and I know it's really hard to hear, but if people can't be bothered to look at the viz you've created because they're bored by it, then you've created the wrong viz. A good visualization is relevant to your user and captivates their attention. It makes them want to ask more questions and sparks their curiosity.

Take the simple but hauntingly beautiful line chart in figure 6.7, for example. Ash Shih created this viz as part of the #MakeoverMonday project in the Tableau community back in 2019, and I haven't been able to get it out of my head since.

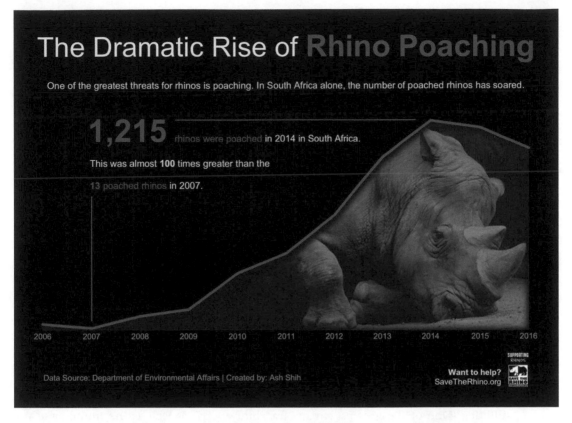

The Dramatic Rise of Rhino Poaching

One of the greatest threats for rhinos is poaching. In South Africa alone, the number of poached rhinos has soared.

1,215 rhinos were poached in 2014 in South Africa.

This was almost **100** times greater than the

13 poached rhinos in 2007.

2006 2007 2008 2009 2010 2011 2012 2013 2014 2015 2016

Want to help?
SaveTheRhino.org

Data Source: Department of Environmental Affairs | Created by: Ash Shih

Figure 6.7   The Dramatic Rise of Rhino Poaching, created by Ash Shih in 2019 for the #MakeoverMonday project. Notice the simple use of color, the way the lines point out the key aspects of the data, and the little touch of decoration, which is the image of a rhino behind the chart, echoing the curve of the line and giving a sense of balance with the callout on the left. I did slightly modify the color of the axis labels and data citation to be a bit brighter so you could see it in print. Check out the original here: http://mng.bz/A8Po. (Ash Shih. Used with permission)

How does one go about grabbing *and keeping* someone's attention? (Emphasis on the "and keeping" because that's a major aspect that sets us as viz experts apart from clickbait scum.) It all starts with a good title. A nice, informative title on your chart (usually at the top) will go a very long way to grabbing a user's attention. Without a title, you won't be able to properly set the context, and your user will be grasping and guessing to figure out what you're trying to tell them. Imagine if Ash's viz in figure 6.7 had the title "Rhinos Poached by Year." That is an accurate title, but "The Dramatic Rise of Rhino Poaching" is, well, dramatic, and it tells you right out that rhino poaching is on the rise. The use of the word *dramatic* tells you it's increased a lot and quickly, and with a title like that, you know what to expect in the visualization that follows. While I love a good twist in a story as much as the next person, this is not the time or place for a twist because you don't want your users to become confused and disoriented. You want them to be driven to action, to ignite their curiosity for more information and more data. And do you know what else enthralls people? A good story.

6.1.3 *Tell them stories*

Let's think about the elements of a good story, or a good plot, for a minute. As with gestalt principles, the number of "essential elements of a story" varies widely based on whom you ask and in what context, but the elements I'm referring to here are *exposition, rising action, climax, falling action*, and *resolution*.

The *exposition* is meant to intrigue you; it's where you get the setting, the main characters, and the overall tone of a story. Think about the opening of Shakespeare's *Romeo and Juliet*: "Two households, both alike in dignity, In fair Verona, where we lay our scene, From ancient grudge break to new mutiny, Where civil blood makes civil hands unclean." That just makes me want to chef's kiss: it's so beautiful and eloquent and tidy, and it intrigues us into wanting to know more. In visualization, this is generally best accomplished with a great title, like Ash's "The Dramatic Rise of Rhino Poaching" in figure 6.7. That catchy title, the exposition, is the hook that grabs your user and their attention.

The *rising action* reels in the reader once they've been hooked. It's the detailed background, the character development, and all the stuff that makes you care about what happens to the characters in the story. It is also here, in the rising action, where the conflict is introduced, like the wedding in *Romeo and Juliet* or Mufasa's death in *The Lion King*. Looking back at figure 6.7 again, I would say that the rising action is the subtitle, "One of the greatest threats for rhinos . . . ," as well as the literal "rise" or increase in the data points, connected by the red line.

We are all familiar with the *climax* in a story, the turning point, the Thing that happens when everything in the story comes to a head, and the conflict is at last resolved. You can practically feel it in your bones with some stories: Juliet and her Romeo each taking their own lives in *Romeo and Juliet*, or the One Ring finally being destroyed in *The Lord of the Rings* trilogy. The climax of a visualization is the main insight, the conclusions drawn from an analysis, and how the situation would end if nothing changed. In the rhino-poaching example in figure 6.7, it's that big callout on the left—that rhino poaching increased almost 100-fold from 2007 to 2014, and the literal peak of the trendline in 2014.

The *falling action* is when the tension generated by the conflict is finally easing. Some loose ends might be tied up, but probably not all of them. This is the wind-down, the afterglow, if you will. Imagine how dissatisfying it would be if the *Lord of the Rings* trilogy skipped straight from Gollum and the Ring falling into Mount Doom, right to Frodo and Bilbo's departure from Middle Earth with the elves? After all the tension of Mount Doom (and Isengard, and Helm's Deep, and Gondor, and . . .), we, the readers/viewers, can't just be dropped straight into the resolution. Instead, we must be unwound gently, as Tolkien does at great length after Mount Doom. In the rhino example from figure 6.7, the falling action is the decrease in the trendline after the peak: it shows that things started to improve, but there was still significant room for more improvement as of 2016. I would also argue that the falling action in this viz includes the background image of the rhino itself, now fully revealed at the end of the line.

Finally, we reach the *resolution*, also known as the *denouement*. It can literally be as simple as, "And they all lived happily ever after," or it can be the montage at the end of every based-on-truth story (and parody thereof), detailing what ultimately happened to the main characters during the rest of their lives. It's the end of *Lord of the Rings: Return of the King*, with Frodo and Bilbo departing Middle Earth with the elves, and Sam going home to his growing family. In a visualization, the resolution is the call to action, the clincher, the answer to the question, "But how do we stop this?" or "How do we keep this from happening?" Turning once again to Ash's rhino poaching example from figure 6.7, it's that "Want to help?" in the lower right corner, paired with the "Save the Rhino" logo.

Now that we've zoomed in on the rhino viz under the microscope of what are the parts of a good story, I want you to zoom back out and look at it as a whole. At the top of the viz, there's the exposition, followed quickly below by the rising action and the climax—the subtitle, the increasing trendline, and the main callout. Following the trendline from left to right across the page, past the point of climax, is the falling action—the rest of the data points and the image of the rhino. Finally, we've reached the bottom right of the page where we arrive at the call to action, or the resolution of our rhino story. Hats off to you, Ash Shih, for taking us all on an incredibly enthralling journey with your simple yet hauntingly beautiful viz about nearly a decade of rhino poaching.

6.1.4   *A good chart is truthful*

So, let's say you've been tasked with analyzing an experiment for which you had really high hopes, but it's looking like the results are inconclusive, or even worse, they're in the totally opposite direction from what you'd hoped. We've all been there.

It could be tempting at this point to either completely fudge the numbers or sweep the conclusion under the data rug, as it were. But both are bad ideas! Above all, it is our sacred duty as data visualization practitioners to *tell the truth*. We are in a position of great power when we wield data to be visualized, and as we all know, with great power comes great responsibility. Our stakeholders, clients, and public trust us to tell them like it is and not to hide or falsify conclusions and results. In this day and age, when even "The camera doesn't lie" is no longer true, we have to be better than that. We must rise above the lies and deceit and be a pillar of trust on which people can always depend.

In case you need me to spell it out for you, here are some ways you can make sure your charts are truthful and not misguiding. This is hopefully the only time you'll see me telling you straight up, "Don't do ____":

- Don't lie in the title. For example, don't say, "Sales are up!" when in fact sales are down.
- While there are legitimate cases for leaving zero out of a *y*-axis (or *x*-axis if your chart is horizontal), those cases are pretty rare. When you choose to do so, make sure you have a good reason for it, and make sure you are very up-front about it. Be extra careful when doing so on a bar chart because we typically compare the sizes of the bars, and those relative sizes don't mean the same thing if you chop off the bottom of each bar.
- Don't use a dual axis to make a chart look like it's telling a different story. I recently saw a viz about military expenditures over time by country where the United States had its own axis on the right, and all other countries were using the left axis. And of course, they weren't synchronized, and 0 was removed from the y-axis only on the US side! Even though the graph wasn't saying anything untrue, it was quite misleading. Very not cool. Please don't do that.
- Stick to the facts and leave your bias out of your visualizations, especially on highly charged topics (hello, religion and politics).
- Maintain a consistent scale and use extreme caution if you're using a scale that is nonlinear (e.g., a logarithmic scale), especially when your audience is the general public.
- Don't hide an insight behind atypical units. This one is a bit less egregious than some others in this list, but it's worth calling out anyway: if, for example, you're working with an organization that reports gains and losses in currency (e.g., USD) and not percentages, then make sure you stick with their norm. You wouldn't want to say, "Revenue was down by 0.3% last year," when they normally report in raw dollar amounts because the 0.3% does make it sound like a bit rosier picture than "Revenue was down by $800,000 last year."

6.1.5 *Ultimately, a good chart gets the point across*

Remember when you learned how to write a paper in middle school (or maybe high school)? My younger self always wanted to keep the reader on the edge of their seat, treating my papers like a work of fiction wherein I would feebly attempt to grab the reader's attention upfront and *never* give away the ending too soon. But, thanks to good teachers and, honestly, thanks to my parents, who are very talented wordsmiths (thank you so much, Mom and Dad!), I learned that's not usually the best way to effectively communicate *information*, especially when you are just learning how to do so. When you set about writing an essay or a research paper or a book, you are most successful (and least likely to tear out your hair in frustration) when you start with an outline, which acts as a kind of *wireframe*, if you will, which we'll get to in a later chapter. That wireframe should have the skeleton of an introduction, a body, and a conclusion, and then you can build it out from there. I usually fall back on the classic *Aristotelian triptych* approach: say what you're going to say in the introductory paragraph(s), say it throughout the body, and then say what you just said in the concluding paragraph(s). As you are learning to make good charts, it helps to follow the same outline: in the title, you tell people what they're going to see, then show them (i.e., tell them, but visually) using gestalt principles and preattentive attributes. Finally, you drive the points home by telling them again what the chart just said, but this time, using data labels, annotations, and callouts. "But Desireé," you say, "what about visualization as data storytelling, which *we just talked about only a few pages ago?* How can you tell a good story after you've given away the ending?"

It might seem like these concepts—that of presenting information and that of telling a story—could never go together or even be related, but think back again to the rhino-poaching visualization in figure 6.7. The title, "The Dramatic Rise of Rhino Poaching," *literally gave away* the climax of that story, and it still totally worked! Ash said what he was going to say in the title, then he said it with the chart itself by way of the trendline, and then he used the callout to say with words what the chart had just said visually. Learning to get the point across in your visualizations requires holding these two concepts—presenting information and storytelling—in a delicate balance simultaneously in your mind (much like Orwellian "doublethink").

Really, though, when it's all said and done, it doesn't matter whether you have followed visualization best practices or obeyed any of the other rules. If you've been truthful with your users, and they understand and like the chart you made, you can pat yourself on the back for a job well done. The best practices and rules are there to help guide you toward viz nirvana, removing the guesswork you'd be doing otherwise, but the ultimate goal is always to get the point across in such a way that it's understandable, and people can take action if they so desire. And you know what? Even after you've gotten really good at it, sometimes you'll still miss the mark. But in those times when you get knocked down a peg (or two), just dust yourself off and jump right back in because, at the end of the day, *you learned something*, and learning is always a good thing. Keep your users' needs at the forefront, keep learning, and you will always be successful. (And you might want to tattoo that to your forehead or plaster it with sticky notes all over your workspace for when you have nondesigner clients and stakeholders who dictate how you should be making your visualizations for them. More on that in chapter 9 on troubleshooting.)

Now that we know what makes a chart good—it's simple, holds a user's attention, is truthful, and ultimately, gets the point across—let's learn some ways in the next sections about how we can make some basic charts a bit better.

6.2 Bar charts that aren't boring

Now that you understand what generally makes a chart good, and maybe you've looked at a visual vocabulary to figure out what kind of chart you want to make, you're pretty ready to make a chart. As you already know, this isn't the kind of book where we'll walk you through making a graph in a particular tool; instead, I'm trusting you to do that part on your own, because all tools function differently, and they all change as time passes. What I will do here, however, is help you make good design decisions—a skill you can port from one tool to the next to the next, from making posters to slide decks to web pages, and everything in between.

Take the humble bar chart, for example. It's close to a "one-graph-fits-all" kind of deal, because bars are just so simple and straightforward. You will make a lot of bar graphs in your time as a viz practitioner, as I have. And you will absolutely get bored with them, as I have. This is one of those times when I kindly thank Tufte for his advice against anything but the basics, and then I set that aside. There are ways to make bar-like charts that are not quite so humdrum as a classic bar, and we'll talk about a few in this section.

6.2.1 Lollipops

One of my very favorite bar chart alternatives is a *lollipop chart*. Instead of a rectangular bar, a lollipop uses a line (or a very skinny bar) with a circle at the end, as in figure 6.8.

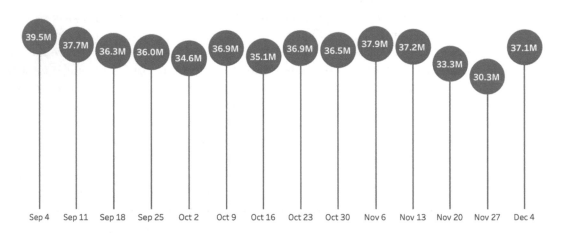

Figure 6.8   A lollipop chart is one fun alternative to a bar chart.

I love making lollipop charts, but I generally don't use them as a stand-alone visual. You might notice figure 6.8 looks just a little off. It's kind of cute, but it just doesn't really seem balanced because the tops of the lollipops are really heavy compared to the rest of the visual. For this reason, I only use lollipops as part of a dashboard with multiple charts on it because then there are other elements to help balance out the top-heavy lollipops. Sometimes, I've found myself making dashboards for stakeholders or clients that are all bar graphs, and I honestly think that looks goofy, too, because you'll likely have different numbers of bars on each graph (so the bars will be different widths), and/or they won't all be oriented in the same direction (e.g., vertical vs. horizontal). I find that it just looks weird, so those are the times I'll whip out a lollipop chart. They get the job done with the addition of just a teensy bit of whimsy, but not too much.

6.2.2   Iconographs

Another fun and interesting alternative to a bar chart is called an *iconograph* because it uses stacks of icons in the place of bars. I haven't used this one very often because it can be a little tedious to set up the calculations (in Tableau, anyway), and the resulting graph isn't very exact because each icon doesn't generally represent a single unit, instead they represent a certain number of units. Check out figure 6.9 as an example, using completely fake data.

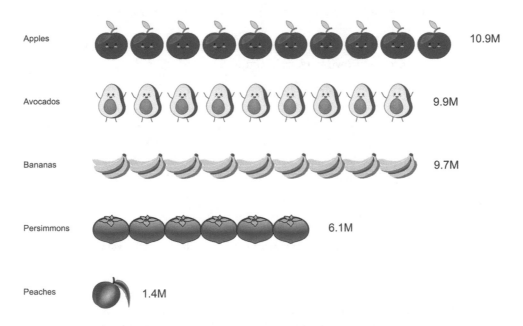

Apples led the way in produce sales

Figure 6.9   An iconograph showing fictitious produce sales, led by apples. (And how cute is that avocado! He was begging to be included, so who was I to tell him no?)

An iconograph is a graph that should be used with care, for the reason mentioned earlier (that it's not particularly exact, which is why I added a label on the end of each stack) and also because it might be too much whimsy, depending on the icons you find/create/use. For example, the happy apples and avocados in figure 6.9

probably wouldn't go over well with business executives, but it could be fun for a personal side project. Still, they're just so darn *cute* that I had to include them here for you.

Is an iconograph made *exclusively* of chartjunk? Yeah, probably, so like I already said, it should be used with extreme caution: know the rules before you endeavor to break them! It does still communicate the message about sales by type of produce, and the labels on the end help with the exactness. It is an otherwise clean, clear, and straightforward visual because I kept the typography simple and everything else on the visualization is pure data.

6.2.3   *Bonus: Revisiting stacked bar charts*

Even though they're not typically boring (because they're just not good from the start), let's revisit stacked bar charts. We've already talked about their less-than-optimal nature and how we can sometimes turn them into line charts instead. But, what about those times when a line chart doesn't work, like when you're not trending something over time or if you only have a single stacked bar you want to show? (Sometimes people can get a little carried away when avoiding pie charts when they want to show parts of a whole.)

One way to handle this, especially in the case of a single stack, is to just split the pieces up into their own bars, as in figure 6.10.

Figure 6.10   A single stacked bar (on the left) is much better visualized as individual bars for each segment (on the right).

Even in the case of multiple stacked bars, the technique of splitting into individual bars as shown in figure 6.10 would still work. The resulting chart is called a *clustered* bar chart, as in figure 6.11, where we have decided to look at this same data, this time split by geography where the avocados were sold. Placing the bars alongside one another in this way enables us to see patterns across the data much more easily, such as which product category is the most popular in each region.

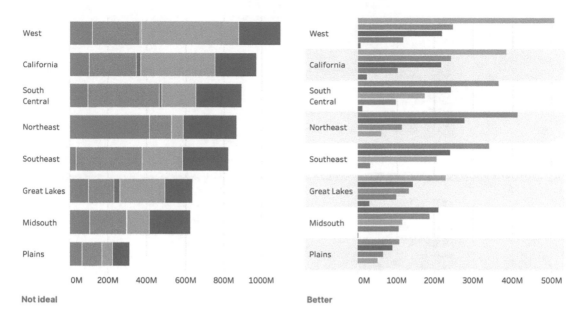

Figure 6.11 The multiple stacked bars on the left can be simply unstacked and displayed alongside one another, as on the right, to better see patterns across the data.

NOTE Normally I would not include the vertical gridlines you see in figures 6.11 and 6.12 because you'd be looking at these charts in a browser, able to interact with them and hover to see the exact value of each segment pop up in a tooltip. (More about designing for interactivity in the next chapter!) However, this is a book, and for print, the gridlines must shoulder the job of cluing you into the approximate value of each segment since labeling them all would get too busy.

Tool comparison: Tableau vs d3.js

I created most of the figures in this chapter using Tableau because I can make them a lot faster that way. Unfortunately, though, Tableau doesn't really shine when it comes to clustered bars because it doesn't directly give you control over the spacing between bars, and it doesn't give you any control at all over the spacing between the clusters of bars (which is why I opted to use the gray "row banding" on the right in figure 6.11). The good news is that d3 does give you these controls, so I've given you a comparison of the two tools in the next figure, with Tableau on the left and d3 on the right, keeping them as similar otherwise as I could reasonably manage.

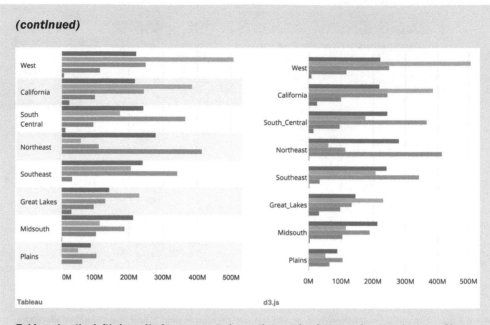

(continued)

Tableau   d3.js

Tableau (on the left) doesn't give you control over the spacing between bars or clusters of bars, but d3 does (on the right). Notice how much less crowded the d3 version feels because there is spacing between each cluster.

The Tableau version feels busier and more difficult to interpret partly because you must rely on the banding in the background to see where one cluster ends and another starts.

One thing that is unreasonably difficult to do in d3 is to do a nested sort of the product categories within each geographical group (as I did on the right side of figure 6.11). *Nested sorting* means that each geographical cluster acts as an independent unit when it comes to sorting the products nested inside it; using nested sorting on a bar graph such as this one results in bars that are tidily sorted from largest to smallest, but the product categories aren't in the same order for each geographical cluster (again, look at figure 6.11 on the right). Nonetheless, in an attempt to maintain as much parity as I could between the tool comparison graphs, I removed that nested sorting on the Tableau side just for this example, though I will admit that this makes it look particularly bad.

One more way you can unstack multiple bar charts is to use one of my personal favorites, a *barbell* or *dumbbell* chart, which you can see in action in figure 6.12.

So far in this chapter, we've learned lots of great things about how to make an individual chart simple yet attractive and maybe even fun. Let's shift gears a little bit and talk about maps because they're a powerful tool that can be very easily misused if not wielded correctly.

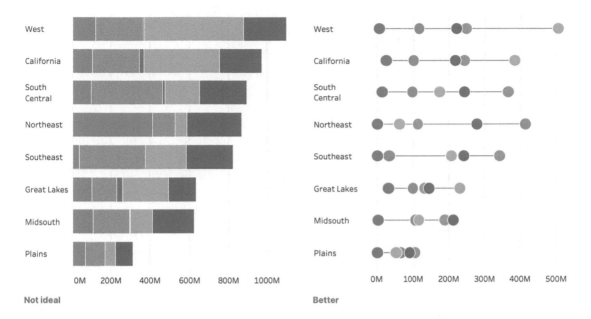

Figure 6.12   I love dumbbell charts, shown on the right, because they are a great way to compare many or few subcategories (product category in this case) across many categories (geographies in this case). While you do lose the context of the total for each geography, I find it much easier to see how the individual product categories differ across the geographies (especially if it was made interactive).

6.3   *Making a good map viz*

If you remember from chapter 1, maps are some of the oldest examples of data visualization. They're great at communicating location information quickly, and personally, I love looking at maps. When my husband and I bought our house in an unfamiliar area where we hadn't been expecting to buy, I spent the weeks leading up to moving day pouring over Google Maps, seeing what stores and restaurants would be available to us from our new digs, how far to the nearest Trader Joe's (only about 10 minutes, thank goodness!), how each of us would get to and from work, routes to avoid the worst rush hour traffic, etc. And whenever there's a wildfire nearby, the first thing I do is go look at the CalFire and air quality maps to see where it is, how far it's spread, and which way the smoke is blowing. Maps are great!

I think we take all the online maps for granted these days. If you're old enough, remember back when you had to own an atlas if you wanted to plan a big road trip? When online maps first became a thing, it was revolutionary: you could print the whole route, with turn-by-turn directions, right from your own computer! Amazing! And now we have the power of the entire Internet in our pockets, glued to our sides, with detailed maps of the entire world a simple swipe away.

The surging importance and popularity of map software are thanks to cartographers and map designers who knew how to make a good, engaging, informative map and pivot their design decisions when they would notice users hitting confusing features or misinterpreting information displayed on the map. When visualizing data on a map, you have great power in your hands: great power to enrapture and enlighten for sure, but also to confuse and confound, or worse still, to deceive and distort. Let's learn how we can avoid the bad and stick with the "enrapture and enlighten."

6.3.1 *Thinking outside the choropleth*

With tools like Mapbox, Tableau, and others, it's easier than ever to slap some data on a map and call it a day. A *choropleth* map, which uses the color of filled-in geographic shapes (counties, states, provinces, territories, countries, etc.) to encode some kind of data, is a simple and popular type of map data viz. However, if you're not careful when choosing the metrics or how you're visualizing them, you very easily run the risk of simply visualizing where the land is, which is fine if you're trying to visualize something like land use, but if you are instead trying to show, say, election results, it's important to be clearer. Have a look at figure 6.13 to see what I mean.

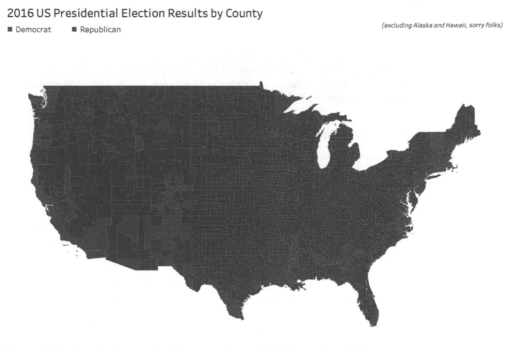

2016 US Presidential Election Results by County

■ Democrat   ■ Republican   *(excluding Alaska and Hawaii, sorry folks)*

Figure 6.13   A basic choropleth (filled) map of the 2016 US presidential election results by county (Data source: McGovern et al. [1])

The map in figure 6.13 shows the results of the 2016 US presidential election, where Hillary Clinton ran on the Democrat ticket and Donald Trump (the winner by electoral votes, but not by the popular vote) ran on the Republican ticket. Looking at this sea of red, one might wonder how Trump didn't win the popular vote—there's so much more red than blue!

While figure 6.13 is a perfectly acceptable map, as it does show which candidate won the race in each county, we can visualize it slightly differently to show that party preferences are more nuanced across the continental United States. Check out figure 6.14, where instead of showing merely who won, we can see the percentage of each county's voters who chose that county's winning candidate.

2016 US Presidential Election Results by County

(excluding Alaska and Hawaii, sorry folks)

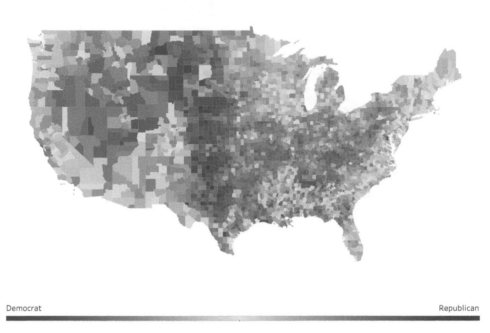

Democrat   Republican

Figure 6.14   A less-bad choropleth map, showing the percentage of voters in each county who voted for that county's winning candidate (Data source: McGovern et al. [1])

Again, figure 6.14 is perfectly acceptable as map visualizations go and tells a more detailed story than figure 6.13. Still, that's an awful lot of red against not very much blue. How did Trump not win the popular vote?

The answer is that *people*, not the *land area*, voted. Much of the United States is very sparsely populated, and rural areas tend to lean more conservatively (Republican) while urban areas tend to lean more liberally (Democrat).

Because of this land-area effect, choropleth maps are not usually the best choice for data visualizations, unless you are literally visualizing something about land, like how land is used (farmland, public park, residential, etc.). Let's dig into some alternatives to choropleths and see how they handle our election results data.

BUBBLES

A *bubble* map, where you place a circle at some latitude and longitude and then use data to size and maybe color the circle, is a fantastic alternative to a choropleth map, especially for something like election results. In figure 6.15, I sized the bubbles by the difference in the number of votes and colored them by the percentage of votes being Democrat versus Republican.

2016 US Presidential Election Results by County

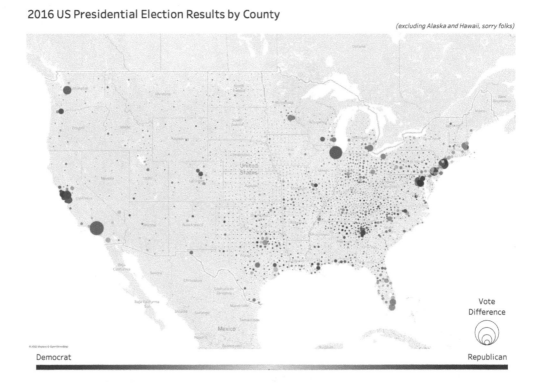

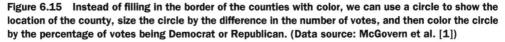

Figure 6.15   Instead of filling in the border of the counties with color, we can use a circle to show the location of the county, size the circle by the difference in the number of votes, and then color the circle by the percentage of votes being Democrat or Republican. (Data source: McGovern et al. [1])

There's one problem with figure 6.15, though: we're relying solely on color to communicate the percentage of Democrat or Republican votes, which we learned from WCAG in chapter 4 is not a great idea. If we make a couple of small changes, we can make a more accessible graph that still gets the idea across.

Rather than relying on color alone to indicate which candidate won the county, we can use a different shape for each party, as shown in figure 6.16. Because the Democratic party is more liberal and is said to be on the "left" while the Republican party is more conservative and is said to be on the "right," that gives us a very handy

2016 US Presidential Election Results by County

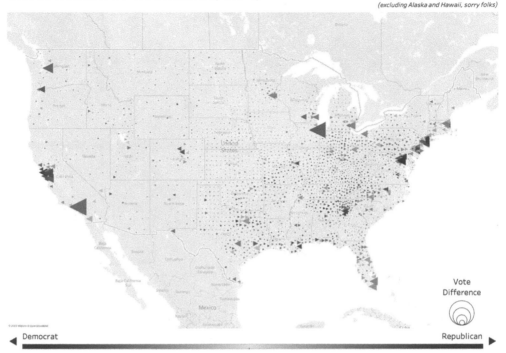

Figure 6.16   To make our graph more inclusive, we can use shapes to denote Democrat votes (left) vs. Republican (right; although you're going to have to trust me because they're all so small) and double-encode the difference in votes on the color, as well as the size. (Data source: McGovern et al. [1])

choice for shapes: a left-pointing arrow for the Democrats, and a right-pointing arrow for the Republicans. How convenient!

DENSITY/HEATMAP

Another decent alternative to a choropleth map is a *density* map, also known sometimes as a *heatmap*, though that can also mean a tabular visualization that uses color to show the data value inside a cell. Density maps are a great option to show the concentration of something, especially when there are clumps of data points, like a map of rat sightings in Manhattan, or population density. Have a look at figure 6.17, which is a map of the locations of harmful freshwater blooms of algae in California observed between 2015 and 2021, which I had made while teaching a data viz workshop at the State of California Water Boards. (We stepped away from the election results for a moment because that data just didn't work nicely with a density map; we really need to see the finer details of that data.)

The color palette on the density marks in figure 6.17 uses darker and more saturated shades of orange for high concentrations of algal blooms, which makes them

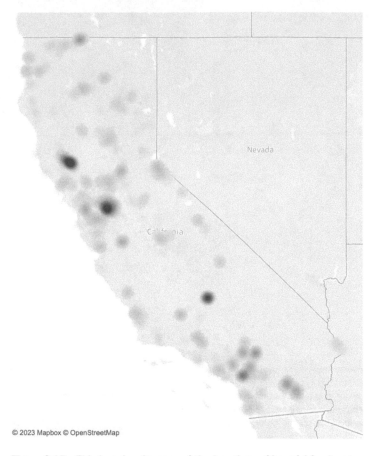

Figure 6.17   This is a density map of the locations of harmful freshwater algal blooms (growths of algae) observed between 2015 and 2021. Thanks to the darker and more saturated colors, we can easily see the few places of high concentration, and it passes the "get it right in black and white" test. (Data source: http://mng.bz/ZR8R, retrieved January 3, 2021, Public domain)

pop out, while the lighter shades for lower concentrations are pushed to the background, and it still passes the "get it right in black and white" test.

Density maps are *not* a great option when it's very important to see the fine details, like with election maps. And speaking of election maps, let's get back to those.

HEXBIN AND TILE MAPS

Sometimes choropleth maps are problematic because of very large areas, and that's when we turn to options like bubble maps or sometimes density maps. Other times, choropleth maps are problematic because of the smaller areas and the fact that those get lost when visualized alongside their larger cousins. In these latter situations, we turn to options like *tile maps*, which place uniformly sized geometric shapes in the general vicinity of the actual geographic location they're representing. This works well when you want to see a regional pattern, allowing you to elevate the smaller components of that region while deemphasizing the larger components at the same time.

Frequently, we see tile maps using hexagonal shapes, which are specifically called *hexbin maps*. Returning to our 2016 US election theme, check out the electoral map in figure 6.18, where we see how the electoral votes from each state were cast that year. Notice how even the tiny New England states are now on the same footing as those west of the Mississippi and how lovely that hexagonal pattern is!

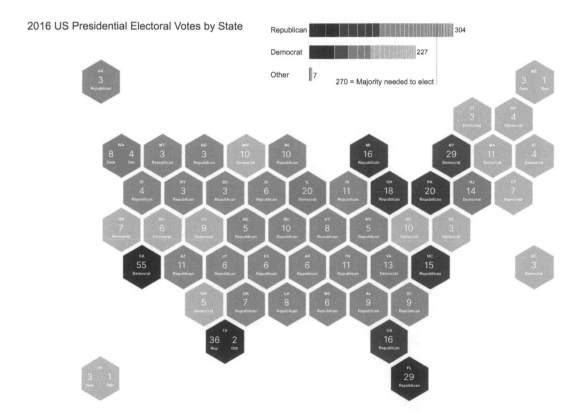

Figure 6.18   A hexbin map of electoral college results for the 2016 US Presidential Election. Each state is colored by which candidate won that state, shaded by how many electoral votes the state has in total and labeled with the number of electoral votes. (Data from Federal Elections Commission: http://mng.bz/RmYZ, publicly available)

As you have noticed in figure 6.18, a handful of states had electoral votes that were not cast for the majority candidate, so those states have multiple labels, showing how many votes went to the Democrat (Dem), Republican (Rep), or Other (Oth) candidates. Finally, the bar graph at the top shows the tally of votes for Democrat, Republican, and Other candidates using the same shading and color seen in the map.

Before we move on, I want to tell you about a very interesting use of a tile map, which is to embed a tiny visualization into each (usually square) tile instead of using a plain hexagon. Think of it as a kind of special case of small multiples, but instead of a rectangular grid, it's in the shape of some geography. The first few times I saw this kind of viz, I was very skeptical. At the time, they seemed overly intricate and unnecessarily busy, but as I got more and more used to seeing them, they started to grow on me. (As Steve Wexler puts it, I'm now a "professional chart looker-atter," so I can handle the more advanced stuff with more ease.) I don't have a great example to put into print because they get very finely detailed, and that doesn't translate well to the limited space we have here, nor would it do the viz justice because they are truly meant for interaction. So, I'll instead direct you to posts on Andy Kriebel's blog tagged with "tile map," which you can find at https://www.vizwiz.com/search/label/tile%20map. (He has made many more tile map vizzes, which can be found by sifting through his extensive Tableau Public portfolio at https://public.tableau.com/app/profile/andy.kriebel, but unfortunately, he hasn't blogged about them all.) If or when you choose to create a tile map with tiny vizzes instead of plain shapes, just make sure it'll fly with your users before committing to it too completely.

6.3.2 *Avoiding the population density effect*

Before we wrap up this section on map visualizations, let's talk about one more thing: if we're not paying close enough attention, our maps might be (accidentally) telling a simple story behind our backs, called the *population density effect.* Let me demonstrate, in figure 6.19, with an election result map showing the number of votes in each county, but with the political party information removed, so maybe you can see where I'm going with this.

The population density effect occurs when a visualizer is trying to tell a story with a map about, say, votes or sales by location (e.g., state, county, city), but what the map really ends up showing instead is merely where the people are. People are doing the voting or the buying, so if you only show votes or sales by location, pretty much the sole insight you can get from that map is where people are more concentrated and where they are not, that is, where the population is dense and where it is not.

To avoid falling into this trap, you'll want to choose your metrics (and your story) wisely. One of the easiest ways to avoid the population density effect is to *normalize* your metric or give it the same scale across all measurements. In practice, this generally means using a ratio instead of whole numbers, such as sales per customer instead

2016 US Presidential Election - Total Votes by County

(excluding Alaska and Hawaii, sorry folks)

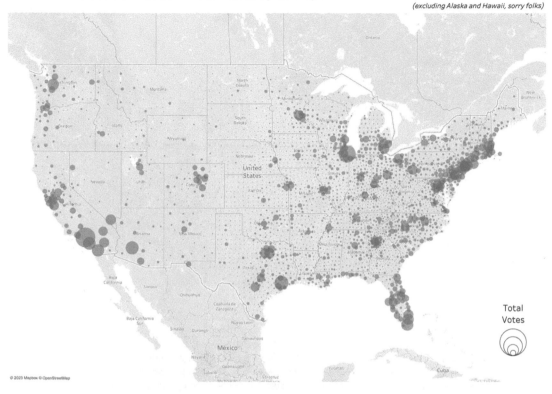

Figure 6.19   While this is a truthful map showing the number of total votes by county in the 2016 US Presidential Election, it's not a particularly insightful one because it's really just a map of where the people are, that is, it suffers from the population density effect (McGovern et al. [1]).

of raw sales, or the percentage of the population who voted instead of the number of votes, which you can see in figure 6.20.

Figure 6.20 is a better way than figure 6.19 to show voter turnout in 2016 across the United States because, in figure 6.20, the playing field is leveled: sparsely populated counties are given equal footing with more densely populated counties. In fact, even though a choropleth tends to emphasize land area, and this one is no exception (those large counties in the western states do tend to draw the eye more than is likely necessary), it works fine in this instance because the insight isn't which side these counties voted for, as it was in figures 6.13 and 6.14. Instead, the insight is about the percentage of the people who voted at all, which is completely unrelated to the land area covered by the county.

Going back to our earlier election results maps that were split by Democrat and Republican votes (figures 6.15 and 6.16), one could say that those technically fall victim

2016 US Presidential Election - Percentage of Population Voting by County

13% ▨▨▨▨▨▨▨ 86%   *(excluding Alaska and Hawaii, sorry folks)*

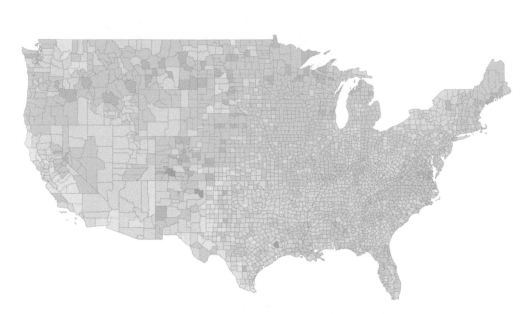

Figure 6.20   Instead of showing a raw number of votes from each county in the United States, it's more insightful to show the percentage of the population in each county who voted in the election or voter turnout. A choropleth is better than bubbles for this because most of the bubbles would be roughly the same size, so it would be hard to see the regional trends. (Data source: McGovern et al. [1], combined with population estimates by the US Census Bureau released to the public in March 2020)

to the population density effect. However, they do show that Democrat and Republican voters are not evenly distributed throughout the counties of the United States. It is especially interesting to know that Clinton (the Democratic candidate) actually won the popular vote in that election, meaning she garnered more raw votes than Trump, the Republican candidate. So, all the red shapes were surprisingly outweighed by the relatively fewer blue shapes. Thus, in this sense, I would argue that those maps did not, in fact, fall victim to the population density effect.

Summary

- When deciding what type of chart to use to visualize your data, you can either look to the preattentive attributes and gestalt principles to guide you, or you can get inspiration from a "visual vocabulary" online, like that from the *Financial Times.*

- Keep it simple, always tell the truth, enthrall users with a story, and ultimately just make sure you get the point across in a way your users will understand.

- The human eye is dreadful at estimating angles, so when using a pie or donut chart, keep the number of segments to a minimum (many say keep it under five, but I say keep it at two or three) and avoid making a user compare these charts to each other.

- Spaghetti belongs on a plate, not a line chart: consider detangling multiline charts into separate *y*-axes but the same *x*-axis (a single column with each line having its own row) or into small multiples.

- Declutter! Remove all unnecessary gridlines, axes, labels, etc. that are automatically generated by your tool of choice, and only add back what you truly need.

- If you want to add whimsy or pizzazz to a viz, first check your motivation for doing so, and then be sure it will be well received. Finally, make sure it won't distract from the message of your viz.

- When using a map in a viz, be sure it's telling the story you mean to tell, not merely showing land area or population density.

7
Designing
for interactivity

This chapter covers

- The basics of designing for interaction
- Using interactivity to enable exploration in a viz
- Designing for some unfamiliar modes of interaction
- Applying WCAG to interactivity

In my very first job out of grad school as a product analyst, I worked for a small company where we used Excel for basically all our reporting. Now, before you judge, this was just before Tableau's popularity really started to take off (according to Google Trends) and a few years before Power BI was first released. After spending a couple of years at that little company, learning the ins and outs of Excel, I landed my next product analyst job at Ancestry, which at the time was about 10 times bigger and had a budget to match. Within a month of starting there, my new boss sat me down in front of Tableau and said, "Make me a dashboard," and it was all over after that—love at first drag-and-drop. I was completely hooked on data viz and quickly developed an unhealthy obsession with interactivity. When I learned about decluttering my vizzes, I took to burying crucial info in tooltips (those little information blurbs that pop up when your mouse pointer hovers on an element). I often made my users toggle or filter between key segments instead of showing them side-by-side—this was what I thought it meant to "make my dashboards cleaner." But don't be fooled: they weren't clean—they were confusing! No one knew what they were looking at, and then I'd get super frustrated when my stakeholders couldn't understand this dashboard that I'd worked so hard to make for them.

In this chapter, we're going to learn how to use interactivity to enhance a viz rather than use it as a crutch or an overloaded pack mule. First, we'll cover some of the basic best practices of interaction design (and how not to build the Norman doors of visualization). Then, we'll dig into a couple of different ways to foster exploration in a visualization. From there, we'll talk about some less-familiar ways of interacting with vizzes and other content across our different devices. Finally, we'll wrap it up with what the WCAG has to say about ensuring our interactivity is inclusive of as broad an audience as possible.

Making a data visualization interactive can be extremely powerful and extend well beyond simply stuffing information into tooltips or slapping on radio buttons and drop-down menus. So, let's get to it!

7.1   *Basics of interaction design*

When you make a viz for an audience, it's a way of communicating with them, and as in all other aspects of interpersonal relationships, communication is *absolutely* key. So far, we've learned to communicate with color and typography, and now we're going to learn to communicate more effectively with interactivity. According to the Interaction Design Foundation, *interaction design* is how we "enable the user to achieve their objectives in the best way possible."

Take the humble door, for example. Why do we so often push on a door when it clearly says we ought to pull, or worse, it doesn't tell us at all how to open it, and we guess wrong? In fact, it's not your fault. It's the door's fault, or more specifically, the fault of the person who designed the door.

> **DEFINITION**   Believe it or not, there's a name for these types of confusing doors: *Norman doors.* Named for Don Norman, the designer who first called out this design faux pas in his book *The Design of Everyday Things,* a Norman door is any kind of door that is confusing to use. To determine whether a door is a Norman door, you can grade it yourself on a pass-fail basis: if your guess of how it opens (push, pull, or slide) is wrong, the door fails. Moreover, if you have any uncertainty at all about how it opens, it fails, and a failing door is a Norman door.

Have a look at figure 7.1 to see three Norman doors (labeled A, B, and C) that I encountered on a single visit to the office recently (and a little donut shop nearby— yes, I might have a sweet tooth).

If you work in an office with conference rooms, chances are very good that you have doors much like Door A in figure 7.1. These doors open out toward the camera, so it's not so bad going in, but coming out of the conference room, you have the same

A   B   C

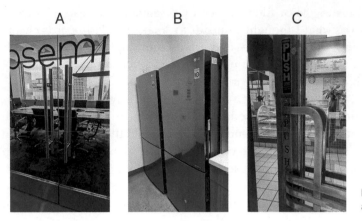

Figure 7.1 Norman doors at work (literally)

exact handles on the other side of the door. Door B is actually two refrigerators in the office kitchen, and unless you look very closely to see where the hinge is on the top of the fridge, there is absolutely no indicator of which side to use to open because they're those reversible doors that the buyer can set to open in their desired direction. The kicker here? These two fridges open in opposite directions, so once I finally figured out how to open the one closest to the camera (I didn't think at the time to look for the hinge, and I'm too short to have been able to see it well anyway), I tried the same side on the far fridge and failed. Finally, door C sure looks like it would open out by pulling, which is why there are not one but two separate signs that say to push. Wow.

So yeah, if a door has a handle sticking out at you, you're highly likely to pull on it because that's just what you do with handles, regardless of how many times it says "push." The form or shape of these ambiguous doors doesn't do a good job of communicating to you what you're supposed to do with them, so someone had to resort to adding labels. But if you remember our preattentive attributes, do you recall how "label" was not among them, but "form" was? Your brain subconsciously notices the shape or form of something long before you read what any labels say. This is interaction design in action, and in this section, we're going to learn some fundamentals to help you avoid making Norman doors out of your visualizations.

7.1.1 Give clues about how and where to interact

One of the most essential elements of interaction design is to give users clues about where and how they can and should interact with your design, that is, to make your interactive elements *discoverable*. If users can't find (or understand, identify, or access) those interactive bits, they will never be able to use them! This includes using *affordances*, the aspects and traits of a thing that determine how that thing can or should be used. For example, a switch is meant to be flipped, or in the case of doors, a knob affords turning—don't you find it weird when you encounter a doorknob that doesn't turn? Don Norman says that when we take advantage of affordances, "the user knows what to do just by looking: no picture, label, or instruction needed." If a door requires a label for a user to know whether to push or pull, it's a poorly designed door.

In visual design and, by extension, data visualization, the affordances available to you as a designer and developer are not quite as ubiquitous as door handles. We do still have things like buttons, check boxes, and toggle switches at our disposal, though, so when you use any of these design elements, make sure their purpose is obvious. For example, if you want someone to click something like a button, try to make it look like a button! A more web-specific example is underlined text: how many times have you seen underlined text on a web page and clicked it as if it were a link, only to find that it's just plain old, underlined text? We have been conditioned to see a single underline on a bit of text as a hyperlink, so unless you're linking your text, avoid underlining it. (Moreover, underlining entire lines of text just doesn't look great—see chapter 5 for better ways to indicate visual hierarchy.) If you don't want to underline links, you can stick to simply changing the color of that text to be some color that contrasts with your nonlinked text (the typical shade, dating back to the mid-late 1980s, is #0000FF in hex—that's full, pure blue; remember from chapter 4?), like in figure 7.2.

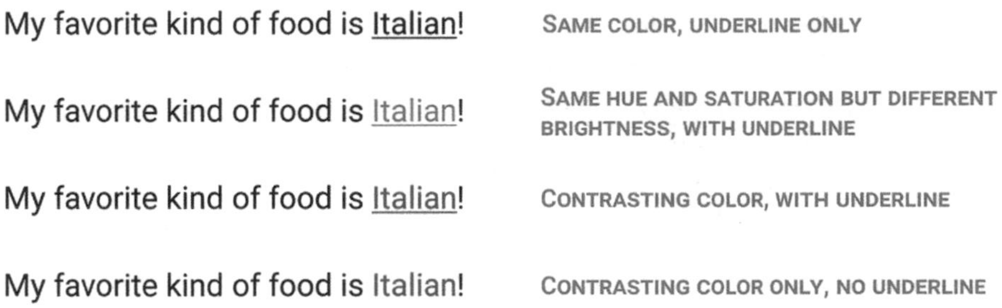

My favorite kind of food is <u>Italian</u>!   SAME COLOR, UNDERLINE ONLY

My favorite kind of food is <u>Italian</u>!   SAME HUE AND SATURATION BUT DIFFERENT BRIGHTNESS, WITH UNDERLINE

My favorite kind of food is <u>Italian</u>!   CONTRASTING COLOR, WITH UNDERLINE

My favorite kind of food is Italian!   CONTRASTING COLOR ONLY, NO UNDERLINE

Figure 7.2   Different ways to communicate that some bit of text is a hyperlink

Hyperlinks throughout the web are typically of the blue and underlined flavor, which works quite well for long documents full of very large blocks of text. In a data viz, however, those pops of blue (or other contrasting color, as long as it has a high enough contrast with the background) might take attention away from the data, so you are welcome to stick with the underline-only version or pair the underline with a change in brightness. Just be sure that the resulting color has a contrast high enough with the background.

We can think of affordances as almost subliminal clues about how and where to interact, but there are also less subliminal ways to indicate interactivity. In BI tools such as Tableau and Power BI, when a mouse pointer enters a data element, a border will appear around just that element to show that it's active or in focus. This serves as a very subtle indicator to the user that the entire viz is interactive; in fact, this type of highlighting interaction pattern dates to the dawn of hypertext itself, predating even the web.

Digging into the early days of the WWW

If you'd like to learn more about the history of interactivity and hypertext, I'd recommend starting with this gold mine of a page at https://www.cs.umd.edu/hcil/hyperties/, and make sure to check out the embedded videos. I hope that you, too, will develop an appreciation and awe for the legendary Dr. Ben Shneiderman and his team from the University of Maryland, who were early innovators in information visualization and human-computer interaction in the 1980s and 1990s. You likely already know some of their work, as they invented the treemap chart type and pioneered work on hyperlinks (in fact, they are the folks responsible for hyperlinks being blue!), hypertext (you know, as in HyperText Transfer Protocol, or HTTP), touchscreens, and even digital photography, to name just a few. Yes, I might have just wasted an embarrassing amount of time diving down a rabbit hole of internet history, not unlike the captain in Disney's *Wall-E* when he's learning about Earth. "Computer, define *dancing . . .*"

Finally, if worse comes to worst, and you're *completely* at a loss for how to subtly hint at what people are supposed to do with your viz, it's okay to simply tell your users how they can interact. We all start out making lots of Norman doors of our designs but resorting to labeling with instructions to pull is better than making innocent people smack their faces into a door when they erroneously try to push. Especially when you're not writing the code yourself, your hands are a bit tied for just how much you can customize the interface, so there's no shame in adding helpful instructions inside tooltips and/or help menus. (This is also a great place to add definitions and descriptions of where the data originated and how metrics are calculated—the more questions you answer up front in the viz itself, the less time you'll spend answering the same questions over and over again.)

7.1.2 *Use familiar interaction patterns*

Allow me to tell you a cautionary tale of some very smart, very motivated users and their struggle with an unfamiliar interaction pattern. My friends and I have been playing *Dungeons & Dragons* (D&D) together for years, and even before the plague time confined everyone to their homes, we had already finished two full multiyear campaigns together online because we're so spread out. Just as the pandemic started, we were beginning a new campaign in a new-to-us virtual tabletop (VTT) software, which will remain nameless to protect the innocent (in fact, that very campaign is still going as of this writing, and my wizard just hit level 17—yay 9th-level spells!). The unfamiliar VTT was a little bit ugly and very difficult to learn to use: my group is full of very smart and tech-savvy people, and there were definitely times when we were all ready to collectively throw our computers against the walls as we got our game and characters set up in the program. One of the main frustrations was, and still is, this very weird interaction pattern that none of us had ever seen before: you'd have to right-click somewhere or on something to make a radial menu pop up, and that was the only place you could access certain tools (e.g., to measure distance or draw circles on a map). Some really important stuff is buried in these radial right-click menus (many of which even have radial submenus) instead of showing up as buttons on toolbars like a sensible program. Because this radial right-click thing is such an unfamiliar interaction pattern, it has taken a long time and a lot of very frustrated web searching until it was finally imprinted on our brains. What's more, those of us on a Mac laptop can't even access a particular dice-rolling feature without attaching an external (non-Mac) mouse: Mac trackpads don't have a true right-click button that can be clicked simultaneously with the left-click button (because the right-click action is fired either by simply using two fingers to click instead of one, or pressing the Command key while clicking). Despite these troubles as we were first learning the program, my friends and I had paid a lot of money for this VTT, and there were many things it did better than our previous choice, so we were highly motivated to stick with it and make it work.

Your users, however, I guarantee will be a different story. Do them a huge favor and don't try to reinvent the wheel: use interaction patterns people already know and love. How do you know what those are? Think about the apps they use regularly (not the apps *you* use regularly, mind you). Compared to all the time your users spend interacting with technology each day, they will spend a minimal amount of time with your visualization—this concept is called *Jakob's Law of Internet User Experience*, coined by Jakob Nielsen of the Nielsen Norman Group (the other half of which is made up by Don Norman—go figure!).

Essentially, what Jakob's Law means is that you don't have to invent new and novel ways for a user to interact with your designs; moreover, you should try to avoid doing that because people like what they already know, and people use things they like more than things they don't. Remember the last time your favorite social media site released a major update and rearranged stuff, or when your local grocery store rearranged all the aisles? People get so up in arms about that, but they usually keep going back because they've already formed that habit. However, when you make something new that's totally out of the ordinary and contrary to everything a person knows, you're not likely to get a lot of traction up front because it's unfamiliar and has too steep a learning curve for them. Had that VTT my friends and I use for D&D been our first exposure to the game, I doubt very much we would have been as motivated.

So, if you have the time, do a little bit of homework on where your users spend their time, both their favorite apps and their favorite data visualizations. For example, if you're making a report for business stakeholders, find out if there are already reports they look at a lot and then take some cues from those. Unless something is an outright terrible design decision, try to use a similar arrangement of where various features appear on the page, such as making a note of where the filters and controls are located and where the help menu is. Next, note what kinds of interactivity already exist on the visualization itself: what information can be found in a tooltip or hover on a data element, and is there any kind of cross-filtering that happens throughout the viz when you click on a data element? One example of such cross-filtering would be that clicking a bar for segment A in a bar graph applies a filter to a line, a donut, and another bar graph so that they all now reflect only segment A's data—this will be demonstrated later in the chapter when we talk about fostering exploration. Stay tuned for chapter 8, where we'll have a more in-depth discussion of this and other homework when you're preparing to make a new visualization.

Overall, especially when you're building a new thing, stick with what your users already know. Then, after that has taken hold, and they completely love your work, you can start slowly introducing other improvements you find in your design travels, but always be mindful of how your users feel about these improvements. If (or more likely, when) you make a change that doesn't land well, you can just revert it, metaphorically dust yourself off, and then get back to that drawing board to try again from another direction.

7.1.3   *Give feedback after an interaction*

Have you ever been interacting with a chart or dashboard, and you're not sure whether something you did worked (e.g., whether anything happened after you changed a filter or switched a toggle)? Such is a textbook example of poor interaction design.

When designing for interactivity, it's best to ensure that the user will know when they've successfully interacted with something by giving them feedback of some sort. This feedback can take many forms, including animation or changing the display of a label:

- *Animation*—This could mean bar heights that grow and shrink or visual elements that rearrange to reflect the new data (Tableau can do both). It could mean displaying a loading spinner while data elements reload (Power BI does this) or something else entirely, such as lines redrawing themselves, bars growing from their baseline, or pies/donuts unfurling around a circle like an old-fashioned fan (all of which are relatively straightforward to do in d3). Feedback to show that an interaction succeeded is a great use of the preattentive attribute of motion, so long as it doesn't slow down the performance of the entire page or become too distracting.
- *Changing the display of a label*—This could mean either changing the label's text itself or making a change to show what data is active and what is not by moving a highlight or changing font styling. See figure 7.3 for an example.

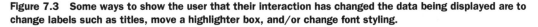

Figure 7.3   Some ways to show the user that their interaction has changed the data being displayed are to change labels such as titles, move a highlighter box, and/or change font styling.

Finally, to ensure the user sees this feedback, make sure there's at least some of this feedback visible on screen at or near the location where they are interacting.

7.1.4 Anticipate errors

If you've ever done the Wordle game from *The New York Times*, you probably know that if you guess a word that isn't a real word, the line of your guess wiggles right to left, almost echoing the motion of someone shaking their head as if to say, "Nope, try again!" It's such a better experience than if they'd decided to go with an alert window that is only closeable by clicking a button, emblazoning your screen with giant red letters that call out the error, or relying solely on the small and unobtrusive text at the top of the page, which says, "Not in word list." Without you needing to look up, that simple and friendly motion communicates that yes, you did submit an answer, but no, it's not a word, so you'll need to try again.

Errors are nearly unavoidable once something is made interactive, especially an open-ended data visualization like an automated dashboard. Instead of leaving people wondering what they did wrong, it's massively important to get out ahead of the errors by putting friendly, helpful guard rails in place. You want users of your vizzes to feel the unadulterated joy of a child whose bowling ball has bounced off the gutter guards all the way down the bowling alley, to ultimately knock down all the pins for a strike, and you want to spare them the embarrassment and self-doubt that I have when I go bowling, and my ball spends more time in the gutter than on the lane itself (okay, I'm not that bad, but I am beyond delighted when I bowl anything over 100). Let's talk about a couple of gutter guards you can set up for your users.

ALLOW ONLY RELEVANT DATA TO BE SELECTED IN FILTERS AND CONTROLS

In some BI tools I know *([cough] Tableau [cough])*, it's all too easy to add a zillion filters to a visualization with no thought for how each will affect the other. Let's take a hierarchy, for instance, which might have data like in table 7.1.

Table 7.1 Biological classification for a handful of species in the *Carnivora* order, which is in the domain *Eukarya*, kingdom *Animalia*, and phylum *Mammalia*—that is, they're all mammals.

Family	Genus	Species	Better known as
Canidae	Canis	Latrans	Coyote
Canidae	Canis	Lupus	Gray wolf
Canidae	Canis	Familiaris	Domestic dog
Canidae	Vulpes	Vulpes	Red fox
Felidae	Felis	Catus	Domestic cat

Let's say we have some data about each of these species and more, and we want to give users the ability to filter down to only the classification they care to see. Throwing on a filter for each of family, genus, and species sounds great, but in *some* aforementioned tools (as of this writing, at least), the default behavior of these filters is that their menus always show all possible values. This means that if you select the species Catus, the viz will filter to only Catus, but the other filter menus will still have all the other values as well, (e.g., the Family menu will still show both Felidae and Canidae!) Not only is this bad UX, but it's also liable to make the user question the data quality, and once you go down that road of distrust, it's really hard to come back. So, it is left to the viz developer to make sure this doesn't happen by setting each filter to "Show relevant values" instead of "All values in database." I realize this is to help with performance concerns because it does slow things down pretty dramatically if there are a zillion filters on the viz, but such is life: data quality should always trump performance. Do yourself and your users a favor and make sure your filters play nicely with each other. (And hopefully, someday, these last two paragraphs will be obsolete because that oversight will have been fixed—a girl can dream!)

In another case, imagine you've made a super-cool viz that has some sort of time dimension to it. Regardless of whether you're displaying a trend over time or pooling it all together, your users may want some way to narrow or broaden the window of time they can see. Naturally, you'd add a filter or some kind of toggle, and oftentimes, this takes the form of a date picker (or pair of date pickers, if you're making both the beginning and end of the time window selectable). When you do make a date picker, it helps tremendously to prevent users from selecting dates that make no sense. As a user using a date picker, this seems like a no-brainer, but as a developer, it can be an easy thing to forget, and depending on the tool you're using, it could be a tad difficult to implement when you do remember. It is well worth the extra development effort, though!

For example, let's say you are making a web-based report about traffic to a website. Why would a user ever want to select a date in the future? They wouldn't! That traffic hasn't visited the website yet, and unless you've got a time machine (all of time and space, anyone?) or some way to see the future, there's no way to know what will happen because there's no data yet. So rather than making your users either feel stupid or get mad at you because they selected a future date and then don't see any data, just make it so they can't select that in the first place. How to do this depends greatly on the tool you're using, but an example for web coders is when you're using a calendar date picker component, make sure to set the min and max allowable dates. Figure 7.4 shows this in the Carbon design system, an open source library of web components by IBM. I set `minDate` to 5/30/2023, and `maxDate` to 6/15/2023, so dates outside that range are shown in a light gray because they are disabled. As a bonus, this picker automatically shows in blue that today's date is June 3.

WRITE HELPFUL ERROR MESSAGES

We've all encountered the massively unhelpful error messages: "An error occurred," "Something went wrong," "A runtime error has occurred," and "Internal server error." Maybe it was the blue screen of death or just a giant mess of seemingly irrelevant and incoherent code. It's the 21st century, people! How are these bad error messages still clinging to life when there are designers and copywriters and product managers and entire departments dedicated to a user-centered product experience? Let's be the change we want to see. Instead of being vague and robotic, be clear and succinct

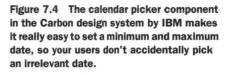

Figure 7.4   The calendar picker component in the Carbon design system by IBM makes it really easy to set a minimum and maximum date, so your users don't accidentally pick an irrelevant date.

about what went wrong, why it went wrong, and what can be done to fix it. And don't be afraid to have a sense of humor where it's appropriate! Just try to keep it on-brand and succinct (and, of course, safe for work). It's not a one-error-message-fits-all world out there, so if possible, try to have different messaging for different errors. While what makes an error message useful varies greatly from one situation to the next, some examples might include the following:

- If the user has filtered out all the data and wound up with a blank screen: "Oops, you've filtered out all the data! Try removing some filters to coax it back."
  - A subset of these errors occurs when a user doesn't have the correct permissions to see all the data. Where possible and prudent, consider including some messaging about that: "Looks like you don't have permission to see all the data. If you think you should, please contact an administrator for help."
- If an API call returns an empty payload: "Sorry, there doesn't seem to be anything to visualize. If refreshing the page doesn't solve this problem, please try contacting an administrator."
- If a database table is empty: "Looks like you caught us in the middle of a data refresh! Please try again in a short while and if the problem isn't resolved, try contacting an administrator."

As you may know and can see from the examples, no matter the data source, it's always a possibility that your dashboard could show up completely empty because of an error when the data was being fetched from wherever it is stored, whether it's the payload of a call to a REST API or an automatically refreshed data extract sitting in a cloud server somewhere. What's more, if you, as the viz developer, don't configure your various filters and toggles well (like if maybe you barely skimmed the previous subsection about preventing filters from tripping over each other), a user could accidentally filter out all the data and be left with a similarly blank screen. How are they to know what happened and which situation got them to the sad, empty screen? Without descriptive and specific error messages, a user may not know whether the blank screen of sadness is something they can fix themselves, or if they'll need administrator help.

There are many more wonderful examples out there than would be suitable to print in this book, so if you're burning with curiosity, go type "Examples of great error messages" into your favorite search engine.

7.1.5   *Make it beautiful*

Once you're sure you've accomplished the other basics of good interaction design, you can and should dedicate some time and resources to making the interactions (and even the static parts of the visual design) aesthetically pleasing. Numerous studies have demonstrated the *aesthetic-usability effect*, which is that when people like the look of a design, they perceive it as being easier to use. And when they think it looks easy to use, they're much more likely to use it, regardless of whether it truly is easy. Looking at that from another angle, it means that users will be more forgiving of usability issues if they like the look of the design.

We've discussed the visual design aspect in previous chapters about color, typography, and making a chart good, but what about interaction? What makes an interaction aesthetically pleasing?

Unfortunately, there does not seem to be a very straight answer to this. Anecdotally in my own experience, it's often about animations being enjoyable and satisfying, but that is horribly subjective and not very quantifiable. I can say, however, that a major contributor to an animation being enjoyable and satisfying is that it is not only fast but also unobtrusive. If I find that I need to wait for an animation to complete, I'm already over it, and I'm sure I'm not alone in this. Beyond animations, though, you'll want to make the interactive pieces themselves enjoyable and satisfying. The worst part in all this is that not only is "enjoyable and satisfying" highly subjective, but it's also a bit of a moving target. As time goes on and the web continues to evolve, so too do user interface design trends. With web design still being such a young discipline, we haven't (yet?) seen the cyclic pattern that we see in fashion (hello, bell bottoms and mom jeans). But, if you go to the Internet Archive's Wayback Machine (web.archive.org) and look up any site that has been around since the late 1990s or early 2000s, you'll unquestionably see a difference in the general aesthetic of the web. In figure 7.5, you'll see a replica of a button from a major online retailer's site in 2001 and a recreation of a typical button from a very widely popular (in 2023) front-end toolkit called Bootstrap.

Replica of 2001 button   Replica of 2023 button

Figure 7.5   How the humble button has evolved in 22 years

As you can see with the buttons, what's considered beautiful and aesthetically pleasing is not constant; therefore, you *must* keep up with the trends if you want your designs to stay relevant. Right now, the trend is toward very minimalistic design, with tons of white space and very clean lines like the 2023 button in figure 7.5, but that doesn't mean it will still be that way 10, 20, 30 years in the future. Even if you don't want to faithfully adhere to the trends, you should at least know what's going on out in the wider design world, so you aren't left behind.

Ultimately, while the aesthetic-usability effect is good news if you like to make things beautiful, it doesn't mean you should become complacent about what's beneath the surface. Pretty visuals and fun interactions will only get you so far: if you don't also put in the work to make sure the viz answers your users' main questions, they will quickly discover that your delightful little viz is completely useless, and that's not a situation wherein you want to find yourself.

7.1.6   *Bonus tip: Give users an out*

Finally, once you've added some beautiful and intuitive interactivity to your already stunning visualization, you'll want to give users a way to back out of any changes made by their interactions like buttons that can undo single changes and/or clear all filters (which would also help with the aforementioned blank screen of sadness problem from section 7.1.4). It's probably obvious to give them a way to revert each change individually, but if you want to make their lives much easier, also give them some obvious way to revert all changes at once with a single click or keystroke. This will help put them at ease as they're starting to learn how to use your viz and interpret the data because they'll feel much more comfortable knowing that any changes made by their interactions are very easy to undo one-by-one or even completely revert (without needing to refresh the page) if they manage to interact themselves into a corner.

Now that you know the fundamentals of designing for interactivity, we're going to discuss how to help your users explore their data using that interactivity.

7.2   *Enabling exploration using interaction*

There are two main types of data visualizations: explanatory and exploratory. *Explanatory* visualizations are the vizzes that relay the results of an analysis, those that outright tell stories, and as such, their data does not change or update: the story is done, and now the viz is there to relay it. *Exploratory* visualizations are meant to help a user find the story themselves by exploring the data and looking at it from many different angles and breakdowns; as such, the data for these vizzes tends to be ongoing and ever-changing. While exploratory visualizations pretty much necessitate interactivity, explanatory vizzes can go either way—they can be perfectly functional as either static or interactive visuals.

> ### Vizzing for executive types
>
> Executives and folks who cannot—or just *will* not—spend a lot of time with your visualization will be unlikely to engage much with a highly exploratory viz. If you're building an ongoing report for an exec, try to make it as explanatory as possible by bubbling up the stuff they care about to the top, which is typically along the lines of the biggest, the best, the worst, and the largest change.

Since we're leaning toward the "everyday" in this book, we'll focus most of our effort in this chapter on exploratory visualizations and their (usually) ever-changing data by discussing a few different approaches to making a visualization interactive. First, and probably most widely known, is the *Visual Information-Seeking Mantra*.

7.2.1   *The Visual Information-Seeking Mantra*

At a 1996 technical conference, Dr. Ben Shneiderman presented a paper titled "The Eyes Have It: A Task by Data Type Taxonomy for Information Visualizations." In this paper, he coined what he called "The Visual Information-Seeking Mantra," which states, "Overview first, zoom and filter, then details on demand." He explains that this mantra had served as a dependable guideline for him when designing systems that a human is meant to use to explore, navigate, and digest vast arrays of information. Lo and behold, that is exactly what many of our visualizations are still meant for today! So how do we apply it to our own work?

When making an interactive viz, be that a dashboard or report or whatever else, one design approach is to first give the user an overview of the data and the key takeaways. Once your users have their bearings and understand what's being presented to them, then allow them to zoom in or out (literally or figuratively) and filter out information that distracts from the main focus of their analytical exploration. Finally, give them a way to drill in to get more details about what remains. Whether you do all three steps on a single page or separate them into three different pages is up to you and your users. What's more, this approach can work well for both exploratory and explanatory visualizations.

In figure 7.6, you can see a highly interactive dashboard I made just for this book (you can visit the live version at http://mng.bz/z0aA), using open data from California's State Water Resources Control Board. This particular data is about the drought risks facing self-supplied communities (which they call "rural" even though many of the communities in the data set are in rather urban areas), as calculated by an assessment performed between 2018 and 2020. Each row of the data is a census block (also known as a *census tract*), so it is very detailed and very ripe for Dr. Shneiderman's mantra.

In the dashboard in figure 7.6, I've plotted the overall risk score on the *y*-axis of a scatterplot against another risk factor that goes into the score, a parameter that the user can choose with a drop-down menu (top left). The data set came with 51 columns,

Water shortage and drought risk in rural California communities

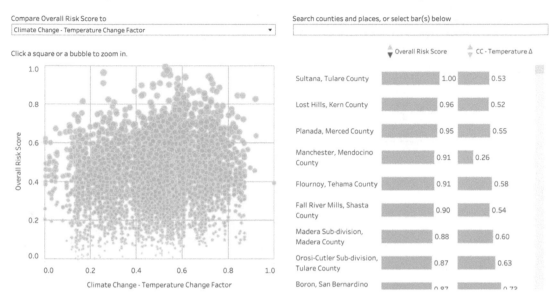

Figure 7.6   This data set is highly complex and very large, so it is perfect for employing the visual information-seeking mantra to help make the information more digestible.

19 of which are used in the calculation of the overall risk score, but most of which didn't have very interesting values for a scatterplot, so I left them out. The scatterplot serves as an overview to show the drought risk landscape across these California communities that supply their own water. This overview is extended by the bar chart on the right that allows the user to see each community's average risk score and the average of the selected comparison parameter and allows them to sort either in ascending or descending order. The next part of the mantra is "zoom and filter," which can be accomplished in many ways on this dashboard: the user can click a bubble or a square on the scatter plot and get a zoomed-in view of just that square. Doing so also filters the bar graph on the right to only the census blocks in that square. Alternatively, the search bar at the top right lets the user search for a particular county or city, which then filters the bar graph and highlights the relevant bubbles on the scatterplot.

Finally, my favorite part of this dashboard is the "details on demand" part of the mantra. Selecting a bar or a bubble on the zoomed-in scatterplot pops up a map in the lower right corner with the relevant census tract outlined. The user can then zoom or pan around the map to see where that census tract is situated in California! Have a look at figure 7.7 to see it at work.

Unsurprisingly, in his seminal paper, Shneiderman relates about the Visual Information-Seeking Mantra that he found himself "rediscovering this principle" across 10 different projects in information visualization research labs spanning government,

Water shortage and drought risk in rural California communities

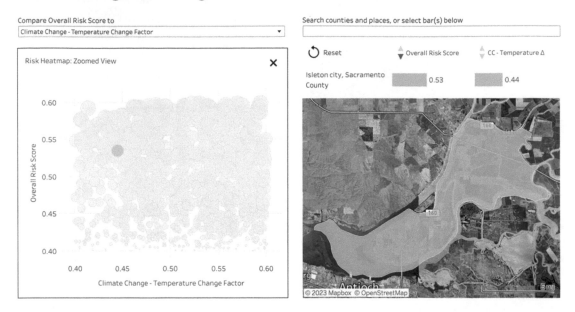

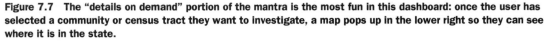

Figure 7.7   The "details on demand" portion of the mantra is the most fun in this dashboard: once the user has selected a community or census tract they want to investigate, a map pops up in the lower right so they can see where it is in the state.

industry, and academia. Though he instructs that the mantra is merely a starting point for one's design, it is nonetheless widely cited and used as a definitive set of instructions. I encourage you to keep an open mind and use it as the guideline it was meant to be rather than a hard-and-fast rule.

7.2.2   *More ways to enable exploration*

Sometimes the decision to make is less about *whether* to show everything and more about *how* to show everything. Every so often we need to visualize the magnitude of some metric alongside where a particular dimension ranks across other dimensions. Confusing? Let's look at an example from Steve Wexler, founder and "chief chart looker-atter" of Data Revelations and an all-around gem of a human. Steve is particularly adept at visualizing survey data, and the dashboard shown in figure 7.8 is one of my favorite examples of his handiwork with a check-all-that-apply type of question, which is an especially difficult type of survey response to visualize. Specifically, the question whose results are shown here stated, "As a doctor, indicate what health indicators you measure yourself; check all that apply." The results are visualized with a breakdown of the doctor's generation. Have a look at the figure and marvel at the amount of information packed into such a small space.

Figure 7.8   The interactivity in this dashboard allows the user to explore multiple ways of segmenting the data set, and as a bonus, it packs a ton of information into a compact space: we learn about the popularity of doctors measuring various indicators themselves across all respondents and respondents broken down by generation, and then we also get a separate breakdown of total respondents by generation. You can interact with it yourself or download it from Steve's blog at https://www.datarevelations.com/howmany/. (Steve Wexler, used with permission)

At the very top right of figure 7.8 is a dropdown menu, showing that Generation is selected for the breakdown. The other options (not shown) in that dropdown menu are Gender, Location (i.e., continent, and yes, even Antarctica shows up!), and how many of the nine items the respondent had checked (from one to eight). Hovering on the question mark reveals a help menu that describes what the dashboard is about and how to use it. Below the header in the left corner, we see a bar graph of the percentage of respondents who chose each of the nine options. Blood Pressure has been selected, so in the upper right, we see another bar graph of the percentage of each generation of doctors who indicated that they measure a patient's blood pressure themselves, gathering the highlighted bars from the viz below into one place. Spanning the middle row, we see generations across the top and row numbers, or ranking, down the left side. The darker, labeled bars indicate that these correspond to the Blood Pressure selection (and are the same bars from the viz in the top right, only now they are shown in context with the rest of the choices for each generation), and the row number indicates the popularity of that choice within each generation. Finally, the bar graph "hanging down" along the bottom indicates the generational breakdown of the doctors surveyed, with baby boomers making up 46% of those surveyed, Gen X making up 35%, millennials making up 15%, and traditionalists (also known as the Silent Generation, born between 1922 and 1945) making up only 4%. (Gen Z was likely still too young to start becoming doctors when this data was gathered.)

Chances are, you would not just give the dashboard in figure 7.8 to someone who's never gotten an interactive report before. You'd have to introduce it to them by adding more guided instruction both in the dashboard and likely by straight-up telling them as you show them how it works. You might even want to make a video or animated gif of how to use the dashboard so they can see how it works.

On the other hand, if you're giving this to someone who's already very familiar with BI tools, it will need less voiceover, and you're probably safe to hand it to them exactly as shown in figure 7.8. Because that person is already familiar with interactive visualizations, then by leaving one of the bars selected like the Blood Pressure option is selected now, they get the messages that those bars are selectable and that they can change the selection if they want.

This understanding of what's going on inside your users' heads comes from knowing their *mental model,* or what they think and believe about the world around them (or, namely, your visualization and how it works). When you understand your users' mental model, you'll be better able to empower them to explore data on their own. We'll talk more about the process of user research in a later chapter, but for now, it's sufficient to say that you'll want to get as much into your users' minds as you can (but please not in a creepy way), so you'll know what they're looking for and what they're used to seeing. The best way to accomplish this is to spend some time with them. We'll cover this in more detail in the next chapter, but ask tons of questions and try to watch them using both a viz that is unfamiliar to them (whether it's an early version of what you're already making or some other viz entirely), as well as one that they already know how to use. If they're okay with it, record the session so you can refer back to it later and not need to worry about taking notes.

7.2.3 Balancing when to require interaction

Interactivity, like the tools of color and typography, should always be added with purpose. As with both of those other design tools, the only reason to add interactivity is to help users engage with and understand the message you're trying to get across to them with your data. Sometimes, especially with explanatory vizzes, you might have very little or even no interaction; that's completely okay if it's what your users would prefer or that's all you can do with your visualization medium or tool. However, in those cases where the web is your oyster, and anything interactive goes, it's all about striking a balance between when to show your cards (putting it all out there) and when to play it closer to the chest (requiring interaction to surface information). In general, the most important and the highest-level information should be immediately visible with no interaction required. After that, there are questions you can ask yourself to help decide what is right for the rest of each viz you develop.

TO LABEL OR TO HOVER?

I used to think that the absolute nirvana state of data visualization was to make something so intuitive that it required no labels or instructions. Thankfully, I have since learned that this is decidedly *not* nirvana and is, in fact, a straight-up *bad idea*. Even Alice, on her journey to Wonderland, was given the instructions to "Eat me" on the magic cake and "Drink me" on the magic bottle. And then, of course, disaster ensued because there was no indicator of what each magical consumable would do to her, so we want to avoid such disasters for our users by giving them the necessary information upfront (and additionally giving them a simple way to back out of disaster, which we talked about earlier in this chapter).

When deciding which information should go in a label and which should go inside a hover or tooltip, here are some questions you can ask yourself:

- How much time do your users have to spend with your viz? This is a hugely important factor in your decision. If your audience is mostly made up of executives and people who want or need everything yesterday, you'll likely want to err on the side of labeling too much rather than not labeling enough.
- What information is required to get the story across, and what is optional or secondary? If there's a bit of information that is a keystone of understanding, that should likely be called out explicitly with a label. If something is secondary, like if you have labeled a bar showing the number of users who did a thing, and you also want to say the total number of users available who could have done the thing, as well as the percentage who did the thing, you'd put that in a tooltip. Check out figure 7.9 for an example.
- What requires a lot of words or full sentences (and isn't very interesting)? If you want to include fascinating background context or key takeaways from an analysis, please don't bury those in a tooltip! However, help text and/or info about where data originated are both fair game. In the case of a dashboard or viz that

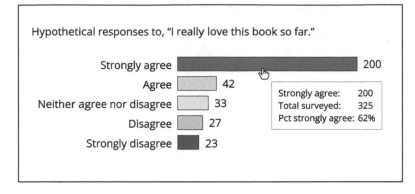

Figure 7.9   If the main point is that X number of people gave a certain response on a survey, you could put that X in a label, and then, if you want to give more context, such as the total number of people surveyed and the percentage who'd chosen that response, you could put that secondary information in a tooltip. This way, users will get the main idea, but when they want to know a little more, then all they need to do is hover on each bar.

consists of more than one chart, I would recommend that this helpful text go as close as possible to its subject matter: either directly in the tooltip on the data or in an informational menu adjacent to the relevant chart. When your viz is a single chart, you can put everything in a single help or info menu that sits off to the side out of the way but is still discoverable—the top right is a great place for this.

- We'll cover this a bit later, but you should also find out whether your users will be able to see hover menus at all, which (spoiler alert) they won't be able to do if they are navigating only with a keyboard.

TO TOGGLE OR SHOW EVERYTHING?

Similar to whether something should appear in a label or a tooltip, there are questions you can ask yourself to help decide whether something should be hidden by a toggle switch or displayed by default.

1   How much time do your users have to spend with your viz? As with the labeling, this is the first question you should ask yourself. If you're making vizzes for executives and people who have no time, I would recommend staying away from toggles except as a very last resort, or in the case of the next question listed here.

2   Do you need to give multiple options for how to view the same data (e.g., giving the option to change temperature units between Fahrenheit and Celsius)? This is a solid use case for a toggle switch, regardless of how you answer the other questions listed here. (Bonus points if your viz can remember the user's selection the next time they bring it up.)

3   Is space a limiting factor? If the size of your visualization is severely constrained, as on a mobile device or when the viz will be embedded in something like an iframe (pronounced like "EYE-frame," this is an HTML element that displays one webpage inside another webpage), then you might need to conserve space by adding a toggle to control when and where certain things are visible. For example, if you're limited to a very small space but you have three charts to show and only room for two, you might put the most important chart on the left or the top and then add a switch to toggle between the other two (less important) charts on the right or bottom. But if space is not severely limited, just put it all out there and don't hide anything.

We've learned a ton in this chapter so far about designing good interactions and when not to make something interactive. Let's take what we've learned and see how it applies to different devices.

7.3   Interactions on different devices

I am so grateful to live in a time when I have the *entire breadth and depth of human knowledge* in my pocket or near at hand at all times. At all times! And when I give it a bit more thought, I'm eternally grateful to those designers and developers who go to the extra effort to make my experience of browsing that knowledge easy and intuitive, no matter how big or small a screen I'm using. In this section, we're going to learn about the different interactions that are available across different devices, starting with the desktop computer. (And unless you've been living under a rock since the early 2010s, you're likely aware that desktop in the context of device types also encompasses laptop computers.) But before we dive into desktop interactions, I'd like to give you a mini primer on how web pages work. If you know it already, feel free to skip to 7.3.2.

7.3.1   A tiny intro to HTML

HTML, which stands for HyperText Markup Language, is the language of the World Wide Web; all web pages are made of HTML, even if they were created using another language such as JavaScript—when the JavaScript (or another language) file is executed, its output is static HTML *elements*, the building blocks which make up a web page. You can see HTML in action if you use a browser on your computer to open any web page, right-click anywhere on that page, and click Inspect (or something of the sort, depending on your browser). The browser will pop up the developer console (and it truly is your best friend when developing on the web), showing the HTML of the page as a navigable tree of nested elements. Pretty cool!

What you'll see is that HTML elements are made of a series of *tags*, which are strings of text surrounded by opening and closing angle brackets, such as `<html></html>`. To display something inside an HTML element, simply place it between the opening and closing tags, like so: `<html><body>Hello, world!</body></html>`.

A simple experiment

Open up a basic text editor like Notepad on Windows or TextEdit on Mac, and type `<html><body>Hello, world!</body></html>` exactly as shown. Save the file to your desktop (or wherever) as `Hello.txt` and close the text editor. Now go find the file and rename it so it has an HTML file extension, `Hello.html`. (This is because some editors try to outsmart you by adding a whole bunch of other HTML if you directly save it as an HTML file.) Now, when you open the file, it should open in your browser by default and look something like this.

Hello, world!

You just made a web page. Good job!

HTML has tags for specific uses, such as `<button>`, `<img>` for an image, `<li>` for list items, and `<a>` for links, as well as tags for containers that organize content, like `<div>`, `<span>`, and `<p>` for paragraph. When a developer wants to make an HTML element change or do something, they must use JavaScript to add a *listener*, which awaits a certain *event* happening, such as the click of a mouse. There are a ton of other events, too, such as the mouse hovering on, entering, or exiting an element, as well as scrolling, double-clicking, an element coming into focus (more on that soon), and many more.

Now that you have a (very) basic grasp of how HTML works, we can talk about interactions on different devices, starting where we're all a bit too familiar: our mobile devices.

7.3.2 *Mobile devices*

Mobile devices are mostly made up of phones and tablets, but smartwatches have gotten quite popular, too, and who knows what will come next? These small form-factor devices are here to stay, though, so we as data viz professionals need to get comfortable with designing for those tiny touch screens and the not-so-tiny fingers that must interact with them. We have a myriad of possible interactions at (and with) our fingertips when we use mobile devices but tapping, pressing and holding, dragging, pinching, and swiping are the stars of the show.

The major limiting factor to consider when designing for a mobile device is screen real estate, and this is further complicated when you make an interactive visual because your user needs space to see around their fingers as they interact with the data. As you likely well know, it's horribly frustrating as a user to try to interact with something on a phone or a watch, only to find that the area for which you're aiming is so tiny that you practically have to stop everything else you're doing so you can concentrate on just tapping that one little spot. So, not only does your viz need to be squeezed into that small space, but its interactive elements need to be quite sizable. The biggest favor you can do yourself is to design for *mobile first*, meaning that you design for the more difficult small screens, and then you can adapt to larger and more complex screens from there.

Here are a few key things to keep in mind when you're planning a mobile design:

- Know your audience. This is still of utmost importance! When you keep them at the front of your mind while designing, you're guaranteed to do a better job than you would when designing with yourself in mind (which is often our default behavior). Make sure your designs are appropriate for their comfort level, both with data and with the device they'll be using. Don't be afraid to do some user testing: ask people to look at your designs or try out your viz to see if everything makes sense to them, take notes on their feedback, and then go make updates as necessary.

- Leave plenty of white space on the left and right sides of the screen between the outer edges of the viz and the outer edges of the screen. This gives users plenty of space that they know is safe to use for scrolling, and tapping there won't cause something in the viz to change.

- Show a tooltip when a user taps on a data point. If showing multiple graphs vertically in a column, synchronize the tooltip across all the charts, like the example in figure 7.10.

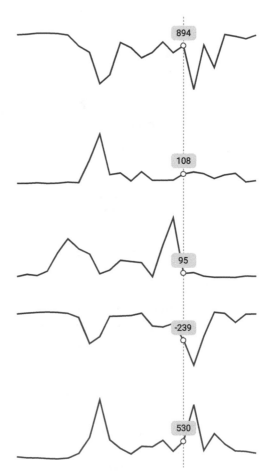

Figure 7.10 When stacking many charts on a mobile device, consider synchronizing the tooltips across all the charts to help the user orient themselves.

- I feel like this should probably be a no-brainer, but when making a viz for a phone, try to fit it within the confines of a single screen, with no need to scroll in any direction to see the edges. It's okay if it has to scroll into view, but once it's there, all four edges of the viz should be able to be visible on the phone's screen at the same time, as in figure 7.11.

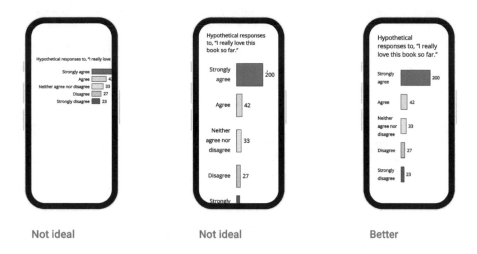

Not ideal   Not ideal   Better

Figure 7.11   Make sure each visualization that is part of your mobile design will fit completely on a single screen without overflowing any of the edges, taking care to leave plenty of space on the right and left sides for the user to scroll.

Now let's switch gears a bit and talk about interactivity on desktop computers.

7.3.3   *Desktop*

As of this writing, most desktop and desktop-like devices don't have touchscreens (yet), so to interact with things on their screens, we, of course, need to use external devices like mice, trackpads, trackballs, keyboards, and whatever you call that little red dot in the middle of an IBM Thinkpad. Designing and developing for a mouse and other pointer-like things (including the red dot) is easy and ubiquitous, so I won't go over it here. However, designing and developing for keyboard-only interaction is far from ubiquitous because, unfortunately, your browser doesn't just magically translate all pointer interactions to keyboard interactions.

The main consideration for a keyboard-only navigator is whether an element on the page is *focusable*, meaning the element can be seen by and receive input from the keyboard. With that in mind, let's talk about the main keystrokes and what they do:

- *Tab*—Jump from one focusable element to the next, where which one comes next is determined by the focus order. In most languages, the focus order, like reading, goes from left to right and top to bottom, but in some languages, it instead goes from right to left and top to bottom. You might see these languages referred to as RTL (for right-to-left) out on the web.

- *Shift-Tab*—Same as Tab, but in the reverse direction.
- *Space*—Toggle the element that is in focus (e.g., open and close a dropdown menu, or check and uncheck a checkbox).
- *Enter*—Activate the element that is in focus, such as a button or link, or submit a form (unless the element in focus is a large text box because then Enter just inserts a normal carriage return). This is usually translated by the browser as a mouse-click event, whether it's because someone pressed Enter on a physical keyboard or used a screen reader to do so (more about that in the next section).
- *Up, down, left, and right arrow keys*—Scroll the (active) viewport (i.e., window or frame) or change the value of an element such as moving a slider or switching between a group of radio buttons.

As you might expect, given that there's a word for it at all, not every element on a page is focusable. Some HTML elements, like links, dropdown menus, and buttons, are inherently focusable, but others, like those meant for organizing content, are not. Next time you're at your computer, try navigating a web page just using the keyboard, and you'll see what I mean. Your tabbing won't bring every single HTML element into focus (remember, the whole page is completely made of HTML elements!), only those that the browser knows to tell the keyboard, "Hey, those things are focusable, so make sure you stop there."

Now, the next thing I'm about to tell you makes me want to cry a little every time I think about it because I genuinely love hover actions.

There is no keyboard equivalent for a hover action. Anything you put in a tooltip that is only triggered on a mouse-related event is completely invisible to a keyboard-only user (and not easily discoverable by a phone user). So sad, right?

What's more, data elements of charts in a data viz are not typically focusable. This means that a keyboard-only user can see your viz, and they can use their keystrokes to click links, toggle switches, move sliders, and press buttons, but they can't hover or even click on a bar in a bar chart. If you need to design and develop for keyboard-only users, you'll have to put in a bit of extra work to make sure they can access all the bells and whistles on your viz. In doing research for this chapter, I happened upon the Accessibility Developer Guide at https://www.accessibility-developer-guide.com/, which is a great resource to demystify all things related to the intersection of web development and accessibility (and can also be found in the appendix). It will mainly apply to those who write code to create their interactive visualizations, but those using BI tools can learn a thing or two as well.

With that, let's talk about screen readers, another way that users can interact with content displayed on a screen, be it desktop or mobile.

7.3.4 *Screen readers*

A *screen reader* is a piece of software that does exactly what it sounds like: it reads out the content displayed on a screen. Most, if not all, modern device operating systems come equipped with some sort of screen reader built into their default accessibility tools. Using a screen reader for the first time can be an overwhelming experience, and I'm sorry to admit that I have not yet fully endeavored to design with a screen reader in mind (nor keyboard-only navigation, at that). Many data viz developers (my past self included) think that if they use a color-blind friendly color palette, they can check off that they're making an accessible data viz. News flash: that's not how this works. I'm not going to lie, designing for a screen reader is like the ultimate data viz challenge mode, which is why past-Desireé didn't try to tackle it in earnest.

But remember to keep your eye on the prize: what is the whole reason we visualize data in the first place? Because it's so difficult and slow to properly digest a table of numbers, and pictures make that digestion much easier and faster. Except, how does that work for people who can't see very well, or can't see at all? Those folks deserve a chance at easier information digestion, too, don't they?

Yes, they most certainly do. So, put on your Big Kid pants, and let's see how we can make it happen.

ALWAYS ADD ALT TEXT WHEN YOU CAN

If you are presented with a chance to add alt text to an image, do it. Yes, even when you post a picture on a social media feed (again, looking at myself here). *Alt text*, short for alternative text, is what displays to users when an image can't be displayed (or hasn't yet been displayed, in the case of slow or unstable internet connections), and it's what screen readers will read out when they encounter said image. For the major BI tools, I know Tableau is starting to give the option of adding alt text to images throughout a workbook, and I also know that Power BI Desktop will allow you to provide alt text for any object on a report. For the HTML coders in the group, the `alt` attribute is required on `<img>` (image) tags, meaning you don't have a choice about adding alt text; for you, it's a matter of making it count.

When you do craft your alt text, keep it short and sweet because a user can't speed up the screen reader. Data visualization accessibility advocate Amy Cesal says, "Good alt text includes: one sentence of what the chart is, including the chart type for users with limited vision who may only see part of it" (http://mng.bz/46NV). Have a look at figure 7.12 for an example.

Amy goes on to suggest linking, not in the alt text but somewhere near the image, to a CSV or other plain tabular format well-suited to machine reading so people can skim through the data with their screen reader if they like. I would add to that a suggestion that if the data is categorical to sort it meaningfully, so they can get the most important numbers first without needing to wade through an entire table.

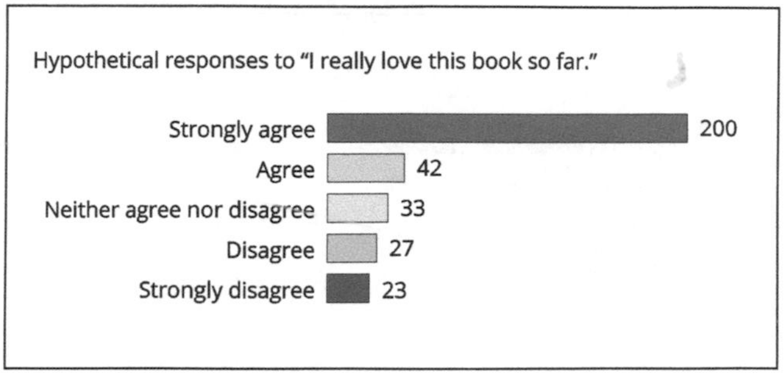

Hypothetical responses to "I really love this book so far."

Strongly agree	200
Agree	42
Neither agree nor disagree	33
Disagree	27
Strongly disagree	23

Not ideal alt text

img0123.jpg

Better alt text

A bar graph representing hypothetical responses to the statement "I really love this book so far," where the bars indicate the number of responses for each category: "Strongly agree" with 200, "Agree" with 42, "Neither agree nor disagree" with 33, "Disagree" with 27, and "Strongly disagree" with 23.

Figure 7.12 Two versions of alt text for the bar graph from figure 7.11, without the tooltip. Even though it is often the default, showing the file name is neither helpful nor necessary; instead, a concise and accurate description ensures accessibility and inclusivity for those using screen readers and other assistive technology.

ACCESSIBLE RICH INTERNET APPLICATIONS (ARIA) LABELS

If you're not a coder, you can skip this little subsection.

Once again, if you're writing code, the world is your oyster. Thanks to our old friends at W3C (the Worldwide Web Consortium, the same body responsible for WCAG), we have options for adding screen-reader-friendly labels to other elements besides just `<img>` tags. These options are specified in the publication called, "Web Accessibility Initiative—Accessible Rich Internet Applications," also known as WAI-ARIA, or just ARIA for short (pronounced just like an operatic solo, "AH-ree-ah").

There are two possible attributes that can be added to an element to give it an accessible name for a screen reader to read out: `aria-label` and `aria-labeledBy`. The difference is subtle: `aria-label` is to be used when the text is not already displayed elsewhere on the screen, while `aria-labeledBy` allows you to pull labels from other objects by referencing their `id` attribute. Both can be used to dynamically generate the necessary labels (great news for those everyday vizzes we love so much!) when your code runs.

Using ARIA labels allows you to ensure that all elements of a chart can be read by a screen reader. As such, they're even shorter and more succinct than alt text, limited to only about three words at most, like the example in figure 7.13, where the ARIA labels for each bar of the graph from figures 7.11 and 7.12 are shown in the yellow box to the right.

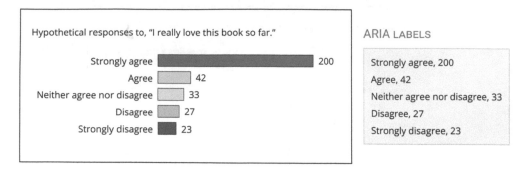

Figure 7.13   Using the graph from the previous two figures, this is what ARIA labels could look like for those bars. Each bar would have its own corresponding label, all of which are shown together in the yellow box to the right.

Since all the text for the ARIA labels in figure 7.13 is already shown elsewhere in the viz, we'd use the `aria-labeledBy` attribute to generate the labels.

WHAT ABOUT WHEN YOUR OPTIONS ARE SEVERELY LIMITED?

So, what about those times when you can't add alt text or an ARIA label to a visual due to limitations in your data viz tool of choice? When all else fails, try to label or caption with descriptive and meaningful text because the screen reader will be able to read that instead, and the user will then benefit from the main takeaways that are so visually apparent. I once listened to an audiobook version of a very prominent data visualization book, and I was astounded at how effective the audio medium could be, thanks to the author's conscientious descriptions of all the visuals in her book. I know these sorts of descriptive labels are very challenging (or impossible) when making the automated and "everyday" vizzes because we developers aren't there to tweak the wording whenever the data changes. But some crazy things are happening in the artificial intelligence (AI) space, and it wouldn't surprise me at all if AI was very soon applied to making visualizations more accessible and inclusive in this way. In the meantime, do the best you can, and when you see those advances pop up in your news feeds, jump on them! And if you need help getting started with writing good alt text, ARIA labels, or captions, that is a great use case for generative AI.

We've talked a lot about accessibility already in this section, but before we wrap up the chapter, let's see what WCAG has to say about interactivity in their accessibility guidelines.

7.4   *WCAG and interactivity*

The main gist of WCAG's guidelines that apply to interactivity is to ensure that a website is usable or operable by as wide an audience as possible, and as such, interaction falls under the principle of "Operable." There are five guidelines under this principle, though only four are overtly relevant to interactivity:

- A website should be accessible by a keyboard-only user, meaning that interactions cannot simply rely on clicking a mouse or tapping a finger but must also respond to keystrokes.
- Users should have plenty of time to read and interact with the content; for example, if automatic scrolling is used, it can be paused and rewound by the user.
- Content should not be designed in a way that is known to trigger seizures or other neurological and physical effects like migraines. Basically, there should be no strobing or flashing effects, and animations should be easily disabled.
- The final guideline is about input methods, but one of its success criteria stands out from the rest: target size. Have you ever tried to tap an incredibly tiny Close button on your phone, only to continuously miss the mark? That's what this target size success criterion is all about: make sure targets are big enough (44 px) so that large fingers and shaky hands will not have trouble finding them.

NOTE If you need a reminder about what WCAG is and why its has guidelines, flip back to section 4.4.2 to refresh your memory.

Summary

- Use familiarity by employing affordances and sticking to familiar (and simple) interaction patterns.
- Make sure users know their interactions have done something by giving timely feedback.
- Be prepared for errors by crafting helpful error messages and displaying them close to their source, both spatially and in time, and allow users to easily course-correct when they get off track.
- The most important information in your visuals should be immediately visible with no interaction required.
- Learn how your users think about a problem because you can better facilitate their data exploration when you know their mental model.
- When designing for mobile devices, think mobile first because it's easier to scale up than it is to scale down, both in size and complexity.
- Don't assume users are using a mouse to navigate a viz. Use focusable elements, alt text, and ARIA labels wherever possible.

Part 3

You have come so far along your journey to visualization nirvana. In this last part of the book, we're going to apply everything you've learned to a fictional case study wherein you've been hired by a (small) client to build a dashboard from scratch. After the case study, we'll go over some scrapes in which you might find yourself in the future and how to get yourself out of them.

Chapter 8 contains the case study, where we'll go over the three main phases of the end-to-end visualization process: research and planning, design, and development. Finally in chapter 9, we'll talk about troubleshooting things like difficult clients and missing data.

Research, design, and development

8

This chapter covers

- A case study about building a dashboard from beginning to end
- Researching and planning what should go into a dashboard
- Designing how the dashboard should look and work and how the data should be modeled
- Iterating to build the final product

Up until this point, you've gotten little snapshots and vignettes of things you can do to up-level visualizations you're already making. I've tried to give you insider information, things I had to figure out on my own because no one ever told me, such as how to pronounce WCAG and how to use different color spaces to tweak a color so it looks just how you'd like it to look. Now, it's time to take a viz from start to finish, from a blank page and clueless users to a clean and beautiful product with happy and informed users. It's time to talk about the end-to-end development of a visualization project, so we're going to walk through a fictional case study using fake hospitality data.

In this chapter, we'll be following a case study about the building of a dashboard from start to finish. We'll go through the three phases of this process: the research and planning phase, where we'll gather requirements and interview stakeholders and users; the design phase, where we'll shape and design the dashboard and our data in tandem with each other; and the development phase, where we'll iteratively take the dashboard from a prototype to its final, beautiful reality, soliciting feedback at every step of the way. The client is waiting, so let's get started!

8.1 The case study

In our case study, we're going to imagine we've been hired by a small hotel group to create a dashboard for their head of housekeeping, Mariette Crewe (she/her). When she's doing the scheduling for her housekeeping staff, Mariette would like to have one place to go to find occupancy information for all three of the properties in the fictional hotel group: The Chord, The Sankey, and The Marimekko.

To accomplish this, we'll be using a (fake) data set that was created in 2020 as part of Mark Bradbourne's "Real World, Fake Data" community project (https://sonsofhierarchies.com/real-world-fake-data/). Specifically, it has a grain of one row per hotel reservation and columns such as stay duration, check-in date, number of adults and children, and the name of the hotel property, among others. Have a look at table 8.1 for a sample of the columns we'll be using.

Table 8.1   A few rows of the hospitality data set, limited only to the columns we'll be using since there are too many to display nicely

Avg. room rate ($)	Reservation ID	Check-in date	Stay duration	Adults	Children	Room type	Property
71.10	779087-Y5-9824-SA	4/15/20	13	3	4	Single	The Chord
71.10	984023-Q0-5015-YG	6/12/20	3	3	3	Single	The Chord
172.38	518066-UQ-2315-FK	2/25/20	11	4	2	Queen	The Sankey
172.38	130339-H9-2116-KE	9/15/20	11	4	1	Queen	The Sankey
98.10	050756-9V-7369-IN	5/26/20	8	2	1	Single	The Marimekko

A project such as this consists of three phases: the research and planning phase, the design phase, and the development phase. Your first task in this project is to do a bit of research to get a thorough understanding of Mariette's needs and wants, which is the beating heart of the research and planning phase.

8.2 The research and planning phase

The research phase of a project consists mainly of interviewing your stakeholders and/or users and informs the *requirements-gathering* process wherein you write down what you are building and why and then get confirmation that you've got it right, as shown in figure 8.1.

Before we start talking to people, though (mainly just Mariette, in this case), let's take a little step back and look at the difference between stakeholders and users.

The Research & Planning Phase

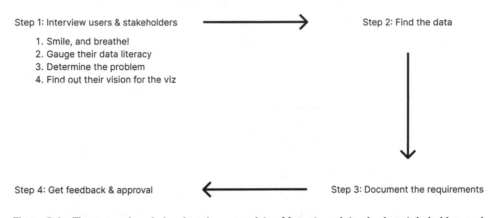

Figure 8.1 **The research and planning phase consists of four steps: interviewing stakeholders and users, finding the data, documenting the requirements, and getting feedback and approval on those requirements.**

When you are asked to do a viz project, the person asking you to build the viz is either a user themselves or asking for it on behalf of others. In either case, this person is a *stakeholder*, a word I've already heavily used, usually synonymously with *users*, but now the difference will be important: the stakeholder is the person (or people) asking you to do the thing; they're calling the shots, and it's usually the stakeholder(s) who will make the final judgment call on whether your project is a success when it's all said and done. The *users*, on the other hand, are the people who will be—you guessed it—*using* your visualization. The stakeholder(s) may or may not be among the users, as shown in figure 8.2.

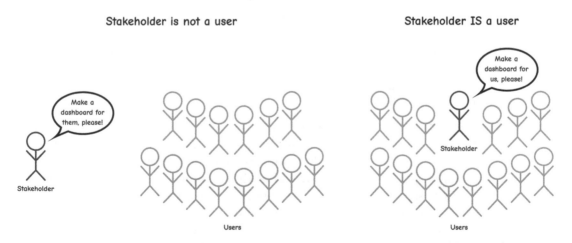

Figure 8.2 **Sometimes your stakeholder, the person asking for the viz, is asking on behalf of others, and sometimes they're going to be a user of the dashboard, too.**

In my experience, the only times I've been on a project where the stakeholder is not also a user are when I'm tasked with building a customer-facing dashboard rather than an internal report of some kind. You might also encounter this situation if, say, someone in management is requesting a dashboard for their team to use, but they won't need to use it themselves. Regardless of why, the dynamic of the entire project is different if your stakeholder isn't one of your users. Though the *process* will largely remain the same when the stakeholder isn't a user, you will likely need to do a little bit of extra legwork to accomplish the following steps in that case. Let's talk about that process, starting with getting to know the users of your dashboard.

All that said, Mariette is both a stakeholder and a user of the dashboard we'll be creating, so let's start by having a chat with her.

8.2.1   *Interviewing stakeholders and users*

To get to know your users, you must start by talking to them. If you don't know who the users are or how to get in touch with them, the stakeholder who asked you to make the viz should have all the information you need. When setting up these interviews, it helps tremendously to have the sessions recorded so you can be all in and concentrating on the conversation. Failing that, have someone else take thorough notes for you, and only if there is no one else to do it, take notes for yourself. You may think you'll remember later, but trust me when I say you won't. As my mom and stepdad used to tell my brothers and me, "A short pencil is better than a long memory."

Once you have a way to record information, you can get down to business. Regardless of whether your users are extremely data savvy, or they run for the hills at the first sign of a bar chart, here are some steps to follow in those first interviews.

STEP 1: SMILE AND BREATHE

It can be a little daunting the first few times you sit down with a user to interview them. While the word *interview* might make you think of a news reporter rapid-firing questions at a press conference, that's really not how it should go. Put yourself at ease, and smile! Users are normal human beings, just like you, who are just trying to make their way in this world. A kind smile can get you very far in life, so don't be afraid to wield one. Also, don't forget to breathe—take a nice, deep breath before you plunge ahead. You've got this!

STEP 2: GAUGE YOUR USERS' LEVEL OF DATA LITERACY

There are two kinds of users you'll work with in your travels as a data viz practitioner: those who are data literate, and those who aren't so much. Your first task when beginning a new project, after taking a deep breath and smiling, is to determine where on this data-savvy spectrum they might be situated because that will be the point of origin on your course to success. I wouldn't come right out and ask, "So, how data literate would you say you are, on a scale of 1 to 10?" but maybe something more along the lines of, "Can you point me to some reports or apps that you use regularly to keep tabs on information that is important to you, particularly quantitative? Some examples could be a sales dashboard or a banking app." Even if they don't give you any links or names, you can do some reading between the lines based on how they react to the question. Are they really excited to talk about their stock investment app? Or perhaps it's something more like, "Oh, well, the last time someone sent me a report was once about five years ago, but I've never bothered to look at it." (Good luck to you if that's what they say.)

As the head of housekeeping, Mariette doesn't spend all day looking at charts and graphs, but she does count herself as more tech savvy than most of her friends, even though she says she's not quite as "with it" as her younger coworkers. You estimate that she's in her 50s, and through conversation, she's told you her kids are grown and out of the house. When you ask her about apps and reports, she tells you she's starting to think seriously about retirement so most of her recent experience with graphs and data comes from time spent on her bank's website. She also tells you that her oldest bought her the latest model of a watch-like fitness tracker for her birthday last year, and while she finds the information interesting, she doesn't engage with the accompanying app very often. (To be honest, you probably won't get that level of personal detail from most users, but because Mariette is fictional, she's particularly forthcoming.)

Upon probing to find out what Mariette likes (or dislikes) so much about the data experiences she named—her bank's website and the fitness tracker's accompanying app—she reveals that it's the interaction patterns and exploration that she values most. She says that she loves using the bank site because it gives her so much freedom to explore, even though the colors are dreadful, and the aesthetic is a bit dated. She goes on to say that the fitness tracker's app is rather the opposite: even though the colors are more fun, and the app has a sleek and modern feel to it, she doesn't use it often because it doesn't give her that same freedom to explore that she loves so much. Now that we know all this, we can use this information to inform our own designs by trying to work in the exploration she likes and avoid the rigidity she doesn't.

At this point in your own projects, feel free to discuss this topic at greater length if it seems like you're getting good intel; once you feel you have a good read on the user's experience and comfort level with data, you can move on.

STEP 3: FIND OUT WHAT PROBLEM THEY'RE TRYING TO SOLVE

Next comes the meat of the interview, and likely, this will be the longest part of the discussion because people love to talk about their problems. Now that everyone's at ease, happy, and comfortable, it's time to find out what information they're lacking, what they need to know that they currently don't, what question(s) they're trying to answer, or what problems they're looking to solve. This time, you can simply ask point blank, "What questions are you looking to answer? What problem are you trying to solve?" Keep in mind, though, it is imperative that you try to keep this as simple as possible because it will serve as your guiding star as you navigate this viz project, keeping both you and your stakeholders on track. If you don't keep it simple, you'll wind up being pulled in a million different directions, and the project will very likely take much longer than anticipated. Staying focused means that everyone wins in the end.

You might be tempted to skip this step since you were told what they needed when you took on the project. *Don't skip this step.* Don't think you know better than the users because you don't. Sure, you might be the viz expert, but they're the ones with the problem (and the power over whether you get paid). In my most recent project at work, I was coerced into glossing over this step, and it made for a very bumpy road. ("We're the experts, and we tell them what the requirements are!" they said. "It'll be fun," they said. *It wasn't.*) Next time, I'll listen to my gut, and my own advice!

So, what does Mariette want in a housekeeping dashboard? She tells you again that she is in charge of scheduling the housekeeping staff and that she wants a single place where she can look at the occupancy metrics for all three hotel properties. The key metrics she cares most about for staffing purposes are number of nights when a hotel is fully booked, number of nights when a hotel is more than 90% booked, number of rooms that stayed over the previous night, and number of rooms checking out each day. When she's doing the schedules, she needs a 30-day view at the very least (with the ability to move that 30-day window), and she says she only does the schedules on a computer, so she doesn't need any kind of mobile-friendly dashboard (in response to which you find yourself inwardly doing a little dance). Also, she's pretty much the only one who will need this dashboard, so there's not really a need to interview more users. Score!

In general, what you're looking for out of this step in the user interviews is a list of all the bells and whistles the user wants in the dashboard. What dimensions do they want to use as filters or breakdowns (also called *slicers*), do they have any need to download the data to a spreadsheet (the answer is almost always yes), do they need to paste screenshots into slides for regular presentations, etc.? Once you have a thorough list full of dashboard features, you can move on to the last step: finding out if they have a mental picture of this dream dashboard.

STEP 4: FIND OUT HOW THEY'RE EXPECTING YOUR FINISHED PRODUCT TO (VERY LOOSELY) LOOK

Now that you have a good understanding of the user's needs, it's time to start thinking about how the dashboard will look. Here, the conversation will differ a bit based on whether you're talking to a user or a stakeholder, but in general, you want to get an idea of what they see in their minds when they think of their shiny new dashboard. Again, it's completely okay to ask it outright: "Do you have any vision of how you want the dashboard to look? Any visual hopes and dreams that I can help make a reality?" If you're talking to a stakeholder, this is a great time to ask about colors, accessibility needs, company branding, logos, font requirements, etc. If you're talking to a user who's not also a stakeholder, you don't have to get quite so specific because they won't know anyway, but inspiration can come from anywhere, and you're making this for them after all, so it definitely can't hurt to know what they want.

What you get out of this part of the conversation will vary dramatically from person to person. You might get specific and strong recommendations about fonts, colors, and layouts, or you might get vague and esoteric blobs that want to be suggestions when they grow up. It could be helpful to have some sort of sketching tools handy (whiteboard and markers, pen and paper, etc.) to give them an easy way to get the ideas out of their heads and into yours. At the end of the meeting, you'll have tons of info to add to your growing list of notes and ideas that we'll start distilling soon. But first, data!

8.2.2 Digging up data

I didn't suggest this sooner because most of the time, the stakeholders don't know much about the data beyond approximately where you will get it and who you should talk to about getting access to it. (And users don't know anything about it at all, so it's no use asking them.) So, before you let your stakeholder get away, have them point you in the direction of the data if you don't already know it.

At this point, I just want you to get a very loose idea of what you're facing in the data realm, and I'll tell you why that's important. I have been on projects where the data set was finalized, set in stone, before I was even brought in to start visualizing, and I've been on projects where the designs are essentially finalized without a thought ever being given toward what shape the data should take (or even whether the desired data exists, but that's a fun and different problem entirely). In both scenarios, all parties involved become frustrated with the added effort of figuring out how to jam a square data peg into a round design hole. Trust me when I say that you should never let one workstream (data gathering, data modeling, or designing) get too far ahead of the other, just like when you're assembling a shelf, and you loosely place and drill in all the screws partially before sinking any of them completely. Thus, at this stage of the game, all you need to do is make sure you have access to the data you need and find answers to the following types of questions:

- What tools do you need to access the data?
- Does all the data exist already, or does some (or all) of it still need to be gathered? If the latter, what does the timeline look like?
- Is the data scattered across many tables, files, or locations? If yes, do you have access to them all?
- Do you have the necessary dimensions and measures to provide what the users need, based on the intel you gathered in the interviews?
- How often is the data updated?
- Do you need to incorporate *row-level security* into the visualization? This means that what a person sees when they open your visualization depends on what permissions each individual has on the underlying data. If so, that will affect how you model the data and will likely look different depending on what tool you're using to access the data and/or build the visual.
- Anything else that springs to mind.

I would then encourage you to, once you do have access, do some light exploring to start getting a feel for what the data looks like. If there is no data yet, as could be the case if you're, say, building a dashboard to visualize survey results, but the survey hasn't been built yet, you could instead get access to the survey tool and create a dummy survey with dummy questions and dummy answers, thus providing yourself with some dummy data. (Stay tuned for chapter 9 where we cover this kind of no-data-yet scenario in more detail.)

For our case study, of course, we have a fake data set that I tracked down and chose because it was interesting and because the three hotels in the data are called The Sankey, The Chord, and The Marimekko (each is a type of chart, and I do so love such nerdy cheek). As is the case with most fake data, it's just a little too clean, as can be seen in some strange idiosyncrasies. For instance, each reservation has adults and children, regardless of the type of room, and when taken all together, the number of children is approximately the same as the number of adults. Furthermore, there doesn't appear to be any obvious seasonality or even variation with day of the week, nor is it obvious what is the capacity of each hotel. Finally, all reservations are in 2020, and as many will recall, there was basically no tourism for a significant portion of that year due to the plague time. But no matter! It's a cute data set and free to use, and Mark Bradbourne (its creator and owner) was very kind to allow me to publish visualizations built on it.

Now, there is one more step in this research phase before we move on to the design phase: we must distill and document all the information we've gathered.

8.2.3   *Documenting the requirements*

By this time, you should have a rather sizable pile of notes you've gathered from stakeholders and users, and a vague idea of how the data looks or will look. It's best practice to gather all of that into a single document that you can then present to the stakeholders to get their approval of what you will and won't do as part of this visualization project. This could be a very formal Business Requirements Document (BRD) or Product Requirements Document (PRD), for which some companies even have templates they want you to use. Or it could be a less formal, nontemplatized document that simply lists these features, most of which will be bulleted lists:

- *The purpose of the dashboard, kept to one or two sentences at most*—This is like the elevator pitch for the viz.
- *The questions the dashboard is aiming to answer*—Remember to keep it simple, three or so main questions at most. The rest is a bonus.
- *The stakeholders and target users.*
- *What's not in scope for the project*—I always call out when I'm not going to include support for multiple languages or multiple device layouts, but you could include anything you're not willing to do. Granted, they might want to renegotiate something later, but you will then be able to point back to the requirements document

to say it was out of scope, and if they want it, then they'll need to reprioritize or renegotiate the timeline.

- *What's in scope for the project*—Here you'll list out everything you plan to build, write, or hand over as part of the project, like build a dashboard with X number of tabs in ABC tool, and it will be published to PQR location to be viewed by the stakeholders and target users. If you are responsible for building an entire data pipeline to feed the dashboard, include that. If you are simply connecting to some tables or an API and won't be doing any heavy data engineering, detail that either here or in the "not in scope" section. Make sure to include that you'll document how everything works!

- *Requirements*—This is where you can, and should, be very specific. You can break this down into sections like Filters and Controls, Visuals, and Interactivity, for example, and include an Accessibility section if that is something you need to prioritize. As far as filtering versus interactivity goes, I know some people prefer to avoid things like dropdown menus and radio buttons in favor of making the data itself interactive, but don't forget the keyboard navigation limitations brought on by not using such stock elements.

- *Metrics*—I like to include this as its own section to make sure the stakeholder sees it and that I have the definitions and general calculation methods right before getting too far into things. This list serves as a source of truth for what must be included, how it is defined, and where each component can be found. By gathering everything into one place (usually a table; see table 8.2), you make it easier for stakeholders to confer and say what they want or need for each metric.

  - It's exceedingly helpful when all metrics are fully defined as early as possible, especially before you go into the data modeling phase (more on that soon) because otherwise it's like trying to hit a moving target. When you're baking cookies, you need to know what ingredients go in before you start baking so you can be sure you have everything and not need to furiously search for "best substitute for butter in cookies" in the middle of the production. Similarly with data, it's good to know everything you'll need to construct each metric so you can be sure you have it before setting about data modeling; for example, for a conversion rate, you'll need a denominator (visits or similar) and a numerator (purchases or something like it). Depending on how your stakeholders want to define conversion rate, you likely also need a way to tie a purchase back to its visit.

  - There are no rules about how this table or list of metrics should look. I've been on projects where there were a dozen or more important metrics, and I've been on projects with only one or two important metrics. Sometimes you need a dozen columns to capture all the important information, and sometimes you only need a few, as in table 8.2.

Table 8.2   A table of metrics that must be visualized in the Housekeeping Dashboard of our case study.

Metric name	Calculation	Does the data exist?	Notes
Reservations checking in	Count of reservations whose stay begins on a particular day	Yes	Can be deprioritized since these rooms will not require housekeeping per se
Reservations checking out	Count of reservations whose stay ends on a particular day	Yes	Trended only
Reservations stayed over	Count of reservations whose stay is not beginning or ending on a particular day	Yes	Trended only
Nights fully booked	Count of nights when all rooms in the hotel are reserved	Yes	Aggregate and trended—most important!
Nights >90% booked	Count of nights when more than 90% of the rooms in the hotel are reserved	Yes	Aggregate and trended—most important!
% Nights fully booked	Nights fully booked/Count of nights in the time window	Yes	Aggregate only
% Nights >90% booked	Nights >90% booked/Count of nights in the time window	Yes	Aggregate only

Sometimes, these tables have many more columns (e.g., source of the data, an example of how it's formatted, etc.) and sometimes fewer. Sometimes they have many more metrics and sometimes only one or two.

Once you have a draft of the requirements document ready for eyes other than your own, it's time to get input from your stakeholders to make sure they agree with and approve of what you've outlined. There might be some back-and-forth here, and that's okay, even encouraged, because if they are engaged, then it means they care, and there should be fewer surprises later down the road. Depending on how available and responsive they are, be sure to allow a few days to a week or more for approval of the document to finally come. I urge you to be persistent about this because getting feedback early and often is the best way to ensure the success of your project.

You've gathered requirements from stakeholders and users, you have access to the data, you know roughly what data is available, and you've gotten stakeholder approval of your plans. Now, you can finally move on to the next phase of the project: the design phase.

8.3   *The design phase*

In this phase of a project, we take our plans from esoteric and ethereal imaginings and put them on paper as designs. An obvious part of the design phase consists of sketching and making mockups, but when you're visualizing data, there's a whole subphase that is easy to either overlook completely or address at completely the wrong time: the data-modeling phase.

8.3.1 Shaping a data model around design

So, before we get too far into our imaginations, dreaming up all kinds of crazy features we can add to a dashboard, we should talk data modeling, so we know what's possible data-wise as we go into the rest of the design phase. Remember, the *data model* is the organizational structure of your data, including the types of data you are storing and how each data point is described. A data model can be made of one or many data structures, be they tables, arrays, or objects. (If I've totally lost you, maybe go back and skim chapter 3.) Usually, a single chart or visual is supported by a single data structure. For now, let's talk tables, with their rows and columns and such, but know that the same sorts of ideas can apply to arrays, objects, and other structures also.

The data you use for a visual will generally be either *tidy*, meaning it has one row per observation and all of its variables are stored in columns, or *untidy*, which is pretty much any other arrangement. If you're using a BI tool like Tableau or Power BI, connecting directly to a wide, tidy table like the example in table 8.3 will give you the most flexibility because such tools make it very easy to aggregate as much or as little as you would like, or as your design requires.

Table 8.3 An example of a tidy table, with a grain of one row per individual fruit eaten (observation) and one column per measure (variable)

ID	Date	Fruit type	Taste score
1	Jun 2, 2022	Apple	75
2	Jun 2, 2022	Apple	25
3	Jun 2, 2022	Kiwi	50
4	Jun 2, 2022	Mango	100

Looking back at table 8.1, the sample rows of our hotel data set, you'll see it's a tidy table like this one, with one row per reservation. Score!

If you're coding instead of using a BI tool, then you should know that Python, R, and d3 all have some very powerful libraries meant specifically for working with such tidy tables (e.g., a data frame in the Pandas library, for Python). But if you aren't using one of those libraries, then it's probably a good idea to do some aggregation first, like the example of an aggregate table in table 8.4. If you're planning to follow along with a coding example, which is often what I do when coding in d3, then matching the structure of your data with that of the example will make your life the easiest and set you up for the quickest success.

Table 8.4 An example of an aggregate table, with a grain of one row per fruit type

Fruit type	Fruit count	Average taste score
Apples	2	50
Kiwis	1	50
Mangos	1	100

Regardless of tool choice, as we discussed in chapter 3, it's easier to start with less aggregated data because you can always aggregate more. It's impossible to disaggregate if the information has been aggregated out of existence—rather like wearing many thin layers for cold weather so you can add or take off as desired, instead of wearing only a thick coat that makes you too hot when it's on, but too cold when it's off.

There are other, very untidy options, such as a very tall table with a single column to house the measure names, and another single column to house the measure values, as in table 8.5.

Table 8.5 An example of a tall (aggregated) table, with a grain of one row per measure per day

Date	Measure name	Measure value
Jun 2, 2022	Apple count	2
Jun 2, 2022	Kiwi count	1
Jun 2, 2022	Mango count	1
Jun 2, 2022	Apple avg taste score	50
Jun 2, 2022	Kiwi avg taste score	50
Jun 2, 2022	Mango avg taste score	100

A table like table 8.5 can be quite difficult to work with, especially if you will need to format measures differently within a single column (e.g., percentages vs. decimals). In such a case, you'd want to either focus on each measure type separately by using filters or instead create entirely separate data structures—one for the percentage measures and one for decimal measures.

While you are well within your rights to jam all measures into one table, I am mainly trying to illustrate that just because you can does not necessarily mean that you should. I have worked with this type of table in practice on multiple occasions, but the only reason you'd even want to consider this for a visualization is if you are subject to very tight resource constraints. In one instance, we needed a way to allow new metrics to automatically flow into the viz without having to touch anything on the visualization side because there weren't going to be any viz developers to do the updating later. In the other instance, there were limited data engineering resources, so as a viz developer, I was forced to use a table like this, which had been built specifically to feed an

Excel report because the client didn't have the bandwidth to maintain a second version of the same data to feed a visualization.

All of that said, take a look at all the information you have from your requirements gathering and user interview sessions, which hopefully you documented so you could get signoff from your stakeholders. With that list in hand, showing all the metrics, filters, slicers, and dicers you'll need, think about what the grain of that table should be; then, if you're lucky, you can hand it all off to a data engineer to gather it up for you, while you move onto the rest of the design and development process (of course staying in close touch with that data engineer in case either of you encounters something unexpected). If you must go cobble the data together yourself, this is a good time to go to the database or other data source to make sure you can pull it together in the shape you need it. Whether you're gathering the data or someone else is doing it for you, if there is information missing at this early stage, then it's more likely you'll have time to either have someone make it available for you or rework your story if that's just not possible.

Now it's time to switch gears a bit, setting aside our "research and numbers" hat and putting on our "drawing and designing" hat. (This is my very favorite thing about doing data visualization: I get to wear both kinds of hats! And I do so love a good hat.)

8.3.2 *To sketch or not to sketch*

I practically felt your eyes screeching to a halt over the word "drawing" in the previous paragraph. Am I good at drawing? No, no I am certainly not (yet?). But using your hands to quickly transfer ideas out of your brain and onto some kind of page can be a very helpful exercise, so let's talk about that.

Around 2019, there was a big push by several prominent members of the data viz community who took a hard stance on the side of using physical media such as pencil and paper or a whiteboard and markers to sketch out a viz before committing to pixels on a screen. These professionals argued that people (users and designers alike) tend to see pixels as a more final product and are less likely to suggest new ideas, tweaks, and iterations when they're looking at a screen than when they're looking at a nondigital drawing. I'm still not sure how right they were, but because I was just starting to break into the design world at the time, I trusted them. Perhaps I'd spent too much time in grad school with pencils and paper—getting the tell-tale dark smudges on the heel of my hand from rubbing across pages and pages of equations all day—or perhaps it was to spare the poor trees, but pencil and paper just aren't my jam anymore. So, I dutifully ordered a six-pack of 8.5" x 11" whiteboards with a colorful set of super-fine dry-erase markers and made sketching the first step in my design process.

In the years since, through the course of dozens of projects, I have realized that sketching in these physical media feels to me like much more of a commitment than using pixels. (Or maybe I'm just lazy because the idea of redrawing a viz element simply because I want to move it from the right to the left side of my sketch is often way too much effort for me.) I would be overjoyed to use my tablet and its accompanying pencil for this, but I have yet to find the perfect (free) app that accomplishes what I want (though I think Figma might be getting on the ball with this soon—here's hoping!), so I will continue to use my whiteboards and markers until something better comes along.

Until that blessed time, my early design process involves roughly sketching ideas using a single color, thinking about them for a day or so, then taking pictures and comparing them all together. Honestly, it hardly warrants the title "process" because it's really just a loose outline of steps that I only sorta-kinda-sometimes follow. If I'm very inspired, I might only sketch about half the idea (if any of it at all) before starting development. In other times, when inspiration is fleeting or there's a lot of information to show in a small amount of space, I try to come up with three separate ideas before choosing one (or having stakeholders choose one, if they're very engaged) to start developing. Not only is it a great exercise to come up with a few unique ideas, but it gives me a couple of backup options in case the first idea doesn't work out. Most of the time these drawings have mainly been for my own benefit, to see my ideas start to take shape and help organize my thoughts, not unlike a visual to-do list. But every so often, it has also been useful to show a stakeholder what I am imagining rather than merely trying to describe it. A picture is worth a thousand words, after all.

On the other hand, some people like to go straight to their tool of choice and start playing with the data (if they already have access to it) so they know exactly how the visuals will look with real data. If you're already a capable developer with your chosen tool, and you're not into drawing, this is a fine alternative to sketching for getting the thoughts out of your head and onto a page—just be sure that you're not spending too much time up front trying to get stuff pixel perfect because there's no need to waste valuable development time. These early-stage versions are *prototypes* because they're not at all meant to go into production use; instead, they help you test concepts and demonstrate potential options to yourself and even stakeholders.

Still other folks (myself included at times) like to go back and forth between sketching and prototyping in one tool or another. Every so often, I'll have an idea that I'm not sure if I can make it work in the tool, so I'll set down the markers and whip up a very basic prototype of the thing. Once I've proven (or disproven) that it's possible, I'll get back to sketching, or if I'm satisfied, then I'll go right into development from there.

So, what is it that you're sketching or prototyping, anyway? Layout ideas!

8.3.3 *Laying out a dashboard*

Regardless of whether you sketch your ideas first, it's time to talk about laying out a dashboard and how we decide what goes where. If you want a refresher on the preattentive attributes and gestalt principles, this might be a good time to go back and skim chapter 2. The main idea to remember for layouts, though, is that generally your most important stuff should go toward the top left, and your least important stuff should go toward the bottom right—this is because that's how we in the Western world read: left to right, top to bottom.

Within that rough guideline, you still have countless options for how things can be laid out on your dashboard, to the point that it can be a bit overwhelming. But you've got to start somewhere, so normally, I start with a very basic layout: I use a size that would (at least mostly) fit on a laptop monitor, put a logo in the top left, follow it up with a title, and then place any filters and controls off to the right. Then the main content goes in the rest of the space, as shown in figure 8.3. Remember to leave plenty of white space between elements and around the outside of the dashboard! I like to start with 20 pixels and then dial it up or down from there as needed.

Figure 8.3   Just a few simple examples of how to lay out a dashboard for desktop or tablet. Notice how there's plenty of space between elements and around the outside of the dashboard.

Of course, there are zillions more ways that content can be arranged on a dashboard, so I encourage you to pay attention to the data around you. You never know from where inspiration will strike, so keep your eyes open all the time, collecting ideas to keep in your viz toolbelt either by taking pictures or by keeping something like a Pinterest board where you can always go to be inspired.

But before you can decide what should go where, you'll need to know what's important to your users. So, this is a good time to take a holistic look at all the notes you've gathered so far during the research phase of your project. Oftentimes designers will use sticky notes, either physical or virtual (using something like a Miro board or Figma's Figjam board), to help them organize their thoughts. The typical process is to look at your research notes and write one idea, request, or concept on a sticky note until you have transferred everything to the sticky notes. You can even add ideas if more come to you while you're going through this process— the sky is the limit! Group the sticky notes together by related themes, and eventually, the biggest and most important themes will bubble up as large groups, while the less important themes with fewer stickies will remain stragglers that can be deprioritized.

I don't typically do the sticky note thing, instead opting for bulleted lists in a note-taking app, as in figure 8.4.

Case Study

Housekeeping forecast dashboard. Housekeeping needs for the next 30 days or 5 weeks.

Questions:
1. What days do I need to schedule the most housekeeping staff because a hotel is fully or almost-fully booked?
2. What days have a large influx or outflux of guests?
3. Are there any days that have particularly many children staying?

Metrics:
- Reservations checking in
- Reservations checking out
- Reservations stayed over
- Nights fully booked
- Nights >90% booked
- Number of adults stayed over or checking out
- Number of children stayed over or checking out

Data needs:
One row per day per reservation (so a 7-night stay would have 7 rows)

Slicers:
- Day
- Room type
- Hotel property

User(s):
- Head of housekeeping
- Person(s) in charge of scheduling the housekeeping staff

Figure 8.4   The method I used to organize my case study user research notes is less visual than one might typically expect, but it gets the job done.

As I sat down with these notes for Mariette's housekeeping dashboard, I quickly saw that the main challenge was figuring out how to visualize several different metrics trended over at least 30 days (not to mention how I would manage to draw something that I wouldn't be humiliated to publish in this book). Less challenging but more important was that I wanted to show the occupancy metrics for all three hotels right up front so that Mariette would know immediately how many days she'd need all hands on deck at each property. With that being the most important data, it would take the most important spot: straight across the top. The trends for the rest of the metrics would then go below. I couldn't decide between one giant view to trend all the metrics and two separate views for trending—the first seemed like it would be overwhelming and busy, while the second seemed redundant and weird. I knew so many metrics could easily make the dashboard rather busy, and that busyness was definitely borne out in my sketches, which you can see in figure 8.5.

As you can tell from the figure, I had an early vision of using donut charts to show the overall occupancy metrics, which I maintained throughout, and once I got the idea to show the stayovers and checkouts on a calendar-like view, I hung onto that too. Because bar charts are so ubiquitous and Mariette isn't particularly data savvy, I tried many different combinations and orientations of bar charts to show the daily metrics, but none of them made me particularly happy. As I feared, it was overcrowded and busy with so many metrics. Still, the show must go on, and progress had to be made, so I took my least-disliked ideas and moved on to wireframing anyway, where a *wireframe* is a simplistic, usually digital, version of what the design could look like later. Generally, there is no color involved, and the fonts are quite basic (I like to use a handwriting-like font, so it's obvious that it's not a final version) because the point of a wireframe is to get a quick, rough idea of whether the design will satisfy its intended purpose. In figure 8.6, you can see my two versions of a wireframe; seeing the design like this helped me eliminate all but one layout option, and it was much easier this way than trying to draw all those tiny chart elements with a marker!

Seeing the wireframe of that many bar graphs, on the left side of figure 8.6, solidified in my mind that this wasn't the way to go with Mariette's housekeeping dashboard. Instead, I opted for the calendar view and the line charts in the option on the right, and I'd figure out legends later. I showed it to Mariette, and she gave me the green light to start building that version.

In a normal design process, the next steps after wireframing consist of making mockups of increasing *fidelity*, meaning that they get closer and closer to looking like a real (digital) product. To be quite honest, the most I normally do is add some color to the wireframe to get the stakeholder's buy-in on the color palette and then call it a day. Usually, I don't have the kind of time necessary to make a very high-fidelity mockup, especially when I'm working with a BI tool, because getting the fonts just right and making the components for radio buttons and drop-down menus that look like the real things you see in the tool is not worth the effort to me. When I'm coding by hand, however, I do find that making a high-fidelity mockup is worth the extra

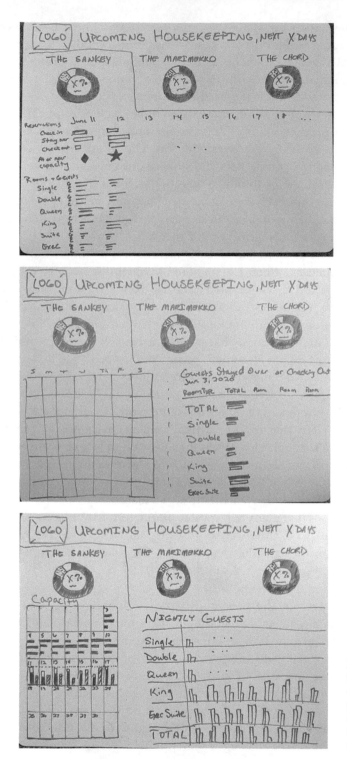

Figure 8.5   My sketches, in order from first to last. I loved the donut charts, so they stayed constant, and once I had the calendar idea (lower left corner of the second and third ideas), I really latched onto it.

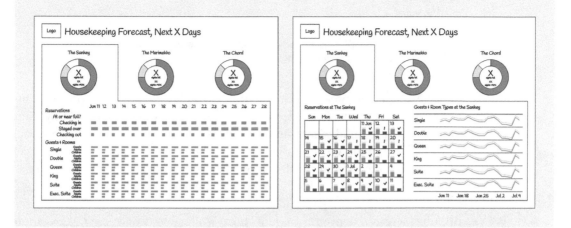

Figure 8.6 **Sure enough in a surprise to no one, a zillion bar graphs (on the left) are overwhelming and busy. Mariette and I decided to go with the concept on the right instead, with a calendar view showing stayovers, check-ins, and checkouts (with symbols to indicate whether a night was fully or almost fully booked), and a line chart showing adults and children by room type (legends to be decided later).**

effort purely because the development itself requires so much more effort. It's all about whether "the juice is worth the squeeze," meaning whether what you put in is worth what you get out.

Has this philosophy come back to bite me? Only once (so far), and truly, that was quite recently as of this writing. If you find that you're working with stakeholders who care a lot about fonts and colors, it's probably worth the effort to make a high-fidelity mockup to get their approval on all that *before* you move from the design phase to the development phase, which we'll cover next.

8.4 The development phase

We started this project with the planning and research phase, where we asked a ton of questions and learned as much as we possibly could in a short amount of time. We gathered all of our learnings into a set of requirements that must be met for the project to be a success and then we made sure that was truly what the client wanted too. Next, we moved into the design phase, where we took those requirements and turned them into ideas, which we then turned into images on a page (or screen, of course). Then we presented those images to our stakeholders and users to make sure their needs would be met. Do you notice a pattern at all? We plan, we build, and then we get feedback. This, my friends, is the *iterative development cycle*, as in figure 8.7, and guess what? We're going to do it again in the development phase.

In the research phase, we planned by asking questions, then we built a requirements document, and finally, we got feedback from the stakeholder. If the stakeholder didn't like something or other in our requirements, we'd have gone back to planning

**Figure 8.7   The three-step iterative development cycle:
plan, build, get feedback, do it all again**

with their feedback, made tweaks to the document, and then gotten feedback again. Once they were happy, we could move to the design phase, where we'd plan by using the requirements, we'd build wireframes and mockups, and then we'd get feedback on those. Round and round we go until everyone's happy, and then we move to development. On the first iteration in the development phase, your build is a prototype.

8.4.1   Prototyping

We've already mentioned prototyping a short while ago when we talked about whether to sketch. Recall that a *prototype* is an early version of a product meant to test a concept or an idea before committing to the real thing. Personally, I love prototyping because I can hack things as much as I want for the sake of speed, the data doesn't have to be perfect, and my code doesn't have to be good (or clean), as long as it runs and does the thing it's supposed to do. I once had a job as a user experience (UX) prototyper and that was some of the most fun I'd ever had at work, before or since!

To make a prototype of a dashboard using your chosen visualization tool, first you'll need some data. It doesn't have to be real data, if you don't have that yet for whatever reason, but it should look something like your real data will look and have the same structure, or as close as you can get. For example, if you're visualizing results of a survey, run through the survey a few times yourself so you have some data points. If you're visualizing something very complex, it might be difficult to come up with random data yourself (truly, it's surprisingly difficult), so try searching the internet for a similar data set: Kaggle is a good start (www.kaggle.com/datasets) as is the aforementioned Real World Fake Data project, or you can use a random data generator (there are zillions out there, so just type "random data generator" into your favorite search engine and go). As we'll discuss in the next chapter, you could also use AI and large language models to help you generate random data.

Once you have your data, just start whipping up your design ideas in your chosen visualization tool! It's as easy as that. Now you can test out the interaction patterns that have been lurking around in your head to make sure they're possible, and you can run them by users and stakeholders to make sure they're useful and delightful.

This is a good time to address the elephant in the room: getting feedback can be difficult, but as you can see from the iterative development cycle, it's an essential part of each phase of a project.

8.4.2   Get feedback early and often

Could you go through development in a vacuum, as they say, without any input from the stakeholders and users until you have a finished product? Sure, you could, but that would be horribly frustrating for all parties involved. There is nothing more disheartening than spending hours and hours over days or weeks toiling with all your heart and soul, only to find that what you made is not even close to what the client wanted. Spare yourself the grief and ask for their feedback frequently! And you don't even have to wait until you have finished one of the build stages—it's completely okay to make sure you're on the right track as you go. I know it is sometimes counter to an organization's culture to show something that is not fully baked or finished, but I firmly believe that if you frame it correctly and set people's expectations ahead of time, all will be well.

Most of the time, though, it's not corporate culture that keeps us from soliciting feedback as frequently as we ought. Instead, it's usually our own fear and insecurity.

OVERCOMING FEAR AND INSECURITY

It's hard to show someone a work in progress, I get it. And it's often very hard to hear critical feedback about something into which we've poured a lot of thought, decisions, and effort, and blood and sweat and tears. It can feel like a personal attack at times, especially if we're not prepared for it.

Oftentimes, creative works are compared to children, and we, as creatives, are told that to put our work out into the world, we have to be okay with killing our babies. In a book that is very dear to me, titled *Big Magic: Creative Living Beyond Fear*, Elizabeth Gilbert strongly cautions the reader against regarding their creative works this way, saying, "This kind of thinking will only lead you to deep psychic pain," because it will be an extra struggle for you when someone critiques your work, or asks you to modify or correct it. For your own sanity's sake and for the quality of your work, you must separate yourself from it emotionally, and I know (believe me, I know!) that's incredibly difficult.

To overcome this tendency toward emotional entanglement with our work, we must simply practice disentangling ourselves. We get that practice by starting small—it's much easier to emotionally accept someone suggesting massive changes to a work when it's still in progress than when it's a completed thing.

If you're the type of person who does well with mock interviews or practicing a talk in front of friends, and if the project isn't confidential, try using those same people as a sounding board for each stage of your next visualization. If you can't show a friend, try a kindly coworker or teammate instead. Tell them ahead of time what you want from them—plenty of praise for things done well, gentle suggestions for how to rectify things done less well—and tell them specifically the kind of feedback you're seeking. If you're looking for a design critique on colors, formatting, and styles, say so, or if you're looking for reactions about the story, layout, and interaction patterns, be specific. It's hard for someone to give you valuable feedback when you throw something in front of them and ask, "What do you think?" so give them some direction. You can start with this simple list and then add on as needed:

- What are you getting from this visualization?
- Is there anything you find particularly confusing?
- What do you like about what you see?

If you're not into the idea of practicing with real people, maybe you're like me, and practicing with other people makes you even more uncomfortable. Instead, when I'm about to go into a session where I'm getting feedback, I give myself a little pep talk ahead of time: "It's not about you, Desireé, it's about getting the job done and getting the point across." As soon as I reframe the situation to be about the data and the story, all pressure is off me, and I can take nearly anything those stakeholders can dish (short of legit personal insults, but I haven't really encountered anyone who's specifically, purposefully, and personally insulted me, not since high school, anyway, and certainly not in the line of my work). Sometimes I even come right out and tell the people from whom I'm soliciting the feedback that they won't hurt my feelings—just saying it out loud like that suddenly and magically makes it true for me.

If you're still beyond nervous and you have the kind of rapport with your stakeholders that allows you to be transparent about your discomfort with getting feedback, go ahead and be real about it. You could also try practicing outside of this work altogether, like participating in a community project such as Makeover Monday (www.makeovermonday.co.uk), or joining the Data Visualization Society's "critique" conversation (which as of this writing is located in Slack: https://data-viz-society.slack .com in the #share-critique channel). Just remember that you can't put proprietary data out into the world, so you'll need to use vizzes you make that can be shared publicly. Eventually, with enough practice, you'll get to the point where you won't be so nervous or uncomfortable anymore, and you can take it all in stride.

BACK TO THE CASE STUDY

Back in our case study, it's time to show Mariette an early version of her dashboard to see how she feels it's coming. In figure 8.8, you can see what I showed her.

Sometimes, our visualizations go through an awkward phase as we're developing them where we ourselves aren't even enamored with how they look. At these times, it can be especially helpful to seek an outside opinion on what could be done differently; else we run the risk of spinning our wheels too long and wasting precious time that could be better spent on how to make the viz awesome rather than just passable. When I finally got up the gumption to show Mariette, she was actually delighted with my progress! That gave me more confidence, and then I was able to discuss with her some of the things I didn't like and the challenges I was facing, like the space for the bar labels in the calendar view. Thanks to her feedback, I felt a renewed vigor for the project as I finally started to see where I could put a legend, better use the space for the calendar and line chart, and how I could add more color and finesse so it wouldn't look so wireframe-ish. You'll see all of this borne out in the final version shortly!

BUT HOW DO YOU KNOW WHEN IT'S DONE?

So, we've gone through the iterative development cycle what feels like a million times, and it seems like we could go through it a million more. Still, at some point, we have to decide that it's done. But how? Well, the changes you're making should be getting smaller and smaller as time goes on and you keep iterating, so you'll eventually reach

Housekeeping Forecast, Next 30 Days

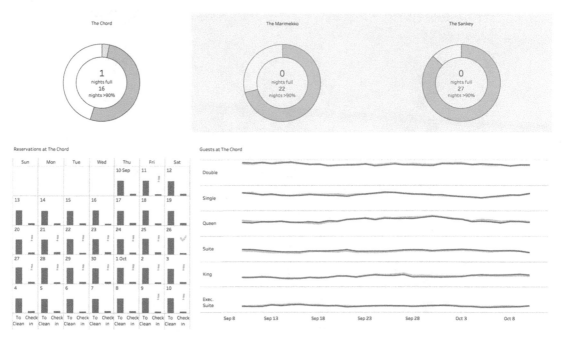

Figure 8.8 The dashboard at this stage took a lot of effort for me to run it by Mariette (and publish here, if I'm being honest) because even I wasn't super pleased with it.

a point of diminishing returns: the time you put into making more changes is not worthwhile given the tiny effect those changes will have, even taken together. When you notice that happening, it's a good sign that it's time to stop and call it "done."

Project deadlines can also help with this conundrum, serving as a hard line in the sand so everyone knows when no more changes can be made. Sometimes, there isn't a hard deadline, though, and we get saddled with a dashboard that we must maintain and tweak for what seems like forever. We'll talk about how to deal with a never-ending project in the next chapter, so for now, let's just pretend that every project has a well-defined deadline at the end.

As you near the deadline, you should reach a point where the visualization satisfies all the requirements, so this is a fantastic time to start pulling out the requirements document during feedback sessions. You can point to the document and show that you're meeting the requirements, so the project is about done, and it's time to stop making changes.

For the housekeeping dashboard, the requirements have all been met, and the changes are getting quite miniscule now, so we're calling it done. Check out figure 8.9 for the final product.

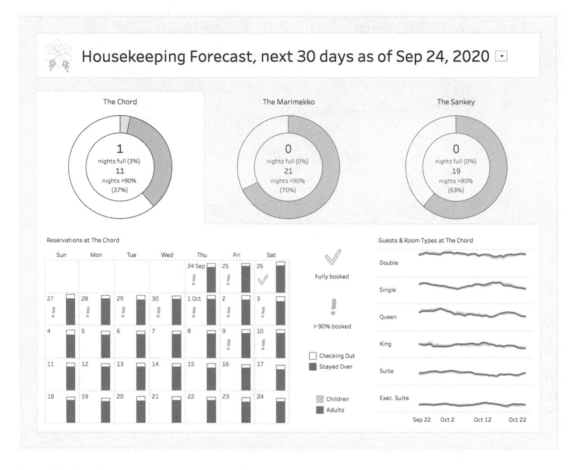

Figure 8.9   The final version of the housekeeping dashboard, complete with legends. Did I hack the daylights out of Tableau to make it outline that white area around the donut chart for The Chord and the bottom section? You'd better believe it. Check out the interactive and downloadable version at http://mng.bz/W1px.

Mariette had suggested that we don't really need to show check-ins on the calendar view because they shouldn't affect housekeeping staffing for that day anyway. With that modification, I was able to put checkouts and stayovers in a single stacked bar that would show the total occupancy from the night previous (which is the night that matters because housekeeping has to clean up after those guests, not before them), and the other side of the calendar day would be for the occupancy indicator symbol. As a delightful bonus, as my husband pointed out, the stacked bars now look like cute little beds—how fun!

Before we wrap this thing up, let's take a closer look at the design choices made around typography, color, and interaction.

8.4.3 Design choices

Since this chapter is serving as a capstone of sorts, I'd be remiss to leave you without a discussion of the design choices I made that pertain to the material that has led us to this point. So, before we get too far away from figure 8.9, I want you to flip back and have a look at it, paying special attention to the typography for the moment.

TYPOGRAPHY

I used the Tableau typeface throughout because it's just such a well-behaved typeface (go back and skim chapter 5 for a refresher if you don't remember what to look for in a typeface for data viz) and kept the color consistent: hex code #333333. The majority of the text is Tableau Book (a weight that is one notch lighter than Tableau Regular) in 8-point size, so thanks to these choices, you should notice only a few places where the typography pops out as different from the rest. In those places, I varied either the size, the weight, or both because I wanted to be very intentional about establishing that hierarchy of importance.

The main header is, of course, the largest because it needs to draw the user's eyes to the top left and serve as a starting point, almost like a "YOU ARE HERE" marking on a map. I used the Regular weight to give it a tiny extra pop. The only other visible places where the typography is different are confined to the donut charts, as seen in figure 8.10: the hotel name is 10 points, and the values of the two metrics are both Regular weight with the top size at 16 points and the bottom size at 10 points, instead of the customary Tableau Book at 8 points.

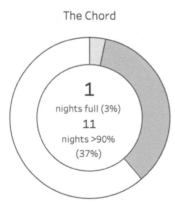

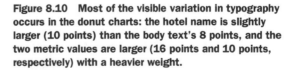

Figure 8.10   Most of the visible variation in typography occurs in the donut charts: the hotel name is slightly larger (10 points) than the body text's 8 points, and the two metric values are larger (16 points and 10 points, respectively) with a heavier weight.

You might have noticed that I specified "visible" a couple times now, and that's because there are also tooltips on this viz, which, of course, you can't see without interacting. In the tooltips, shown in figure 8.11, again I used the Tableau typeface in the same color, #333333, but the default size is 10 points here to aid in readability and lean into giving the tooltip that "zoomed in" effect. Meanwhile, the emphasized text has a weight of Medium while the other text maintains the same Book weight we see in the other body text in the viz. You'll notice the pattern of emphasis is a bit different in each tooltip, but that's because I wanted to only add emphasis where it was really necessary, not just to maintain symmetry. Sometimes you need to maintain that translational symmetry, but these tooltips are simple and different enough that it wasn't really necessary here, though you are welcome to disagree with me if you'd like. Check it out in figure 8.11.

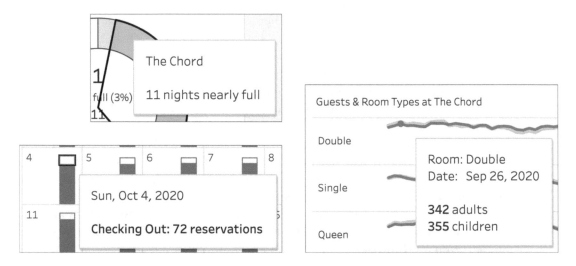

Figure 8.11   Because the attention given to tooltips is different than the rest of the viz, so too the typography pattern is a little bit different. I still kept the text the same color and maintained the Tableau typeface, with Book being the default weight. Emphasis was added only by using the Medium weight, which is one notch heavier than Regular. I increased the size to 10 points instead of 8 for better readability and to lean into the effect of zooming in.

COLOR

Moving on from typography, let's look at the colors I chose for the hospitality dashboard. To create a palette of colors, I took the two colors from the little logo (which happens to be part of the logo for my own consulting business, designed by a close friend) and plugged them into the Coolors tool, which you can find in the appendix—one of its main functions is to randomly generate one or many colors, with or without a set of starting colors, and you can randomly generate as many times as you'd like until you find something you like. I then used the built-in color blindness checker in that same tool to make sure my final colors were color-blind-friendly. Since they looked acceptable in the simulations of the most prevalent color vision deficiencies, and we didn't have any explicit accessibility needs for this project, that sufficed for me. Have a look at the full palette in figure 8.12.

I then made the two logo colors the most important colors in the dashboard, assigning each to one of the two most important metrics: nights fully booked and

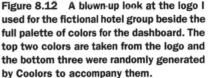

Figure 8.12   A blown-up look at the logo I used for the fictional hotel group beside the full palette of colors for the dashboard. The top two colors are taken from the logo and the bottom three were randomly generated by Coolors to accompany them.

nights at least 90% booked. These colors maintain their same definitions throughout the dashboard, which makes it easy for a user to remember what each color means.

Finally, I made the background of the dashboard a lighter version of the blue in the logo, so that I could emphasize the foreground information by surrounding it in literal white space. This employs the gestalt principles of enclosure, as well as that of figure/ground (which we didn't talk about in chapter 2, but which tells us that our brains are instinctively good at distinguishing foreground objects from their background).

INTERACTION

Next, we come to the interactivity, which we all know is the most difficult aspect to demonstrate in print, but I will do my best here.

Mariette really enjoys the interactive and exploratory nature of her banking app, but because this dashboard is for housekeeping scheduling and not for, say, financially planning out the rest of her life (i.e., the stakes are a bit lower and simpler here), we were able to get by with minimal interaction. The only true requirement is that you select a hotel by clicking on the name above the corresponding donut chart and that will filter the visualizations below.

> **NOTE**   While the date selector on this dashboard, which can be found in the dropdown menu in the upper right corner beside the year, is static in real life because of the static nature of the underlying data, if this was a real project, then I would have set the default date showing to always be the date you open the report. Then if Mariette wanted to go forward in time and look at another date, that's when she'd have to select another date, but if she just wanted to see the next 30 days then she wouldn't need to do anything.

While it wasn't strictly necessary, I added a couple of interactions that I thought Mariette could maybe find helpful sometime down the road: I set the two visualizations on the bottom of the dashboard to cross-filter and cross-highlight each other, as shown in figure 8.13.

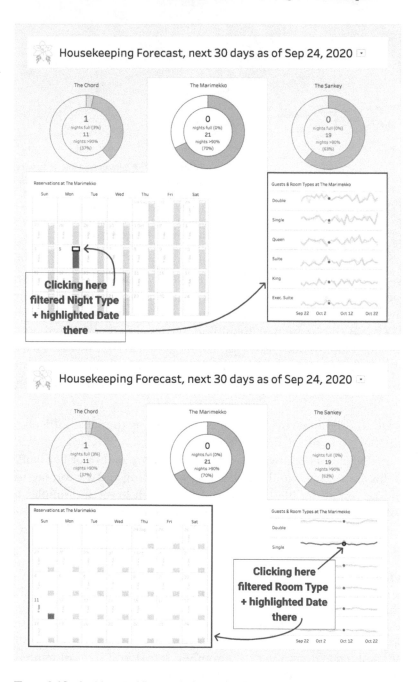

Figure 8.13   In this set of figures, I changed to The Marimekko hotel to demonstrate how that looks. In the top figure, you can see that I clicked on a white sliver on the Reservations viz, which filtered the Guests viz to only "Checking Out" and highlighted October 5. In the bottom figure, you can see that I clicked on a date in the single-room type on the Guests viz, which filtered the Reservations viz to only single rooms and highlighted that date, October 11. (I masked the legend area to improve readability just for these screenshots, but rest assured it's still there in the interactive dashboard.)

Alright, now that we've gone over most of my design choices, let's get back on track and wrap this thing up with documentation. In your own projects, you'll see the finish line like a light at the end of a tunnel: depending on how the rest of the project has gone, it could be either an oncoming train or truly the end of the tunnel, but one way or another, it's time to document the living daylights out of this thing.

8.4.4   Documentation

I'm not going to lie or candy-coat it: documentation is one of the most annoying parts of project-based work like this. I haven't met anyone who likes it (except for maybe technical writers), but it has to be done, so I'm here to help you through it.

Documentation can take on many forms. It can be comments in your code, an automatically generated wiki page, a painstakingly and manually created document that lives in some shared drive somewhere, or anything that will house descriptions, instructions, and explanations about what you did, why you did it that way, and how someone can change it sometime in the future.

As a developer, I find it most useful to rely on well-commented code, be that in actual code like Python, JavaScript, or SQL, or comments inside calculations in a BI tool. A supplemental document giving me the general lay of the land is also pretty handy to have, and stakeholders love having a document that tells them how something works. I swear they'll almost never use it, but I'm sure that the few times they do use it, they'll find it so helpful that it makes all your hard work on it worthwhile.

Before you jump in and start writing pages and pages of docs, check to see if there is a template you can use or a standard you should follow. Ask around! Check with your stakeholder, your manager, your teammates, the IT department, the analytics team, software developers, and anyone else that comes to mind. If no one has anything to offer, try the internet. If you're allowed to do so, you can even employ generative AI and large language models to help write the documentation—this is an especially good idea if you're writing documentation in a language that isn't your first, or if you're just not that great of a writer for whatever reason (no judgement here, writing is not for everyone!). You can also reuse some of the requirements document to help you fill out whatever template you find.

Now, not all documentation templates and standards are created equal. Regardless of whatever you find out there in the world, here are some aspects you should be sure to include:

- *What questions is the viz aiming to answer*—Tell people why they'd want to use this dashboard.
- *Metrics*—At a high level, explain what each metric means and how it's calculated. No need to get extremely detailed here, but help people understand what they're seeing.
- *Frequently asked questions (FAQ)*—Even if no one has asked you anything yet, you can probably anticipate some of the most common questions you'll get, though what those are will depend on your viz subject matter.

- *Key information about the data source(s), filters, and other controls*—Does the data source only get updated by hand when the moon is full in a cloudless sky? Did you set the filters to show only the relevant values? Did you set the filters to show everything, regardless of whether there's data for it? Write it all down and explain why you made those choices.

This is far from an exhaustive list of things you should include in documentation, and you should also consider the audience for the documentation you're writing. It's best to include two sets of documentation, in fact: one for the end-user of the dashboard, and one for more technical folks who might need to make changes in the future. Don't skip the technical docs, even if it's only going to be you maintaining the dashboard! You'd be surprised how much you can forget over time about why you chose to calculate something in a certain way, and of course, none of us are guaranteed tomorrow, so throw posterity a bone and explain your logic in a way that someone besides yourself will be able to understand.

Finally, make sure people know how to find the documentation you've worked so hard to write! Great documentation means nothing if people can't find it. You could put a link to it in the report itself, put it in a shared drive, or on the company wiki—just make sure its location makes sense to your users and stakeholders.

Summary
- Find out what your users like and don't like in a data visualization so you can incorporate that into your designs.
- Take thorough notes and then put all the requirements for your viz project into a single document for your stakeholders to give their signoff that you have understood what is needed and that they understand what's in scope for the project and what's not.
- Craft your data model in tandem with your designs and chart choices to save yourself a ton of headaches while developing your viz.
- Sketch your layout ideas if it helps you stay organized or if it would help your stakeholders grasp what you'll be building. Make a wireframe (also or instead) if you would find that helpful as well.
- Don't be afraid to whip up an early prototype to prove concepts to yourself, your stakeholders, and even your users.
- Get feedback early and often.
- "Done" is better than perfection.
- Document everything, even if it's not fun, and then make sure people know where to find it.

Troubleshooting

This chapter covers

- Making the most of data with holes of any size
- Responding to requests (or demands) that you do Bad Design Things
- Managing a project whose finish line is a moving target

In this final chapter, we're going to talk about what to do when things go wrong, when the cow manure hits the combine blades. We'll talk about what to do when there are a few holes in your data, when there are more holes than data points, and how to report on data that doesn't even exist yet. Then we'll discuss what to do when your client or stakeholder asks you to go against your intuition for visualization and design. Finally, we'll wrap up by going over some reasons why a project's finish line might be continuously getting farther away instead of closer, and how to manage each.

It's the last chapter, and you've made it so far—push on with me just a little further to the finish line. So, let's jump into missing data!

9.1 How to handle missing data

In the chapter about interactivity, we talked about treating your users to well-crafted error messages in the event that they are suddenly faced with no data, either because they filtered it all out or because there was an issue in the underlying data source. Now, we're going to talk about two other cases where you might need to deal with missing data: missing data points and not-yet-existent data.

9.1.1 *Missing data points*

Sparse data is a not-super-fun fact of life with which we all have to cope at times. There's not much to be done about it because that's just the way the cookie crumbles occasionally, but there are a couple things to keep in mind when you're faced with it: don't hide the holes, and give it room to fill in.

DON'T HIDE THE HOLES!

We've talked about trending data with both line and bar charts, and in both cases, we need to make sure that missing data points are evident to users. Let's say you're trending some data by day using a line chart. A plain line, whether it's curved at each data point or not, can make it difficult to interpret not only where the data points are but also where they aren't. To avoid this problem, I like to add a dot at each data point so the data is more obvious. If the dots wind up making the viz too busy, then I either reconsider the whole chart, try filtering to a smaller set of data, or try merely making the dots smaller. Going one step farther and breaking the line when there's missing data then seals the deal. Check it out in figure 9.1.

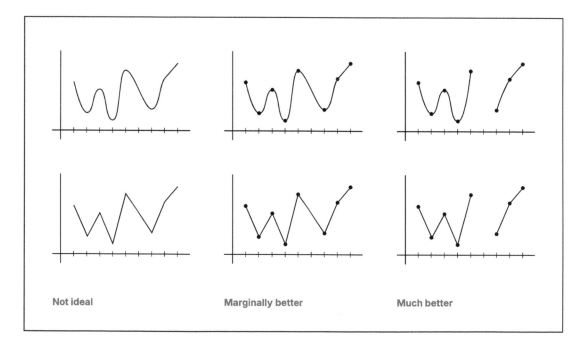

Not ideal   Marginally better   Much better

Figure 9.1   When trending data in a line chart, I like to make it more obvious where the data points are by adding a dot at each point. Not only is it easier to understand, but it's also more apparent when there's data missing. Breaking the line on missing data points further drives the point home.

For bar charts, this should probably go without saying, but I'm going to say it anyway: if you're making a trended bar chart—say it's trended by day—make sure there are empty spots for the missing days so it's really obvious that those days are missing, as in figure 9.2.

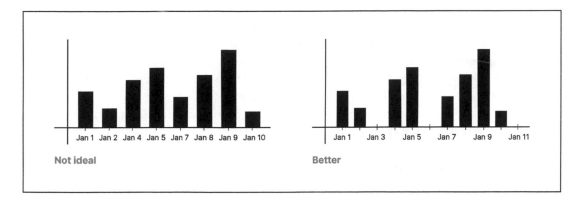

Figure 9.2 Don't hide the holes in your trended bar charts. Make sure those missing days (weeks, months, etc.) are obvious.

Basically, make it obvious when there are holes in your data. If you don't, and someone is not looking closely enough, it could be very easy for them to draw the wrong conclusions, and that's the last thing you want. Remember from chapter 6: a good chart tells the truth!

GIVE IT ROOM TO FILL IN

So, there's kind of sparse data that has a hole or two here and there, and that's what we just talked about. Then there's very sparse data that has more holes than data, which usually arises at the beginning of data collection, when data is just beginning to trickle in. It can be tricky to anticipate how things will look when the data is more mature, but this is another case where making a little effort is better than making no effort at all. This anticipatory effort is called *future-proofing*.

Oftentimes, the mindset I've encountered in tech is to deal with what you have now and don't put too much, if any, work into anticipating what's to come (i.e., future-proofing). The purpose of this perfectly reasonable mindset is to save time and resources because there's no way to anticipate every possible outcome or edge case, and sometimes, product roadmaps can take unpredictable turns, resulting in your hard work having been completely in vain. Thus, it's often best to just get something out there even if it's not perfectly airtight.

However, there is, as always, a delicate balance that must be struck if you don't want to spend a boatload of time fixing a zillion design issues right out the gate, especially issues that could have been easily avoided. The key word there is *easily*: if it would be faster to implement a preventive measure than to fix a resulting problem later, then by all means, please implement the preventive measure! In these times when "an ounce of prevention is worth a pound of cure," that's when future-proofing is in order.

Most of the future-proofing for very sparse data has to do with allowing enough space, as in literally leaving enough room in the viz for data to fill in later. This means having room for all categories to fill in a table or bar chart, or ample space for a meaningful amount of time to be displayed in a trend. Alternatively, or perhaps additionally, it means configuring as much as you can to allow elements to automatically fit themselves into the view. How this auto-fitting is done and how much control you have over it depends greatly on the tool you use, so I won't cover it here, but suffice it to say that it's usually possible on some level in most tools.

In the case of a trend, future-proofing might also mean limiting how much data can be displayed at once so the trend doesn't get too crowded after a long time has passed, or configuring the *x*-axis to suppress some labels so what does show will still be readable down the road, like in figure 9.3.

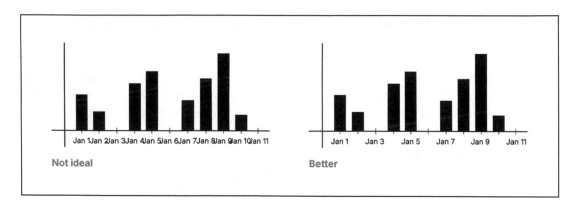

Figure 9.3   A bar chart similar to the one we saw in figure 9.2, where each bar had been labeled. This was fine when there was enough room for all the labels, but adding more bars means that the *x*-axis will soon become overcrowded and that some labels should be suppressed to maintain readability.

In some tools, the default treatment for axis labels when they become overcrowded is to tilt the label or even rotate it 90 degrees, but I would argue that it's a better experience for the user if you suppress some labels instead (though, of course, this only works for a trend, not for categorical data). Have a look at figure 9.4 to see what I mean.

You might notice that the tilted labels at the bottom of figure 9.4 aren't so bad, but I contend that's only because they're so short. If they were any longer, like if the entire month's name was spelled out as in figure 9.5, it then becomes difficult to read. So, I like to steer completely clear of rotated *x*-axis labels altogether.

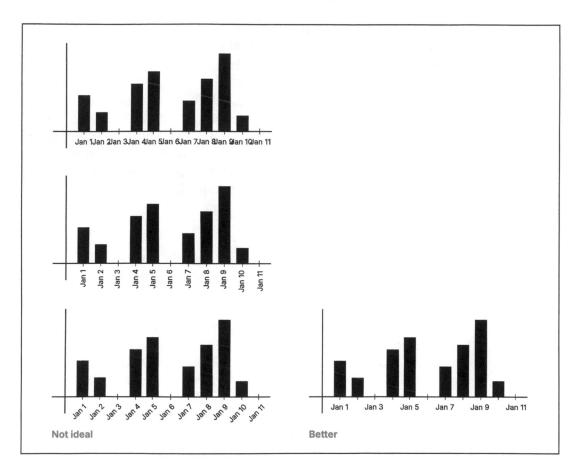

Figure 9.4 Why resort to making users turn their head to read vertical labels when it's much more readable and still just as understandable to leave some out (at regular intervals, of course)? And while the diagonal labels aren't horribly offensive in this case, it's only because these particular labels are quite short. To spare users of neck injuries, I still like to entirely avoid rotating x-axis labels.

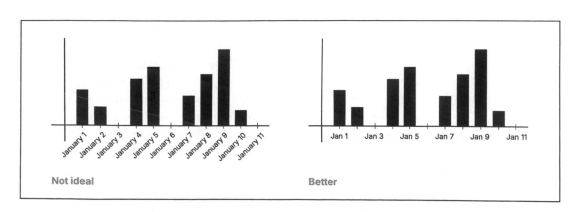

Figure 9.5 While I don't like rotating any labels on an *x*-axis, long labels look even worse than short labels.

NOTE   When you have categorical data whose labels won't all fit horizontally, or the labels are just too long, remember that you can always flip the axes so that the labels are down the *y*-axis, and the bars extend horizontally instead. See figure 6.5 for a refresher.

There are many ways to future-proof your visualization, but the best and most foolproof way to ensure your data viz still looks good when the data is no longer sparse is to check on it frequently in the early days as the data collection is ramping up. Set reminders for yourself if necessary, or if you're on a short-term project, consider baking it into the contract that you'll check back after some time has elapsed to make sure everything still looks good and is working as intended. That add-on might even win you the contract in the first place!

9.1.2   *Not-yet-existent data*

So far, we've discussed how to handle sparse data, whether it's only a little sparse, missing a data point or two here and there, or it's very sparse so that there are more holes than data. Now we're going to back up even further, to the prototyping process, and talk about how to work with data that doesn't even exist yet.

I used to work with a very experienced data architect, and one of my favorite things he used to say was, "I refuse to report on data that does not exist." He was referring to not inferring and making decisions based on data values that do not actually exist in a real report because, believe it or not, there are product managers out there who regularly do this. While I totally agree with my architect friend, we do sometimes need to build a report for data that does not yet exist. But how does one do that?

The very best way to build a report for data that doesn't yet exist is to figure out how the data will be generated (surveys, click tracking, e-commerce transactions, something else) and test that thing out a few times yourself so you can use that test data in your prototypes. How you do this will look very different depending on the tech stack or what tools and technology platforms are used between the person or system generating the data and your visualization, as shown in figure 9.6.

There are infinite different configurations of tech stacks, so there's no way to say definitively, "This is exactly how you generate and use test data," but generally, these are the steps:

1   Do the thing to generate some test data. For example, take a survey, click some buttons, or use a fake payment method to go through an e-commerce flow (talk to the developers who work on the flow because they will surely have ways for you to test it out without needing to put down your own credit card).
2   Find where that data lands, be that in a database table, output from an API, or somewhere else.
3   Hook your visualization tool up to that data source or find a way to get a one-time export of the data and drop that into your viz tool.
4   *Et voilà,* you now have test data for your prototypes!

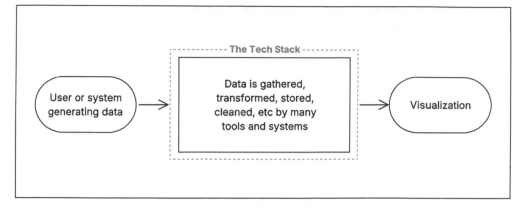

Figure 9.6 How you generate and access test data to populate your prototypes will depend heavily on the tech stack being used to collect, store, clean, and serve up the data between generation and visualization.

The advantage of this approach to getting test data is that it will likely be in the same shape as the real data when it finally does exist.

Sometimes, though, we don't have that kind of luxury, and we have to make do with a less optimal solution. If there is no way at all for you to generate test data using the real systems that will ultimately generate the real data, you do have some other options:

- Search the web for data sets about the same or a similar topic.
- Use a random data generator. There are zillions out there, and they're pretty much a dime a dozen.
- Use a large-language model (LLM) or other generative AI, like ChatGPT. For example, I told ChatGPT to generate two random survey responses for a survey containing three questions by telling it the questions, the structure I wanted, and the column names. It took a couple of tries, but eventually, it gave me a comma-separated list of what I wanted, as shown in table 9.1.

Table 9.1 A simple example of a survey with three questions and two respondents, generated by ChatGPT

Respondent	Question text	Question response
1	"On a scale from 1 to 5, how likely are you to recommend our app to a friend?"	4
1	"Please rate the app on a scale from 1 to 10."	7
1	"On a scale from 1 to 10, how much did you enjoy your breakfast this morning?"	8
2	"On a scale from 1 to 5, how likely are you to recommend our app to a friend?"	3

Table 9.1　A simple example of a survey with three questions and two respondents, generated by ChatGPT *(continued)*

Respondent	Question text	Question response
2	"Please rate the app on a scale from 1 to 10."	6
2	"On a scale from 1 to 10, how much did you enjoy your breakfast this morning?"	6

What's really nice about using something like ChatGPT, or any of its successors, instead of a random data generator tool is that you'll have a lot more control over the values and structure of the randomly generated data. Getting realistic data is your main objective here because then, your designs will better suit the real data, and you'll have to do less work when that real data finally starts coming through. Do yourself a favor and spend a little bit of extra time with the LLM to fine-tune your test data:

- Make the set of columns realistic, such as dates, times, names, addresses (if you will need those), etc.
- Make the values in each column realistic, like if your data points will all live in a single state or country, or all your dates are supposed to be in the future, etc.
- Make the distribution of values in each column realistic. For example, if you need a column for how much someone spends purchasing a subscription, tell the LLM to use the right values. Or if you have a column for something like the sale price of a house, tell the LLM that you want a random distribution around the average sale price in the geographic region in question.

If you don't do that extra leg work, and the test data winds up being too different from the real data (especially structurally), you might not be able to swap data sources at all and instead have to rebuild from scratch. It's not the end of the world if that happens because it might be unavoidable, and on that second time around, it won't be so difficult because you'll have a better idea of what you need. I find it better to do a little extra work (like tweaking the data with the LLM) than to do a lot of extra work (like rebuilding everything I already built once).

Okay, now that we've exhausted how to handle situations where data is missing for any number of reasons, let's talk about how to handle situations where you're asked to go against what you know about design.

9.2　*What to do when you're asked to ignore your viz-tuition*

Notice how the title of this section is not "What to do *if* you're asked" but instead is "What to do *when* you're asked" to do something against your viz-tuition. It's a guarantee that you will have stakeholders who want to see things a certain way, and that certain way will sometimes be exactly counter to everything you've learned about making a good visualization, both in this book and out in the wild. That's not because you're being misled by your educational resources, but more because your stakeholders don't know what they need or even sometimes what they want (or they do, and they're dead set on it).

The first line of defense in these cases is to try to figure out why they're asking you to do Bad Viz Things. Once you know the goal, you might be able to present them with an alternative that all parties will find viable: win-win!

If that fails, then in general, the way I like to handle these situations is by giving the stakeholder what they're requesting, but in parallel, I'll build or design the thing that I believe will look better and be more suited to their needs. Then I present the client with both options. Most of the time, they are completely enamored with my way, but sometimes they still like their own way, and then you have to acquiesce. It's their dashboard, their visualization, after all, and if they want a particular(ly terrible) aesthetic, even though you've offered them something better, it's on them.

While there are a great many kinds of these situations that could arise, let's look at two specific examples that you're very likely to encounter and then work through how to handle each.

9.2.1 *When asked to visualize a zillion categories in color*

Hands-down, I 100% guarantee that you will one day be asked to visualize way too many categories, using a different color to encode every single one. So, what do you do? How do you handle that kind of request?

First, I recommend that you attempt to gently dissuade the requester from this line of thinking. Try something along the lines of, "Are you sure about that? It will be quite overwhelming and look very messy to have 30 (or 20 or even 10) colors in a single visual, and it will be very difficult to make sense of what the graph is trying to say. Would you be open to considering other options?" Most reasonable people will acquiesce to such a polite request, but even if they are insistent, you don't have to give up hope (yet).

As already mentioned, my favorite way of dealing with this type of short-sighted insistence is not only to give the stakeholder what they are requesting but also build something better in parallel. Here you can bust out an idea like small multiples, which we discussed in section 6.1.1 as an option for un-spaghetti-fying a tangled mess of a line graph by breaking the graphs into small grids (like in figure 9.8, even though I'm stealing my own thunder a bit here). Or you can try something like figure 9.7, where you make all categories the same color and weight, and then use an accent color and heavier weight for the main or focus category.

If you have interactivity available to you, you can make the focus category in figure 9.7 changeable based on a selector of some kind, like a drop-down menu or radio button, so the user can choose which category they want to see at the forefront.

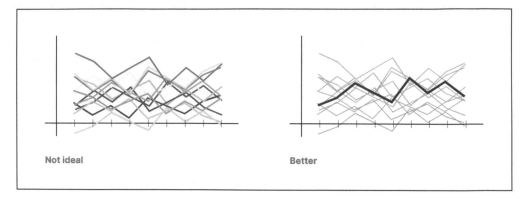

Figure 9.7   If the stakeholder is requesting that all categories be shown together, you can use color and form to push all non-interesting categories to the background and bring the main or focus category to the forefront. (Also, this is only 12 categories—imagine how bad 20 or 30 would look!)

9.2.2   *When asked to use someone else's suboptimal design*

Sometimes, when you've been brought in to do a visualization project, the client tries to save your time (and their money) by working on the design themselves so you can focus on the build. This can, of course, have a few different outcomes, where that design can be anywhere between great and abysmal. If you encounter this, I do encourage you to keep an open mind. We can learn a lot even from suboptimal designs—no one sets out with a goal of making a bad visual, so when you're met with one, take a leap and ponder all angles of it to see what does work in addition to what doesn't.

I had this happen to me once, where the project had taken a while to get going, so the client had tried to save time by creating their own wireframes before I had come on board. They had mocked up a total of nine dashboards, one for each of their key metrics, where each dashboard had its metric sliced and diced by a number of dimensions, like geography, product type, marketing channel, etc. I affectionately and rather crassly referred to this as a *vomit of dashboards* in my own internal monologue because if I built the dashboards to their own specs, it was going to be a giant mess, and no one would be able to find anything, nor would they want to touch it with a 10-foot pole. I gently and tactfully expressed my concerns to the stakeholders (you never want to be condescending), but they wanted me to proceed anyway, using their designs.

Skeptical as I was, I quickly did as they asked, but because I worked quickly, I was able to sneakily make my own mockup on the side for a dashboard that would follow the Visual Information-Seeking Mantra of "Overview first, then zoom and filter, then details on demand." My idea was to have an overview dashboard that would show each of the company's key performance indicators on a card (shown at the top of figure 9.8), and upon clicking one of the cards, the user would be taken to another dashboard that was focused only on that metric. There, they could use a dropdown menu to choose how they wanted to break down the metric into segments, and it would then break down into small multiples with the total of the metric showing in a lighter color on each pane (shown at the bottom of figure 9.8). This would allow the user to understand the context of the segment in relation to the total, unsliced metric, which is usually why people like to try to show a zillion lines on a single chart anyway—they want to know how that segment relates to the others. See figure 9.8 for a demonstration.

Figure 9.8   When asked to use someone else's suboptimal design, I gave the client what they requested, but then, on the side, I whipped up a quick wireframe of something I thought would satisfy their needs better: a dashboard following the visual information-seeking mantra of overview first (top), then zoom and filter (lower left), then details on demand (lower right).

After I showed the new wireframes to the stakeholders, they liked it, but they were still skeptical and preferred to proceed with their own ideas, so I took a big risk and tried one more thing: I quickly started building a prototype of my design with their real data. Had the stakeholders been more adamant and insistent, I wouldn't have tried pushing my own design a third time, but they were hesitant, and I knew I could deliver quickly, so I went for it, and it was all worthwhile. When I finally showed them something functional with their own data, they loved it and wanted me to go forward with my design. When all was said and done, the final dashboard turned out a bit different than what is shown in the wireframes in figure 9.8, but it was very close, and the client was very happy, saying that I'd shown them the "power of visualization." They were incredibly grateful for the clean and powerful dashboard I gave them.

Your stories won't always have the same ending as this one, and in fact, all of mine won't either, but that's okay. Sometimes we have to take a risk here and there, sticking our necks out a little bit if we want to push ourselves and others toward greatness. Even if it doesn't pan out, and we don't get our own way, we can still learn and grow by making the most of the design-hand that is dealt to us.

9.3   *Dealing with scope-creep and the never-ending project*

Do you remember that song from your childhood, "The Song That Never Ends," because it just goes on and on, my friend? (And you're welcome for that little earworm.) In all likelihood, you will probably find yourself someday in "The Project That Never Ends," but it almost certainly won't be presented to you as a project with no conclusion. Instead, it will start as any other project would, but as time goes on, you'll find that the end keeps getting further away instead of drawing closer. When requirements are continually added throughout the project like this instead of just sticking to the original plan, it's called *scope creep*. A little bit of scope creep is usually pretty acceptable because you easily might not have anticipated everything at the outset. However, when the scope has crept up so much that it starts to dramatically affect the outcome of the project or push the end of the project out by weeks or months, that's when it's a real problem. But how does that even happen, and more importantly, how can you hit the brakes when it does? Its different causes require different mitigation methods, so let's look at each separately.

9.3.1   *Requirements gathering wasn't thorough enough*

As we have discussed, gathering requirements and getting stakeholder buy-in at the very beginning of a project is of paramount importance. Thus, as with many other things in life, if you do a shoddy job of laying that firm foundation, then you will reap the consequences later.

To avoid this problem in the first place, you must be specific nearly to the point of being pedantic when scoping the project. Your requirements document needs to be as airtight as you can make it, listing what is in scope and what isn't (i.e., what you will do and what you won't), including all features, filters, controls, parameters, visuals, accessibility, etc., and all the data necessary to power everything.

The main way to be specific during requirements gathering is to make sure you thoroughly interview enough stakeholders and users. If you're hearing that a particular person or department is going to be the main consumer of your dashboard, you'll want to put their needs at the very top of the priority list. Try to get at least 45 minutes to an hour with them. This should give you ample time to get at the heart of their wants and needs, and it will also allow a bit of a buffer in case they are late for your meeting (the calendars of important people are always very booked).

This is not to say that you can entirely avoid unexpected requirements popping up somewhere down the line. No one is perfect, and no one can foresee every single possible circumstance, but just do your best. Whenever changes do arise, be transparent about the effect they will have on the finish line as well as the bottom line. If fulfilling the new requirement(s) will affect the end of the project or the final cost, tell the stakeholders in no uncertain terms. They can then decide if it's worth the change or whether some other feature(s) can be deprioritized instead. Remember, it's ultimately their project, so they should be the ones to call the shots.

Another way to be specific is to do some preliminary legwork to make sure you'll have everything you need. For example, let's say you're making a report about team productivity. In one system, you have a table that has a column with the team names and another detailing what area of the product they oversee. Meanwhile, in a table from a separate system, you have a different column with the team names, a column containing a list of people who are assigned to that team, and a column detailing how much work each team member completed in a given week. To report how much work is done each week on each area of the product, you'll need to join those two tables together. You might think it sounds crazy, but you'd be surprised at how differently something as simple as a team name can be stored in different systems, as in figure 9.9.

If it was just a matter of formatting the team names on the left in figure 9.9, it would be possible to join the two tables with some light data cleaning. Unfortunately, though, since the names aren't even structured the same across the two systems, there's no hope of programmatically fixing this problem. If you have any hope of linking them, you must come up with some kind of key, a table that has a mapping of how to link the two tables.

It might seem farfetched to you that this situation would ever arise, but it's based on a real situation I encountered with a client. It's not enough for the client and stakeholders to say that all the data exists; someone must go one step further to make sure that what exists is all usable. Otherwise, when you eventually discover that you can't do what you'd planned with the data that you have, you're going to be sent on a panic-stricken wild goose chase that will likely end in one of two ways. First, you might find someone who can create a link for you, but it will need to be prioritized with their other work, and they might not be able to get it done in time for you to use it during your project. Second, there might be no one who can help you; thus, the task will be

```
System A                    System B

THE-AVENGERS               avengers, the
MEWTOO                     team mewtoo
TEAM-AWESOME               TEAM-AWESOME
TINY-CODERS                Tiny Coders
PLATFORM                   Platform team
PAYMENTS-TEAM              payments-team
ART-TEAM                   ART-Awesome Reporting Team
```

Figure 9.9   System A stores team names in the format on the left, uppercase with no spaces, while system B on the right doesn't follow any particular format. If you try to join these tables on System A's team name equals system B's team name, you might, at best, get a few results, but certainly not all of them. You'll need to find some way to link them.

impossible. Nothing can help you in the second outcome, but if you do your due diligence during requirements gathering, you'll be better able to work with the first outcome, saving yourself time and heartache down the road.

9.3.2   *Too many or not enough cooks in the kitchen*

Another cause of scope creep is having too many stakeholders or, as I like to say, "too many cooks in the kitchen." If you've ever tried to cook in a kitchen where too many others are also trying to cook (say, for a holiday get-together with family), then you'll know the frustration of having too many cooks in the kitchen.

So, it is when there are too many stakeholders: stakeholder Lizzy says she likes everything the way it is, but stakeholder William says he doesn't like the font you used because he thinks it looks too much like Comic Sans (even though it looks nothing like Comic Sans and is, in fact, a great font), so he wants everything converted to Arial instead. Meanwhile, stakeholder Georgiana would have the final say, but she is on her third vacation during the four-month project and won't be able to give her opinion until she's back to work 10 days hence. Spoiler alert—when she does come back, she'll decide that she no longer wants the highly specialized filter menu that you spent several days getting to work properly. (Did this exact thing happen to me on a project? Maybe.)

When there are too many people calling the shots, not only does it become impossible to get them all in a room together to make decisions, but it takes them forever to finally make those decisions. To make matters worse, they also tend to feed off each other's displeasure. When you can't get them all together to give their sign-off on your work, you might make changes to suit one stakeholder only to get completely opposite feedback from another stakeholder later. This makes your job both infuriating and impossible to do, and it eats up valuable project time (and money).

Sometimes, the opposite problem arises, and instead of too many people being too involved, no one bothers to call the shots or give guidance about what you're doing. Here's what it might look like: you're merrily chugging along through the iterative steps of the design and development process, making stuff, then showing the stakeholders for feedback, and then making more stuff, when eventually you notice that it's taking longer and longer to get responses from those stakeholders. Or maybe the responses are getting less and less effusive until, eventually, you realize your stakeholder is hardly paying you any mind at all.

As with most interpersonal issues, the problems on each side of this coin are best solved with communication. Talk to someone in charge of your stakeholder(s) or of your project and tell them about the issues you're having. If you can't find someone who can help you, you might have to put on your big kid pants and go talk to the stakeholders yourself. If there are too many people pulling you in too many directions, then calmly and rationally explain what is happening as a result of having so many approvers. Keeping your wits about you is important here; you don't want to lose your temper because that can cause you to sound like a petulant child, and that's no way to keep the respect of your clients. If the problem is that your stakeholder(s) are checked out and not paying attention to you, ask if they still have time to field the project and your requests and, if they don't, see whether there's someone else whom they might want to tap who can lend their opinions and expertise. (I would not recommend suggesting that they put the project off or wait until later because, oftentimes, later will never come, and you're liable to lose the project that way.)

Clear, calm, and rational communication is the key to success in all relationships. Learn how to do it well, and the world (and each of your visualization projects) will be your oyster.

9.3.3 *You're trying too hard*

Finally, you might notice the project scope getting out of hand if you've been too eager to please, sometimes known as "doing too much." It's easy to land in that position, especially when you're trying to impress a new client or charm a new boss. Of course, you want to do a good job and be asked back to do another project, so sometimes you might try your hand at overdelivering, going the extra mile, or making it a habit to say, "Yes, sure!" when the stakeholder makes a new request. But one day, you will find that you are nearly out of project time and close to burnout, and yet the client requests are still coming.

To avoid this, balance is the key; it's best when you start out balanced rather than scramble later to stabilize a wildly rocking boat. Learn when to draw the line and say no. There's a time and place to go the extra mile, and there's a time and place to rein it in and be happy with meeting expectations instead of exceeding them. Part of being a professional at anything means learning to set good boundaries and then knowing when to stick to them and when to bend them (ever so slightly) to buy yourself some goodwill. It does not mean doing every little thing that's asked of you without questioning. If you do good work, your clients and stakeholders will respect that—people generally prefer someone who will partner with them and help make them better over someone who just blindly does whatever is asked of them.

9.4   *The last word*

If you've gotten this far, I can't tell you how grateful I am that you chose to come on this journey with me. It is my deepest hope that you have found this book enjoyable and useful and that you've been inspired by data as I have. The best part of my job as a data visualization practitioner is giving people that "Aha!" moment, so I hope you've had many yourself throughout this book and will take what you've learned in these pages to go and make beautiful, insightful, and usable visualizations of and for the world around you. Happy vizzing, friends!

Summary

- If your data is sparse, don't hide that. Instead, make it obvious so people don't accidentally draw the wrong conclusions.
- The best way to make sure your viz looks good as a flow of data starts to ramp up is to check in on it periodically—set alarms to remind yourself if you have to!
- When the data doesn't yet exist for a report you need to build, try to find some data that will be as real as possible so that the designs will fit the real data.
- When a client dictates that you make design choices you don't agree with, gently try to guide them to the better choices by giving them what they're requesting but also by whipping up something quickly that will be more along the lines of what they truly need. If possible, try to make a working prototype because that will be the best and most convincing demo.
- If you find that the finish line for your project keeps getting pushed out further instead of getting closer, don't be afraid to communicate about why that's happening and what can be done to finally wrap things up.

appendix
Further resources

This appendix contains links to some of my favorite online resources. I chose to include these links as an appendix because, as we all well know, the internet is a very fluid place, with links changing, websites getting rearranged, and entire domains retiring every day. As the publication date of this book slips further into the past, you, as a reader, might have to get more creative when looking for these tools, but I'm sure you're quite resourceful and will be able to manage. Good luck, and happy vizzing!

A.1 My code repo

First of all, you can find all the code used to generate most of the images in this book on my GitHub: https://github.com/callmedeeray/everyday-data-visualization-illustrations. I make no apologies for my hacky code.

A.2 Where to find open data

In chapter 3, I told you to open your favorite search engine and query for your topic, plus the words "open data" to help you locate data sets about the thing you want to viz. Sometimes, though, you don't have a topic in mind already and you just want to cruise for what's out there and see if inspiration strikes, so here are some places you can go to find such data sets.

KAGGLE
Some of you are likely already familiar with Kaggle for their competitions targeted at data scientists and practitioners of machine learning, but you might not know it as a great source for open data sets. Check it out at https://www.kaggle.com/datasets/.

REAL WORLD, FAKE DATA

If you are looking for a clean, ready-to-use data set for a business dashboard, have a look at the Real World, Fake Data project by Mark Bradbourne. Start with the introductory post on his blog, which tells you about the project and also has links to each data set, hosted on Data.World: https://sonsofhierarchies.com/real-world-fake-data/. Spoiler alert: I used one of his data sets, about hospitality, for the case study in chapter 8.

DATA.WORLD

Speaking of Data.World, it's an enterprise data catalog platform, meaning that it helps large organizations by, in the site's own words, making "data discovery, governance, and analysis easy, turning data workers into knowledge superheroes." But, it also houses an incredible amount of open data—nearly 130,000 data sets as of this writing! Sound too good to be true? It's not: they're a Public Benefit Corporation, and a Certified B Corporation to boot. Check them out here: https://data.world/datasets/open-data.

A.3   Tools for colors

There are lots of tools out there for colors, like accessibility checkers and color palette generators as well as a few other miscellaneous color tools. We'll start with an accessibility checker.

A.3.1   Accessibility checkers

Hands down, my very favorite accessibility checker, or color checker, is https://accessible-colors.com/, which you can see in action in figure A.1.

What I love about this color checker is that if your text-to-background color ratio fails the selected compliance level, it will suggest both a different text color and a different background color by changing the saturation and lightness, maintaining the hues. It's incredibly cool, and I've not seen any other tools that do this, so if this tool ever dies, you can bet I'll be in mourning for a long time. Note that as of this writing, it is based on WCAG 2.0, and there are no guarantees that it will be updated to use later versions of WCAG as they are released. But I will remain ever hopeful!

Also, to use this for colors of visualization elements or big chunky things (larger than 3 pixels wide at the smallest point), like bars, pies, donuts, etc., put your intended bar/pie/donut color in the Text field, keep the font size at 18px, and then change the weight to Bold and proceed with your checking. This ensures that you'll be using the correct guidelines, as they're a bit looser for larger elements than dainty text, as you may remember from the last section of chapter 4.

Another color checker I quite like is Viz Palette, created by Elijah Meeks (co-founder of the Data Visualization Society and venerable author of *D3.js in Action*, which is how I got started with D3) and Susie Lu (another incredible trailblazer in the world of data viz, whose "Re-viz-iting the Receipt" absolutely blew my mind when she

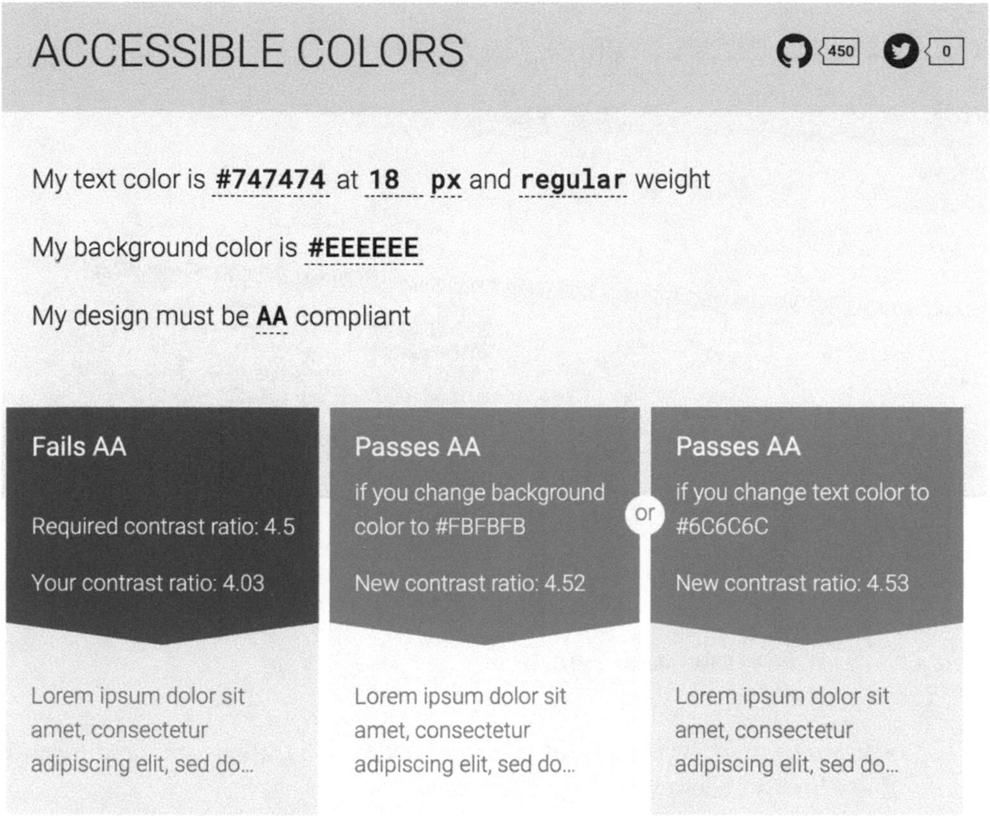

ACCESSIBLE COLORS

My text color is **#747474** at **18 px** and **regular** weight

My background color is **#EEEEEE**

My design must be **AA** compliant

Fails AA	Passes AA	Passes AA
	if you change background color to #FBFBFB	if you change text color to #6C6C6C
Required contrast ratio: 4.5		
Your contrast ratio: 4.03	New contrast ratio: 4.52	New contrast ratio: 4.53
Lorem ipsum dolor sit amet, consectetur adipiscing elit, sed do...	Lorem ipsum dolor sit amet, consectetur adipiscing elit, sed do...	Lorem ipsum dolor sit amet, consectetur adipiscing elit, sed do...

Figure A.1   My very favorite accessibility checker, in action.

tweeted about it in 2019). You can find Viz Palette at https://projects.susielu.com/viz-palette; see what it looks like in figure A.2.

   To use this tool, either edit the predefined colors or paste in your own list of colors and click Replace to replace the default palette. You can use named colors (e.g., `"red"`, `"green"`, `"blue"`), hex codes (e.g., `"#ff0000"`, `"#00ff00"`, `"#0000ff"`), RGB colors (e.g., `"rgb(255,0,0)"`, `"rgb(0,255,0)"`, `"rgb(0,0,255)"`), or HSL colors (e.g., `"hsl(0,100%,50%)"`, `"hsl(120,100%,50%)"`, `"hsl(240,100%,50%)"`). It seems to work best if you enclose each color in quotes and the entire list in square brackets, like `["hsl(0,100%,50%)", "hsl(120,100%,50%)", "hsl(240,100%,50%)"]`. Once you have input your palette on the left, you'll see some sample random-data visualizations using your palette on the right. You can make a few changes to the settings to get the sample vizzes as close as possible to your own plans, and then you can also simulate what your palette will look like to people with different types of color blindness. Finally, at the bottom right, you'll also get a little report about how much or little your colors conflict

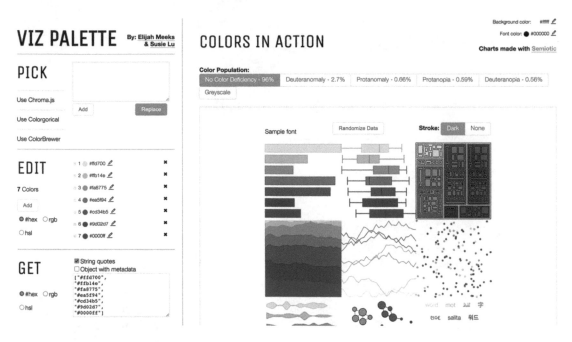

Figure A.2   Viz Palette by Elijah Meeks and Susie Lu

with each other, by shade and by name. It's an incredibly useful and lovely little tool that I highly encourage you to check out.

A.3.2   *Color palette generators*

There are zillions of color palette generators out there, and as I was going through my bookmarks, which I've been collecting over the years since I started doing viz, I had to remove at least three links that had died. So, last caveat: these links might die. Nonetheless, here are some that are still alive as of this writing. I'll group them by section in section 4.3.3, which is where we talked about these kinds of color palette–generating tools. Within each little section, I'll order them by usability, from easiest to most difficult.

Tools that choose based on color theory

As I was doing some research for this book, I happened upon the Data Color Picker at https://www.learnui.design/tools/data-color-picker.html and wondered where it's been all my life; check it out in figure A.3.

Data Color Picker uses the HSB color space to generate a palette from a gradient based on a single input (for a single-hue gradient) or two inputs (to pick from either a diverging or nondiverging two-hue gradient) and then shows you an example of what

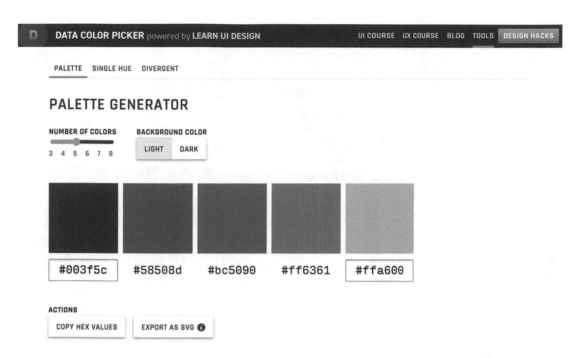

Figure A.3   Data Color Picker

the resulting palette would look like when applied to both a pie chart and a choropleth map. Finally, it even allows you to choose how many intermediate colors to generate, and then you can copy the resulting hex codes into your tool of choice.

Another color-theory-based option is to use a color wheel. Paletton, at https:// paletton.com/, is a great tool for this; see figure A.4 for what it looks like.

I find it wonderfully satisfying to click and drag the little circles around the wheel on the left and watch the palette change on the right. You can choose from complementary, analogous, triadic, and tetradic (four colors) with the basic settings, or you can jazz things up a bit with split complementary and others by hitting the gear icon. You can preview the palette in action on some example web pages or artwork, and you can also simulate different kinds of color vision deficiencies. This one is a little more difficult (for novices) to export than the others, as you only get the RGB or hex codes, but there are tons of options for the more design-heavy users out there.

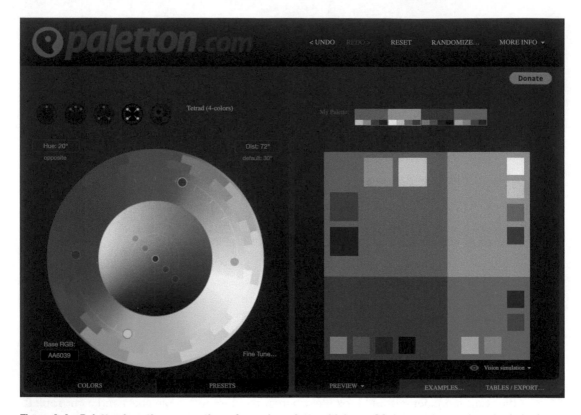

Figure A.4   Paletton in action, generating a four-color palette with hue = 20 degrees (remember, that's in the realm of red/orange) as the base.

Our last color-theory-based palette generator is Colorgorical, at http://vrl.cs.brown .edu/color. I find this one to be the least intuitive, but it seems very powerful as palette generators go. Figure A.5 shows what it looks like.

Colorgorical has many bells and whistles, but basically you select how many colors you want to generate and how different you would like them to appear. Then you can use the hue circle to filter out any hues that you don't want, and then you can select your desired lightness range and starting colors (not shown in the screenshot in figure A.5). You can use the settings at the top of the main section on the right to change the color space used, the format of the output array, and on what types of charts you'd like to see your palette in action. Finally, when you're done, hit the Generate button back up in the top-left corner of the screen, and you'll see the graphs populated on the right as well as an array of your colors, which you can copy and paste into your data viz tool of choice.

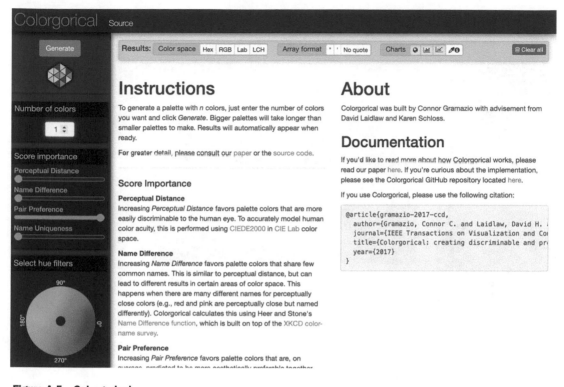

Figure A.5   Colorgorical

TOOLS THAT CHOOSE COLORS FROM A PHOTO OR AN EXISTING PIECE OF ARTWORK

As I mentioned in chapter 4, tools that choose a palette of colors from a photo or work of art are some of the coolest out there and the ones I've used the least. But the one I used on my sunset picture was a Google Arts Experiment called Art Palette, which you can find here: https://artsexperiments.withgoogle.com/artpalette/. After the little intro finishes, you will be presented with two options. The first option allows you to change the colors that are showing, and doing so will cause the tool to surface images that use the palette you just made (so cool!). Your second option is to upload an image (or you can skip past the intro and go straight to uploading by following this link instead: https://artsexperiments.withgoogle.com/artpalette/images), and this is what I did with my Maui sunset picture, shown in figure A.6. Almost immediately, you'll see little circles appear on your image and the background will change to show those colors.

You can move the circles to pick out different colors if you so desire, and when you're happy, you can click View Artworks With This Palette, which will show works of art and other images with your same palette. From this screen, you can hover on the colors at the top and copy the hex codes, or you can pull them out of the URL generated

Figure A.6   **My Maui sunset picture in Google's Art Palette, with the default colors it picked**

when you use the sharing button in the top-right corner. Neither is a great way to export the colors, but hey, otherwise it's super nifty!

TOOLS THAT CHOOSE FROM A BASE COLOR OR COLORS AND GENERATE RANDOM COLORS TO ACCOMPANY
One of the first color palette generators I ever found was Coolors, at https://coolors .co/ and shown in figure A.7. This one can also generate a palette from an image, but I've only ever used it to specify one or two colors and then have it randomly generate the rest of my color palette.

Coolors can handle anywhere from 2 to 10 colors (though to generate more than 5 you'll need to pay for a Pro license): to add colors, simply hover in between two colors and hit the + button that appears; to do fewer colors, you can hover on one of the colors and hit the x that appears. From that same hover menu, you can also select a different shade, drag it to another position, copy the hex code, or "lock" that color in place. To change a color that is showing, simply click on the hex code and replace it with your own. Then to see the real magic, tap your space bar, and Coolors will randomly generate colors for you in the unlocked slots. It's, dare I say, very *cool*.

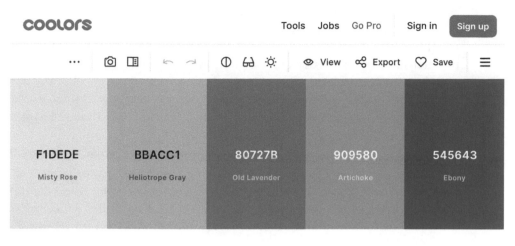

Figure A.7 Coolors

A.3.3 Other miscellaneous color tools

With color being such a broad and technical topic, of course, it's challenging to categorize all the color tools that exist out there, so here are a few others that either I used in this book or that I thought you might find useful.

A TOOL TO HELP YOU PICK A TEXT COLOR BASED ON WCAG

While this tool doesn't actually generate an entire palette for you, it definitely deserves an honorable mention because it can help you pick a text or viz element color that passes WCAG 2.0 guidelines, based on the specified background color. Color Safe can be found at http://colorsafe.co/ and looks like figure A.8.

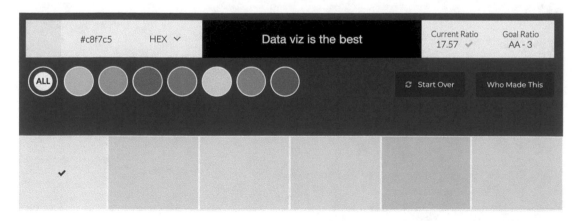

Figure A.8 Color Safe helps you pick a text (or viz element) color with a WCAG-approved contrast ratio against the background color you specify.

When you open Color Safe, you're asked to specify the background color and the font family, size, and weight of your text; you can also change the sample sentence to one you like better. Then when you click Generate, the tool will serve up a plethora of colors that have the necessary contrast ratio with your background color for the font specified. You can narrow these colors by hue or scroll through all of them. Selecting a color will change the sample text so you can see how it works against your background. To export your chosen color, select either Hex or RGB in the upper left and then copy the color's code into your data viz tool.

TOOLS THAT CONVERT BETWEEN COLOR SPACES

As I was writing the section in chapter 4 about the CIELAB color space and creating the graphics for it, I had to resort to a color converter because neither Figma's nor my Mac's color pickers had an option for CIELAB. So, I used the tool called Colorizer, which can be found at https://colorizer.org/ and shown in figure A.9.

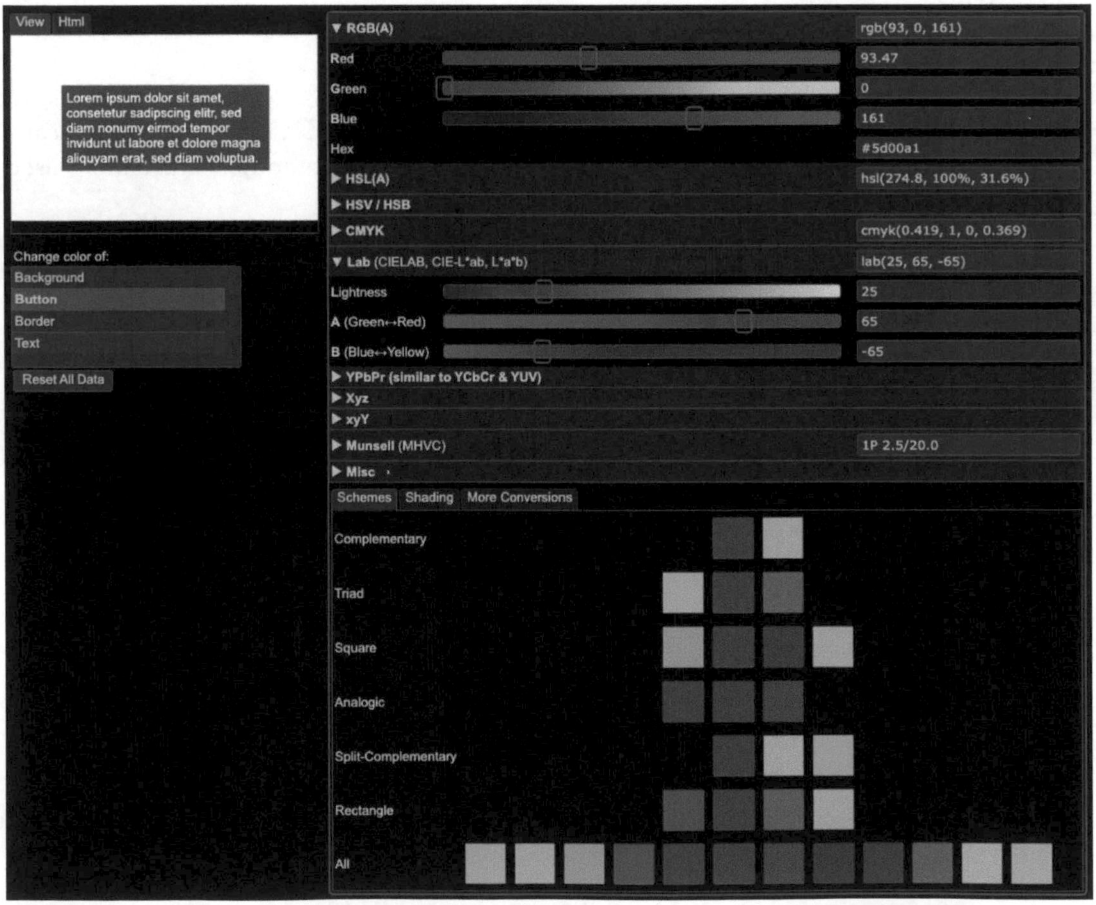

Figure A.9 Colorizer in action, changing the color of the button behind the text box on the left. You can see at the bottom right that it even gives you color wheel–based palettes based on the color in focus!.

So while it can be a little tedious to go back and forth between a converter and your design or data viz tool (tell me about it—I did it 50 times for those two CIELAB images in chapter 4!), the effort is worthwhile if you want to be very precise in your color work. And, after all, as designers, isn't our attention to detail one of the great things that sets us apart from the rest?

BONUS: THE XKCD COLOR SURVEY

Finally, if you're a giant nerd like me, have enjoyed all this information about color, and also love the XKCD webcomic, you might enjoy the results of the color survey XKCD did in 2010, available here: https://blog.xkcd.com/2010/05/03/color-survey-results/ [beware the not-safe-for-work (NSFW) language]. It's a great read.

A.4   Tools for choosing chart types

In the text of chapter 6, I already gave you the static Visual Vocabulary poster created by *Financial Times* at http://ft.com/vocabulary and the interactive version built in Tableau by Andy Kriebel, available on Tableau Public at http://mng.bz/BAJ1. But, I have a couple of other resources I like to use when I'm looking for viz-spiration in my own work, whether for professional or personal use. These flow charts or decision trees are a great way to help you pick a chart type when you're having a bit of vizzer's block.

CHART SUGGESTIONS: A THOUGHT STARTER

This PDF has been in my bookmarks list nearly as long as it's been in existence (it's copyrighted 2009, which is incidentally why it's not reprinted here). You can find it at http://mng.bz/46Nw.

FROM DATA TO VIZ

Winner of an Information Is Beautiful award in 2018, this beautiful page not only has flow charts to help you make good decisions (see figure A.10), but it also includes some caveats to help keep you from making bad decisions.

A.5   Tools for accessible interactivity

In chapter 7, we talked all about interactivity, what to do with it, what not to do with it, and how to make vizzes interactive for some less-conventional interaction devices and methods. I already told you about the Accessibility Developer Guide at https://www .accessibility-developer-guide.com/ and the DataViz Accessibility Advocacy and Advisory Group at https://github.com/dataviza11y. If you are a heavy user of Microsoft tools, check out their guide for how to add alt text on visual objects across their product line: http://mng.bz/OZAK.

What kind of data do you have? Pick the main type using the buttons below. Then let the decision tree guide you toward your graphic possibilities.

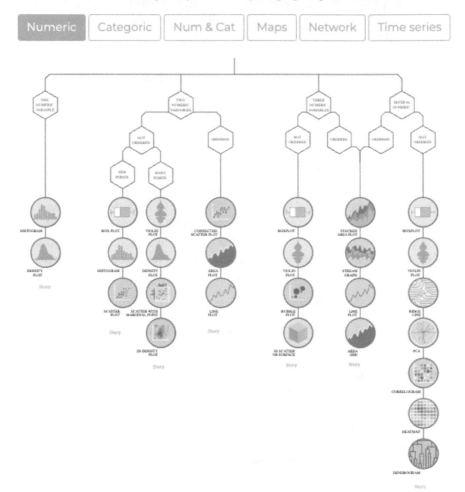

Figure A.10   The interactive flow chart on From Data to Viz

references

Chapter 4

1 Went, L. N., & Pronk, N. (1985). The genetics of tritan disturbances. *Human Genetics, 69,* 255–262. https://doi.org/10.1007/BF00293036

2 Sharpe, L. T., Stockman, A., Jägle, H., & Nathans, J. Opsin genes, cone photopigments, color vision, and color blindness. In K. R. Gegenfurtner & L. T. Sharpe (eds.), *Color Vision: From Genes to Perception* (pp. 3–52). Cambridge University Press, 1999.

Chapter 5

1 Lyon, G. R., Shaywitz, S. E., & Shaywitz, B. A. (2003). A definition of dyslexia. *Annals of Dyslexia, 53*(1), 1–14. http://www.jstor.org/stable/23764731

2 Peter, B., Albert, A., Panagiotides, H., & Gray, S. (2021). Sequential and spatial letter reversals in adults with dyslexia during a word comparison task: Demystifying the "was saw" and "db" myths. *Clinical Linguistics & Phonetics, 35*(4), 340–367. https://doi.org/10.1080/02699206.2019.1705916

3 Duranovic, M., Senka, S., & Babic-Gavric, B. (2018). Influence of increased letter spacing and font type on the reading ability of dyslexic children. *Annals of Dyslexia, 68*(3), 218–228. https://www.jstor.org/stable/48693795

4 Jackson, J. E. (2015). Toward universally accessible typography: A review of research on dyslexia. *Journal on Technology & Persons with Disabilities, 2*(16), 155–165. http://hdl.handle.net/10211.3/133383

Chapter 6

1 McGovern, T., Larson, S., Morris, B., & Hodges, M. (2020). tonmcg/US_County_Level_Election_Results_08-16: US County-level Presidential Election Results (v1.0). Zenodo. https://doi.org/10.5281/zenodo.3975765

index